THE
SHEPHERD'S
BUSH
MURDERS

Also by Nick Russell-Pavier

The Great Train Robbery: Crime of the Century

THE SHEPHERD'S BUSH MURDERS

NICK RUSSELL-PAVIER

arrow books

3 5 7 9 10 8 6 4 2

Arrow Books
20 Vauxhall Bridge Road
London SW1V 2SA

Arrow Books is part of the Penguin Random House group of companies
whose addresses can be found at global.penguinrandomhouse.com.

Penguin
Random House
UK

First published in Great Britain in 2016 by Century

Published by Arrow Books 2017

www.penguin.co.uk

A CIP catalogue record for this book is available from the British Library.

ISBN 9781784751890

Typeset in 11.48/16.57 pt Baskerville MT by
Jouve (UK), Milton Keynes
Printed and bound in Great Britain by Clays Ltd, St Ives plc

Penguin Random House is committed to a sustainable future for
our business, our readers and our planet. This book is made from
Forest Stewardship Council® certified paper.

For Dennis Russell-Pavier
9 March 1921 – 3 May 1966

Photographic Acknowledgements

Preface

I first became interested in the Shepherd's Bush Murders when I stumbled across a black and white ITN archive interview with James Newman, a nine-year-old boy. On Friday, 12 August 1966 he was standing alone on the corner of Braybrook Street, East Acton, next to Wormwood Scrubs Park when two cars pulled up a short distance away. He thought a film was being made when he heard a gunshot and saw one man fall to the ground, another chased and shot in the back and a third shot in one of the cars. It was hard to make sense of what he was witnessing. Fifty years later it's still difficult to understand what took place without following closely the journey that took six men to Braybrook Street that day.

Some readers of a true-crime account are only interested in the actual event. They grow impatient and restless if the story ventures into the smaller particulars, wider context and provenance. But, as the saying goes, the devil is in the detail. Without a clear sense of the nature, preoccupations and motivations of the participants and an awareness of the times in which they lived, it's impossible to see how and why things happened as they did, feel the shock wave created by the events, understand the mindset from which they sprang and the legacy they left in their wake.

This story is about a crime that shook Britain in the summer of 1966 and had a profound and lasting effect on the way millions of people felt about the changing country in which they lived. It's the story of how in just a few minutes something was changed for ever in the hearts and minds of the British people. It's a story of life and death, of personal tragedies and of how a series of small steps can lead incrementally to disaster.

Chapter 1

On Thursday, 27 November 1958, Police Sergeant Cyril Mercer and Police Constable Capp from Highbury Vale police station went to 42 Burma Road, Stoke Newington in response to a call at 14:25 from Mary Millicent McDonald reporting a burglary.

There was nothing remarkable about the quiet tree-lined street of Victorian terraced houses – it was like many all over London. Domestic burglary was commonplace in the area and its investigation was a familiar routine for the two police officers. Mary McDonald answered the door. She explained that she was a lodger in the house and had called the police after discovering that her room had been ransacked and various possessions were missing. She led Sergeant Mercer to a rear room on the ground floor. PC Capp knocked on the other door in the hallway but got no response. He opened it, looked inside and shouted to the sergeant.

Lying on the floor in the front room was an elderly man. His legs were bound together at the ankles with string and his arms were tied behind his back, the wrists bound. He was gagged and was bleeding badly from a deep gash on the back of his head. The string around his wrists and ankles was wound so tightly that Mercer struggled to cut it with his penknife. The gag was so constricting that the sergeant could not insert the blade of his knife behind it without risking further injury to the victim.

While Mercer struggled to free the old man, PC Capp phoned for an ambulance. Sergeant Mercer and Mary McDonald did what they could by way of first aid until the ambulance arrived. McDonald said the man's name was William Gaylard; he owned the house and was her landlord.

Once Gaylard had been safely sent off to hospital, Mary McDonald told the police officers what she knew. She and her future husband had been having lunch with her upstairs neighbour, Mr Jarry, on the first floor. At about two p.m. she had returned to her room and had found it plundered. She noticed things missing – two bracelets and a three-strand pearl necklace. The items, which she valued at around twenty-five shillings, had been in her room when she'd gone upstairs before lunch.

Retired baker William Gaylard, 79 years old, was admitted to the German Hospital in East London at 14:50 on that Thursday afternoon and was seen by senior house officer Dr Mardho Bradshad Vaidya who found him covered in blood. Gaylard's multiple injuries were extensive and included a deep laceration two inches long at the back of his skull, a second two-inch laceration on the front of the skull, a ruptured blood vessel in his left eye, a laceration about half an inch long and another laceration about one and a quarter inches below the left eye, bruising to both ears, bleeding from his nostrils and a graze below his knee. An X-ray revealed a fissured fracture of the skull on the left side.

Some newspapers reported that William Gaylard's finger had been cut off so that the thieves could steal his wedding ring. However, that was untrue: such a severe injury and loss of blood would have been reported by the two police officers who first discovered the elderly man tied up in the front room of his home and would have been noted by Dr Vaidya when he examined him. In his statement to the police William Gaylard said that the ring had been in his pocket.

Later that afternoon Detective Inspector George Gladdish from the Fingerprint Branch and Detective Sergeant Charles Dickenson from the Photographic Department, New Scotland Yard, arrived at 42 Burma Road. Dickenson took four photographs. The first shows the passageway leading from the front door. The second shows the sideboard in the front room. The third shows the spot where William Gaylard was found and the fourth shows the combined sitting room/bedroom and kitchen that he occupied. DI Gladdish took possession of two items of evidence, a piece of glass from a broken decanter and another glass decanter that was on a sideboard. The following day Gladdish took the piece of glass to Dickenson and asked him to photograph a clearly defined bloody finger-mark.

Back at the German Hospital William Gaylard's wounds were sutured as necessary, cleaned and dressed. When he was recovered sufficiently he made a statement to the police and explained how he had been robbed and attacked in his home. 'I own that house and I occupy two rooms on the ground floor, a sitting room and a bedroom. On Thursday, 27 November 1958 around 1:15 p.m. someone knocked on the front door. I opened it and saw two men there. I'd seen them on the Wednesday before when they asked me about my income-tax papers. On Wednesday I took them into my room and talked to them about my income tax and then they left saying they'd look through their books and come back on the Thursday.

'On the Thursday when they came I took them into my front room and I'd no sooner turned round to put something down on the sideboard when wallop and down I went. They cut off every bit of clothing I had. I shouted for help but they gagged me. I had two black eyes and for four days afterwards I didn't remember anything about it. I had about twenty-five shillings in my pocket when they came in and a ring in my pocket as well. On the dressing table in the front room there were two glass decanters. They hit me on the head with one and it all broke in pieces.'

*

On the evening of the vicious assault twenty-two-year-old Margaret Roberts, a newly-wed and five months pregnant, was at home in her mother-in-law's council flat at 21 Kendal House, Augustus Street, NW1 when her husband Harry returned with another man. Both men were covered in blood and said they had been in a car accident.

Margaret put Harry's trousers in the sink to soak overnight. But the blood wouldn't come out so the next day she took them to the cleaners. When she called at another shop on the way home her attention was caught by a picture of an elderly man on the front page of a newspaper. The report said he was dangerously ill in hospital after being beaten up and robbed at his home. Margaret instantly recognised the man in the photograph. Before she'd got married she'd lived with an elderly couple in North London. When the wife died she stayed on to look after the old man, William Gaylard. She continued to visit him even after she married and used to take him something for tea on Sundays. Her husband Harry sometimes went with her.

As far as Margaret Roberts knew her ex-soldier husband was charming, kind and thoughtful, an honest hard-working man who had no history of criminal activity. She'd married him nine months earlier, shortly before he was discharged from the army after completing National Service. The first crack in their new married life appeared in December when Harry was suddenly dismissed from his job for 'irregularities' concerning thefts from the warehouse of his employers, Wright & Co. (Kings Cross) Ltd. Roberts was subsequently arrested, charged with the thefts and granted bail until the case came before the Essex County Quarter Sessions at Chelmsford in January 1959.

Margaret was shocked by this new side of her husband, revealed here to her for the first time. The more she thought about the robbery and the brutal attack suffered by her old landlord and friend, the more certain she became about who was responsible. She later confronted Harry with it and he admitted it. For several weeks she wrestled with her conscience. She was his wife and carrying his child. She did nothing and told no one.

A few weeks later Margaret and her husband went out for a drink. She said later: 'He wasn't working at the time, but seemed to get money from somewhere. All his quiet manners had gone, only his tidy habits and neat dressing remained. He didn't seem to care how he got money as long as he got it. It was as though he felt the world owed him something and that he was free to take it. One night we walked through Park Lane in Mayfair – there were a few prostitutes hanging about and he said, "See if you can get a man and I'll keep watch. You can make a packet and so can I."'

The couple argued until late that night and the following morning Roberts apologised. Later in the week they went to the New Cabinet Club, a hang-out for underworld and other dubious characters, in Gerrard Street, Soho.

'We were both very drunk,' Margaret Roberts recalled,

'and again he suggested I should go on the streets. I refused again and he knocked me off my stool onto the floor. He punched me and kicked me and while I was lying there with a mouthful of blood he took our wedding certificate out of his pocket and tore it up. Then he scattered the pieces on the floor. I staggered out of the club and walked until I found a telephone box. I called up West End Central police station and told them about the robbery. A car came to the box and they took me to the station where I made a statement.'

On Tuesday, 27 January 1959 Detective Inspector Thomas O'Shea arrived at the premises of George Moss, a firm of builders in Camden, where Roberts had found a new job as a labourer.

O'Shea told Roberts who he was. Then he said, 'On 27th November 1958 two men attacked an old man at 42 Burma Road, N16 and stole some money. He was left severely injured. I have reason to believe you were one of the two men concerned.'

Roberts replied, 'Not me – I don't know anything about it.'

'Have you ever been to 42 Burma Road?'

'I don't know where it is.'

'Do you know a man named William Gaylard?'

'No, I have never heard of him.'

'Can you remember where you were on 27th November 1958? It was a Thursday.'

'No. Driving a van, I suppose.'

'You will be taken to Highbury Vale police station and charged with robbery with violence,' O'Shea cautioned Roberts.

'Then you'll have to prove it, won't you?' Roberts replied curtly.

And prove it was exactly what Detective Inspector Thomas O'Shea intended to do. Later that same day he went to Kendal House and in the presence of Roberts's mother, Dorothy, he took possession of some items of Harry's clothing including a suit and a raincoat.

The following morning DI O'Shea went to Chelmsford where Harry Roberts was due to stand trial for the warehouse thefts from his former employer. Before Roberts attended court O'Shea showed him the clothes he had obtained from his mother's flat and said, 'I've taken possession of this clothing from your address. I've been informed that it belongs to you. The clothing will be submitted to the police laboratory for examination.'

O'Shea cautioned him and Roberts replied casually, 'The plastic mac isn't mine, I don't think. What are you looking for – bloodstains?'

Roberts then appeared in court, was found guilty of the warehouse thefts and sentenced to eighteen months' and three months' imprisonment consecutively. After the hearing O'Shea escorted Roberts back to his cell.

Facing the prospect of prison for a relatively minor crime was one thing but there was a more serious matter on Roberts's mind as he walked back to his cell with DI O'Shea. He was still trying to work out how the police had connected him with the robbery at 42 Burma Road and there was only one conclusion.

Roberts said, 'Who grassed on me?'

O'Shea reminded Roberts that he was still under caution but he ignored it. 'Look, I did hit the old man but I didn't mean to hurt him. What a fool I am. But this is what's worrying me. What can a person get for putting a job like this up?'

Chapter 2

The day of reckoning came for Harry Roberts on Tuesday, 10 March 1959. He was brought from Wormwood Scrubs prison to the Old Bailey on a charge of robbery with violence.

With Justice John Cyril Maude presiding, Counsel for the Prosecution was grammar-school-educated thirty-year-old Richard Dillon Lott Du Cann. Representing Roberts were solicitors Peter Rusk & Co, who appointed thirty-seven-year-old Ali Mohammed Abbas as counsel for the defence.

Had he but known it, Roberts was fortunate to have such an eminent defence counsel assigned to him. After Abbas's death in 1979, a plaque was erected by Camden Borough Council in his memory at his former home at 33 Tavistock Square in Bloomsbury. It reads: *Ali Mohammed Abbas 1922-1979 Barrister and one of the founders of Pakistan lived here 1945-1979.*

Conversely, Harry Roberts had drawn the short straw with fifty-seven-year-old Justice Maude. He was old-school Establishment through and through – Old Etonian, Christ

Church Oxford, called to the bar at the Middle Temple in 1925. He was not the most progressive or liberal-minded judge to encounter: in 1948 he had voted against the suspension of the death penalty on the grounds that the 'long drop' was deeply feared by criminals.

Following his arrest, Margaret Roberts next saw her husband at the Old Bailey. She was nearly eight months pregnant when Harry Roberts was brought up to face the case against him. He was charged 'with feloniously robbing William Gaylard of approximately £1.5s.0d cash and a ring valued at £11.0s.0d, property of the said William Gaylard and two bracelets and one pearl necklace valued together at £1.10s.0d, property of Mary Millicent McDonald and at the time of such robbery did use personal violence.'

When it came to his trial and the process of law, Roberts's violent crime resulted in four separate indictments and, as is the usual custom at the start of proceedings, the clerk of the court stood and read aloud each one to the assembled courtroom.

DI Tom O'Shea was in no doubt that he had arrested the right man. But convincing a jury in court that Roberts was guilty was by no means easy. The other man who was with Roberts on the day of the robbery was never identified and Gaylard was unable to identify Roberts as one of his assailants. Most crucially, what members of the jury didn't know and would not be told was the incriminating information first given to the police by the defendant's wife, Margaret Roberts. Nor would they hear her side of the story. For although Margaret was sitting in court for all to see, as the spouse of the defendant she could not be compelled to appear in the witness box as a prosecution witness to give evidence against her husband and it was highly unlikely that anything would have induced her to do so voluntarily.

For there to be no reasonable doubt, the evidence that O'Shea and his forensic colleagues had gathered would need to be skilfully presented by the prosecution counsel and all pieced together clearly, logically and in meticulous detail.

Counsel for the Crown Richard Du Cann who, despite being just thirty years old and lean and spare in his appearance, commanded the attention of the court. He announced that he would be calling a number of witnesses, or presenting their sworn depositions: William Gaylard; Mary Millicent McDonald; Dr Mardho Bradshad Vaidya; Lawrence Henry Collins, a jeweller; Adrian Lawrence Drew, a prison officer at HMP Wormwood Scrubs; Detective Sergeant Charles Dickenson of the Police Photography Department, New Scotland Yard; Detective Inspector George Gladdish from the Fingerprint Department, New Scotland Yard; Brian John Culliford, Senior Scientific Officer, New Scotland Yard; Police Sergeant Cyril Mercer and Detective Inspector Thomas O'Shea, of 'G' Division, based at Highbury Vale police station.

The Shepherd's Bush Murders

The physical evidence comprised twelve exhibits:

1 Ring
2 Glass Decanter
3 Receipt
4 Fingerprint form
5 Four photographs of the ground floor of
  42 Burma Road
6 Piece of broken decanter
7 Photograph of a mark in blood on Exhibit 6
8 Photographic enlargements of Exhibit 7 and left
  middle finger impression on Exhibit 4.
9 Suit
10 Raincoat
11 Sample of glass
12 Sample of head hair (William Gaylard)

The connection between this diverse collection of exhibits was explained to the jury through the various statements made by witnesses. First, the gold ring stolen from William Gaylard had been traced to a jeweller's shop in Baker Street, and had been sold on 27 November 1958, the same day as the robbery. Jurors might have wondered how this rather miraculous piece of sleuthing was achieved since no explanation was given, but it can only have been possible as a result of information supplied by Margaret Roberts.

Although William Gaylard was able to identify the ring

as the one stolen from him, the manager of the jewellers, Lawrence Collins, could not identify Harry Roberts as the man who later sold it. Collins did produce a receipt for the purchase, which was presented by the prosecution as Exhibit 3.

I, E.A.Mason, 32 Lancaster Gate Terrace, WC2, do hereby declare that I am absolutely and solely possessed of the property consisting of a 18 ct gold ring now sold by me to Messrs Roberstons (London) Ltd of 108 Baker Street, W1, for the sum of £3.12s.0d and have lawful power and authority to dispose of the same, the above mentioned goods being my own property and that the said goods are not now on hire or charged or encumbered in any way or manner whatsoever.

However, when police detectives tried to trace E.A. Mason at the given address he proved to be non-existent. It was not the kind of decisive evidence the prosecution was going to have to come up with. It only established that the ring stolen from William Gaylard had ended up being sold by someone other than him on the afternoon of the attack while he was being treated at the German Hospital for the head injuries he'd suffered. But it didn't prove that the defendant, Harry Roberts, had had anything to do with it.

Adrian Lawrence Drew, Prison Officer, HMP Wormwood Scrubs was then called to the witness box and confirmed that he had taken the fingerprints of the defendant, Harry Maurice Roberts, and the fingerprint form was now Exhibit 4. This paved the way for more compelling evidence from the photographic and fingerprint specialists from Scotland Yard.

Detective Sergeant Charles Dickenson of the Photographic Department said that he had received a piece of broken decanter, Exhibit 6, from Detective Inspector Gladdish. He photographed a finger mark in blood on the glass fragment and also the left middle finger mark on the fingerprint form, Exhibit 4, and mounted them side by side for comparison, which he produced as Exhibit 8.

Detective George Gladdish, Fingerprint Branch told the court, 'I received from Dickenson the photographic enlargements, Exhibit 8, and on each of these enlargements I have marked 16 ridge characteristics which are in agreement. I have been engaged for over 23 years on the identification of persons by means of fingerprints and I have never known impressions of different fingers to agree in the sequence of ridge characteristics. From my experience I have no doubt that the mark on Exhibit 6 was made by the same finger that made the left middle finger impression on Exhibit 4.'

The case for the prosecution seemed to be gathering momentum when Senior Scientific Officer Brian John Culliford provided further forensic facts. 'On 30 January 1959 I received from Detective Inspector O'Shea a quantity of clothing including this grey suit, Exhibit 9, and fawn raincoat, Exhibit 10, and also a sample of glass, Exhibit 11, and the decanter, Exhibit 2. On 12 February I received from the same officer a sample of head hair, Exhibit 12. The left sleeve of the jacket and the back of the waistband of the trousers on Exhibit 9 and the right sleeve lapel and left front of the raincoat, Exhibit 10, were all stained with blood. I cannot tell if it is human blood or not.'

In 1959 there was no DNA testing and the bloodstains he found on clothing taken from Roberts's home could not be linked to William Gaylard. Culliford wasn't even sure that it was human blood.

Detective Inspector O'Shea was then called to give his evidence. He recounted the conversation about the 42 Burma Road robbery that took place between himself and Roberts on 28 January when Roberts was facing charges of store breaking and stealing from the warehouse of his former employer. However, conclusive as these remarks might have appeared to members of the jury, it was explained to them by the judge that these spontaneous responses made to Detective Inspector O'Shea were not sufficient proof of guilt. But for the sake of clarity and completeness, and no doubt because Richard Du Cann knew the impact they would have on the jury, O'Shea was asked to recall subsequent exchanges he'd had with Roberts.

'I asked him if he wished to make a written statement regarding the offence with which he was charged. He said, "No – not yet. Anyhow, I'll think about it and let you know."

'27 February, the defendant was charged with the offence as it now stands. He was cautioned and made no reply.'

And so it was that the prosecution case was painstakingly presented without the benefit of Margaret Roberts's evidence. The display of exhibits was worthy of an Agatha Christie novel – a decanter from the sideboard, a few strands of hair from the victim's head, a bloodstained suit and mackintosh, and a piece of broken decanter with a single finger-mark in blood. But despite what Roberts had allegedly said when he'd been arrested, there was nothing to link him to the crime except that single middle-finger mark on a fragment of glass. He was never a gambling man but he must have been hoping that the odds were in his favour. The evidence didn't prove conclusively that he was the person who'd attacked William Gaylard. There was nothing to prove he had stolen anything from him.

When the jury retired to consider their verdict after hearing directions from the judge, Harry Roberts's immediate future hung on a single item of admissible evidence. It took the jury less than an hour to reach a unanimous conclusion and when they returned the foreman announced that they found Harry Maurice Roberts Guilty of all four indictments.

At the age of twenty-two it was Roberts's fourth conviction and his second appearance at the Old Bailey. His darker side, concealed behind a grin, thoughtful manners, kindness to those he knew and comradeship with fellow soldiers, had been laid bare. It only remained for Justice John Cyril Maude to pass sentence. His comments to the neat, tidy and quiet young man standing in the dock were concise and damning. 'You, acting together with another man, brought death pretty close to this man of seventy-nine. You yourself have come close to the rope. You are a brutal man. It is to be hoped you do not appear before us again.'

In the few published accounts of Harry Roberts's violent robbery of William Gaylard it has been said that Gaylard died one year and three days after the attack on him in Burma Road. This was just two days beyond the time limit for which Roberts could have stood trial for his murder and, if found guilty, hanged. But this is untrue. Despite his ordeal and serious injuries at the hands of Harry Roberts in November 1958, William Gaylard was still alive aged 87 in 1966, and was a resident at Tooting Bec Hospital in South London. A short clip of him can be seen in an ITN documentary film entitled *Reporting '66* made in December that year.

But on 27 November 1958, Harry Maurice Roberts had been heartless, opportunistic, callous and brutal during a robbery from which he got twenty-five shillings, one gold ring – and seven years in prison.

Chapter 3

At the end of Harry Roberts's 1959 trial for the robbery of and assault on William Gaylard, Margaret watched her young husband of less than a year taken down from the dock at the Old Bailey to the cells below. It was a profoundly shattering moment. She had every reason to feel betrayed by the man who had promised so much but done so little to make their life together a success. 'It was the last time I saw him. Everything suddenly went black and I woke up in an ambulance on my way to hospital. Soon afterwards I knew I had lost my baby.'

Roberts was taken in a black prison van from the Old Bailey to HMP Pentonville on Caledonian Road, London N7. Known as 'The Ville' by those familiar with it, Pentonville Prison is a daunting fortress of a place. Behind the façade were a central hall and four radiating wings with three floors of suspended metal walkways running the length of each side and visible to prison staff in the hub. The cells measured 13 feet (4m) long, 7 feet (2m) wide and 9 feet (3m) high, each one housing two inmates sleeping in bunks and with small windows overlooking internal yards.

In his first days and weeks at The Ville, Harry Roberts was monitored and assessed so that decisions could be made about where he should serve the rest of his time in prison. The most likely destination for a prisoner sentenced to five years or more was the infamous Dartmoor jail in Devon.

With feedback from prison officers and his fellow inmates it did not take great powers of deduction for Roberts to work out where he was most probably headed. It was perhaps this bleak outlook stretching in front of him that prompted his pleasing manner and cooperative nature to resurface and improve his prospects. He behaved so well at Pentonville that after a few months his prisoner status was reclassified. The prison authorities decided that, rather than punitive incarceration, Harry Roberts should be sent to a prison that offered training and humane treatment geared towards bringing about a convicted man's rehabilitation. As a result, instead of Dartmoor Roberts was transferred to Wormwood Scrubs.

By guile or ingenuity and maybe with a bit of luck too, Roberts was given a chance to reform his ways, perhaps to emerge from jail more balanced and make something of himself away from the vicissitudes of minor crime. Gilbert Hair, the governor at Wormwood Scrubs, was regarded as a visionary, promoting rehabilitation in place of old ways of prison life where men were employed in mindless labour, suffering harsh regimes, confinement and brutality. He believed that with support, encouragement and training it was possible for a convicted criminal 'to take his freedom with courage and pursue an honest future'.

The routine and discipline under which Roberts had thrived in the army were found again in the progressive opportunities at Wormwood Scrubs. In many ways Harry Roberts had escaped *into* prison. His disjointed working life, failed marriage, lost child, broken promises, casual violence and string of petty thefts could all be left behind outside the high brick walls.

It wasn't long before he became a Blue Band trusted prisoner and began a course in bricklaying at which he worked with singular concentration. In his cell on 'D' Wing, he read books from the prison library about building and architecture. Away from the uncertainties of life as a free man, Roberts brought focus and determination to passing his City and Guilds examination, which eventually he did – top of his class. Next he signed up for a plumbing course and applied himself with the same unswerving commitment.

It would be a mistake to imagine that Roberts had been transformed miraculously into a star prisoner and had turned away from any notions of crime. Immersed in the culture of prison life and the company of criminals, the inevitable regular topics of conversation were criminal activity, past deeds and risks taken, plans to pull off 'the big one' and – of course – how to get away with it.

Roberts knew his assault on the elderly William Gaylard

would not enhance his standing with his fellow prisoners. Instead, he said that he'd been charged with GBH (grievous bodily harm) because he'd kept a brothel and had had to deal with a difficult customer.

To while away the tedium and keep fit most of the younger prisoners were keen on playing football or cricket, but Roberts had no interest in or talent for either game. On the rare days when he was persuaded to play he would act the clown, falling about and pushing other players off the ball, which amused spectators but annoyed those other players. He enjoyed being the centre of attention but disliked doing anything at which he could not shine.

Roberts played his part, or perhaps he felt he needed to play a part: the tough guy, the courageous guy, the funny guy, the clever guy, the man of action, the man other men would respect. To build the perception that he was a hard man Roberts talked of his time in Malaya, making no secret of the fact that he liked guns and was a qualified marksman. The stories he told – and he had a reputation as a good storyteller – provided some entertainment and amusement but few of the other men shared his interest in guns. Most of his fellow inmates had also been called up for National Service and had had some weapons training but, because of the increased penalties, they were not in favour of using guns when it came to crime.

The concern of the older, more experienced prisoners was not simply that using guns made a crime more grave, but that if you took a gun on a job there was always a chance you'd actually use it in the heat of the moment. Nevertheless, one or two prisoners shared Roberts's love of guns and the power they thought it gave them to intimidate victims and get what they wanted more easily and quickly. One of them was Joseph Edward Martin, a labourer who was two years older than Roberts. Martin and Roberts, like most young men, thought they knew better than the oldsters.

But in 1965 Martin would not only shoot but kill. On 18 December that year Joseph Martin, accompanied by Francis Michael O'Connell and Bernard Beatty, carried out an armed robbery at the United Dairies Depot in Wood Green, stealing £886.2s.6d. (about £12,000 in today's money) and 3,060 milk tokens. They were armed with a shotgun, a revolver and iron bars, and were wearing stocking masks when they burst into the cashier's office. As they were making their escape the alarm was set off and 51-year-old Alfred Philo, who lived on the premises, dashed across the yard to try and cut them off by closing the gates. Philo did not know the raiders were carrying guns and in the ensuing panic he was fatally shot by Martin. The gang rammed the car of a local schoolteacher as they made off in a stolen vehicle. She was later able to identify the driver when Martin and his accomplices were traced and arrested. The resulting charges and sentences at their trial in the spring of 1966 offer important comparisons when it comes to the trial in December that year of the three men arrested for the Shepherd's Bush murders.

Harry Roberts's mother regularly visited her son in Wormwood Scrubs prison. In the unusually warm summer months of 1959 he would sit with her at the edge of the cricket field and buy her tea and cakes. When he became entitled to more privileges she bought him curtains for his cell window, an expensive red rug for the cold concrete floor and a radio. With help from a fellow prisoner who was an electronics engineer Roberts devised a cunning plan to increase his popularity.

Using a sewing needle and wire pilfered from the prison workshops Roberts connected his radio to the electrical bell system designed to call a prison officer in case of emergency. The bell system linked every cell in the block and could be used as a radio relay. Roberts connected his radio output to one wire of the bell by inserting the needle into the bell push and used the metal conduit to deliver the second connection. To pick up the service other prisoners had to obtain a sewing needle, a length of wire and also a telephone earpiece from the prison workshop that was engaged in salvaging parts from old telephones. It was then a simple matter to connect the earpiece to the metal conduit and bell push on the wall of their cell. It was a neat trick and for a time the whole block could listen to the radio to pass the long hours after lock-up in the evenings.

In the company of most other men in 'D' Wing, Roberts joined in another popular pastime. He built a home-made telescope so that he could watch the windows of a nearby nurses' home. With the prison cells in darkness the nurses had no idea that they were being observed in their rooms when they were going to bed. Between the prisoners there was an agreed system of signals to indicate which windows to watch. Five knocks on the heating pipes followed by three knocks meant the fifth-floor third window.

But such anecdotes can create a false impression. Years spent in a prison are not like the romanticised depictions of men in captivity portrayed in novels and films of the time. Prisons are not populated by rough, tough, non-conformist anti-heroes who look like Stanley Baker, Sam Wannamaker, Paul Newman or Burt Lancaster. Convicted criminals are by nature antisocial, narcissistic and unrealistic. Dysfunctional behaviour and personality disorders abound.

Ex-convicts who have served long prison sentences say prison time is slow time: physical and mental horizons close in, days blur in mind-numbing routine. Incarceration can trigger paranoia, heated arguments, sudden violence and even murder over such trivial things as an accidentally spilled drink, whose turn it is to do a daily chore or just the way someone looks at you. The all-pervasive prison culture takes hold and over time it's impossible to prevent some part of the human spirit surrendering to institutionalisation.

During association periods with other prisoners, Roberts

would sometimes play cards or join the discussions. He proved a proficient player at card games like brag, whist, bridge and poker and was capable of eloquent debate, but he lacked patience. When things weren't going his way he could erupt suddenly, become aggressive and his eyes would glisten with barely suppressed violence. After such episodes Roberts could be silent for days before returning to his usual good humour and amiability and behaving as if nothing had happened.

Chapter 4

Of the faces of the six men whose lives collided in the Braybrook Street killings on Friday, 12 August 1966 that of Harry Maurice Roberts is the most publicised and notorious. It has appeared in countless TV news bulletins and on newspaper front pages over the last fifty years. By his own admission he was the instigator and prime mover of the bloodshed. As a result, except for during the first five days after the shootings before Roberts was publicly identified, the Shepherd's Bush murders have almost never been mentioned in the press or other media without the accompaniment of this photograph.

The enduring image of Roberts is a single black and white photo, a head-and-shoulder's shot. He is in his late twenties and is wearing a dark jacket and a white shirt. There is a kind of lopsided smirk on his face that gives his right eye a slight squint. The left eye looks straight into the lens of the camera with a pinprick of light in the upper part of the pupil that makes the stare penetrating. It isn't possible to make out the half-inch scar below his left eye or the small scar on his left eyelid. The nose is straight and quite small. His unusually thick eyebrows, arching high over his top eyelids, were once described as like those of the famous music-hall star George Robey. Roberts's hair is full, thick and dark, parted almost in the middle, cut quite short for the time and with a slight wave to it. Sometimes the photo is shown as a reverse mirror image, but the effect is the same. It is a picture of a young man who appears troubled, perhaps a little upset or annoyed. But it's hard to judge this photograph objectively because it's impossible to look at the image and not recall the associations that it always carries.

Harry Roberts was born, overdue and weighing 11lbs 2oz, at eight p.m. on Tuesday, 21 July 1936 in Wanstead, Essex. The medical staff at the fourteen-guinea-a-week Maycroft private nursing home were very concerned about his thirty-five-year-old mother for some time afterwards and it took several days for her to recover.

Roberts was the only child in a comfortable home. His parents, Harry Maurice (senior) and auburn-haired Irish-born Dorothy Blanch (née Harries), ran the George Hotel not far from Epping Forest, where armed police were to hunt Roberts thirty years later.

He was named after his father, an ex-Guardsman, but the dominant influence in his life was to be his mother. She said in later life that her son 'never wanted for anything'. But in 1941, at the age of five, Roberts was parted from his parents when he was evacuated to

South Wales. In that same year his parents separated, his father was called up and Harry Roberts never saw him again.

Roberts's new home was Llanbradach, a Monmouthshire mining village, ten miles north of Cardiff beyond Caerphilly, where he lived with Mr and Mrs Hopkins. Seven hundred London children escaped from the Blitz to Llanbradach. Many of their names can still be found in local authority records, but not that of Harry Roberts because, as his mother was keen to point out, her son was evacuated 'privately'.

Not that it made any difference to five-year-old Roberts. In Wales he went to the village school with everyone else. Despite the obvious trauma for a child of that age when they were separated suddenly from their parents and looked after by complete strangers, he seems to have settled in well and his school reports were good. But by now his father was becoming a distant memory and his mother saw him just on her fortnightly visits and took only a passing interest in his welfare.

Roberts lived in South Wales for four years until the war ended. At nine years old his routines and that sense of home and security so vital to children were again turned upside down when he was returned to his native London – but not to his mother and home. He was sent to a boys' boarding school in the south of England set up and run by the De Salle Order of Christian Brothers. It had a good academic, sporting and disciplinary reputation. The school's alumni include two former Lord Mayors of London, Sir William Dunn and Sir John Gilbert. The only record of Roberts's time there is a note that he was confirmed as a Roman Catholic on 15 December 1946.

When he went home in the school holidays Harry Roberts was a boy apart. His mother said they seldom 'associated locally'. Asked if she thought that her son's separation from his parents and home influence had had any effect on him she replied theatrically, 'Oh dear, no. Not at all. No. I don't think so. Not in the least.' She said he was 'work-shy' and 'mixed in the wrong company'.

Leaving aside psychological theories about how boys may be affected by the loss of a father and a consequent lack of paternal nurture in their formative years, Roberts's separation from home, evacuation to Llanbradach and time at boarding school certainly altered the trajectory of his life.

When talking about his early life Roberts said that he first became involved in crime as a child, helping his mother sell rationed and stolen goods in the thriving postwar black market, a sideline she'd developed originally as a publican who had ready access to goods and customers as both passed through her bar. Roberts's parents left Wanstead at the start of the war, moved to North London and bought a café from which Dorothy Roberts sold unlicensed rationed foods such as tea and sugar, sometimes actual ration books, and anything else that came her way.

When Roberts was thirteen he began pleading with his

mother to become a day boy at his school. Dorothy Roberts eventually gave in and agreed. The boarding fees were expensive and she considered that her son was old enough to travel back and forth across London and look after himself when she was working.

She said that she had no idea he was playing truant until she got a telephone call from the headmaster at Roberts's school asking why her son had been absent. Dorothy had also noticed that her son was regularly pilfering from her handbag. She arranged that the headmaster would call her any morning when Roberts didn't turn up for school. She made sure, too, that she didn't leave her bag lying around the flat. 'Every time my boy got into trouble and I tried to thrash things out with him, I got nowhere. I just couldn't seem to get through to him, somehow. He always knew better than anybody else. He was very clever – too clever for his own good, I used to tell him.'

At fourteen Roberts's behaviour led to him being expelled from boarding school. He then attended a London County Council school at Medburn Street, NW1. His new school was just a fifteen-minute walk from Varndale Street where he lived with his mother but this change and school life closer to home did nothing to improve the adolescent Roberts's attitude or make him behave more maturely. At the end of April 1951 he was expelled for poor conduct and left school three months before he reached fifteen, the minimum legal age for ending secondary education at the time. He had no academic qualifications.

With his mother's help Roberts found employment, earning two pounds, five shillings (£2.25) per week as a capstan lathe operator in Camden. He left of his own accord after eight months.

On 22 November 1951, now fifteen, Roberts appeared before Stanford House Juvenile Court charged with receiving stolen electrical fittings valued at £10. He was placed on probation for two years.

Just over a mile south of Roberts's home in Camden Town on Wednesday, 21 May 1952 notorious villain Billy Hill pulled off Britain's biggest post-war cash theft, known as the Eastcastle Street Robbery. It was the first of a new type of crime, meticulously planned and executed with ruthless precision and speed. The raiders sandwiched a Post Office van between two cars. The first car pulled out of a side street, causing the van to slow down, and a second car pulled up behind. The GPO driver and his two colleagues were dragged out and coshed and the van was driven away by Terry Hogan, a close friend and criminal associate of the Great Train Robber Bruce Reynolds. The Post Office vehicle was later found near Regent's Park with eighteen of the original thirty-one mailbags missing. They contained £287,000, over £7 million in today's money. The gang responsible included Billy Hill, Hogan and George 'Taters' Chatham, although at the time none of the gang was ever apprehended or prosecuted.

The nationwide publicity, unprecedented amount of money stolen and the fact that the men responsible got clean away fuelled the ambitions of many aspiring young criminals growing up in Britain's capital with its burgeoning crime rate. And no doubt such stories of daring and bravado and easy money did not escape the attention of the young Harry Roberts.

During the next two years Roberts could not hold down honest employment and by the end of the summer of 1954 his fragmented, fledgling working life had nosedived. At the age of eighteen he found himself on remand in 'A' Wing at Wormwood Scrubs and it gave him his first glimpse of prison. He later described his introduction to Wormwood Scrubs. 'It was just like you see in the old black and white films – wrought-iron railings with rows and rows of heavy locked doors. But the thing that struck me most was the silence.'

On 10 September 1954, at the Central Criminal Court, Roberts was found guilty of assault with intent to rob after he'd used an iron bar to attack a shopkeeper during a robbery. He was sentenced to nineteen months' training at Gaynes Hall borstal in Cambridgeshire. In a strange twist of fate, the borstal stood on the site of what is now HMP Littlehey from which Roberts would eventually be released sixty years later in November 2014 as one of Britain's longest-serving prisoners.

A week after leaving Gaynes Hall, on 11 January 1956 Roberts's life was suddenly transformed when he was called up for National Service. A remarkable change took place in the attitude of the alienated youth who had a record of petty criminality when he joined the Rifle Brigade, The Royal Green Jackets, at Peninsula Barracks in Winchester. Private Roberts, number 23275960, was no longer the wayward boy apart. The army provided a secure structure and a place to fit in. His former platoon corporal, Brian Woods, said of Roberts, 'He turned up with a pretty hard London crowd. But he seemed the odd man out, not really tough. Mostly he was a good soldier, a useful shot with a rifle and Bren.'

Roberts was assigned to 5 Platoon, B Company, and qualified as a marksman. He was quickly promoted to corporal and served in Kenya during the Mau Mau Uprising and then in the Far East, in the Malayan Emergency. He returned to Britain at the beginning of 1958.

He claimed that the army taught him to kill and that he personally had killed at least four men. However, when his ex-army colleague Len Hardy, who had served in the Malayan jungle with Roberts, was asked, 'Did he in fact ever kill a terrorist?' Hardy simply replied dismissively, 'No.' And in army records there is nothing to show that Corporal Harry Maurice Roberts ever had to fire a gun in action.

Roberts allegedly told people that he reached the rank of sergeant but his army discharge papers tell a different story and refer to him as Corporal Roberts. Under the heading Military Offences they state that he was, 'severely reprimanded and forfeited 35 days' pay by Royal Warrant by the Commanding Officer on 21 February 1958 for being absent without leave from 16 Jan to 20 February.'

Despite this misdemeanour, at the end of his time in the army Roberts's military conduct is described as 'very good' and his discharge testimonial is surprising when viewed in retrospect.

Corporal Roberts has thoroughly deserved his two stripes. Above average intelligence, he has worked consistently well engaged in jungle operations. He is reliable and trustworthy. For a considerable period, he was in charge of the Company Tracker teams. He is a marksman on the BREN – could be a reasonable instructor if he attended a Methods of Instruction Course. Recommended as an infantry section Commander. Corporal Roberts is hardworking and conscientious. He is perfectly capable of working without supervision. He is loyal and has a pleasing manner. Strongly recommended to his future employer.

Aged twenty-one, Roberts left the army in March 1958 and went back to live with his mother at Kendal House, North London.

'I've been told to shoot or be shot, Mum, in Malaya. I've been told that. But you didn't know there was a war on, Mother,' her son told his mother as she later recalled in a press interview.

'No, I didn't,' was her response.

'We went out for training, as far as this country is concerned, Mum, for training, to shoot or be shot. It's a lovely country, but shooting or being shot is a terrible thing.'

Shortly before his army discharge, Roberts met a blonde, diminutive – four foot, ten inches – 22-year-old Nottingham girl, Margaret (Margo) Rose Crooks at a party in Chelsea. At the time Margo had a job behind the bar at the Shamrock Club in Whitechapel. The couple married just six weeks later at St Pancras Registry Office. The witnesses were Mr and Mrs Colin Howard, the only people other than his mother that Roberts remained in contact with for any length of time.

Now a married man, Roberts began working as a van driver, with a weekly wage of £7.14s.1d for Wright & Co (Kings Cross) Ltd on the Caledonian Road, North London. It was a job, true, but not one worthy of his abilities. It was unfulfilling and menial work after the adventure and responsibilities of his National Service time and the glowing endorsement that the army had given him.

The couple began their life together in his mother's flat. Years later, asked if she was happy about the marriage Dorothy Roberts replied 'No', paused for a moment and said 'No' again, quietly.

'Was it because you were very possessive of your son?' the interviewer suggests.

'Oh dear, no,' she says indignantly. 'Not at all.'

Margaret Roberts's memory of the situation is different.

The two women in Roberts's life never got along. Margaret said that her husband was dominated by his mother.

When she met her future husband he was 'handsome, very smart, very smartly dressed and a very kind nature, very kind. He made a woman feel like a woman.' She recalled the jungle stories that he told her in those early days in which there is a recurrent theme. 'He had to fight, sort of kill or be killed. And I know that at the time he was in the thick of it. I know he killed people then, but he was in a war then, when he came home he told me that he'd had to kill in the jungle, or be killed. When he finished his service, he was proud that he'd been in the army. But at the time I wouldn't have thought that he'd have killed otherwise.'

The kill-or-be-killed words echo her mother-in-law Dorothy Roberts's remarks about what her son had told her about his time in Malaya. But that was all Dorothy and Margaret Roberts had in common. The tightly wound triangle of mother, son and newly-wed daughter-in-law in the pressure cooker of Dorothy Roberts's small Camden Town flat was not an easy or happy one. By the end of the year, with Margaret five months pregnant, Harry Roberts was in trouble again; this time his robbery of and vicious assault on the elderly William Gaylard was more serious and it gave him his first real taste of prison.

Chapter 5

The restless, changing nature of the late 1950s and early 1960s had little influence on the hermetically sealed microcosm of life at Wormwood Scrubs where men were insulated from everyday challenges, wider interests, and participation in the outside world and its concerns. To some degree this may explain why, while many young men in Britain were feeling optimistic about their future and were inspired to reach for something better, Roberts's view remained inward-looking, short-term and limited.

As the years slipped by Roberts was transferred to HMP Maidstone and then to Horfield prison in Bristol. In March 1963 he was selected for a hostel scheme that allowed him to live outside the prison as a trustee and go to work.

Roberts was found a job as a bricklayer for the building firm George Wimpey and Co. Ltd. The condition of his day release was that he had to return to the hostel by 10:45 p.m. For some men the temptations of the scheme were too great and they came back drunk, broke other rules or simply disappeared. But Roberts didn't waver and, besides, he was never a big drinker. At the weekends he'd have a few pints at the local pub, the 'Vic' in Gloucester Road, ten minutes' walk from Horfield prison. It was here that he fell into conversation with Lilian, the estranged wife of a former local policeman, forty-year-old Anthony Frederick Perry. She lived fifteen minutes' walk away in the other direction at 63 Filton Grove.

Four years and eight months after his sentences of eighteen months for attempted store breaking, three months for theft from his employer's warehouse, plus the longer stretch of seven years for the robbery of and assault on William Gaylard, Harry Roberts, now twenty-seven years old, was released in November 1963, having earned full remission.

Roberts took lodgings at Lilian Perry's terraced house in Filton Grove. He progressed to another job for Wimpey at a building site in Weston-super-Mare, Somerset, where he worked for six months. He proved conscientious. Workmates who were later interviewed by the police and press, said he drove himself to the limit to earn as much overtime and bonus money as he could, taking home as much as £70 a week.

Qualities of character that had been noted by the army in his discharge papers as '. . . *hardworking and conscientious. . . perfectly capable of working without supervision . . . loyal and has a pleasing manner*' were in evidence once again and impressed his new employers. Roberts was promoted to chargehand with a basic wage of over £40 a week.

Harry Maurice Roberts was on a roll and appeared to be living proof that his visionary governor at Wormwood Scrubs, Gilbert Hair, was right. Training, humane treatment, support and encouragement could bring about complete rehabilitation.

And it was almost as if Harry Roberts was trying to prove his old guv'nor's theories correct, perhaps prove something to himself too. He was making more money than he'd done in his life and a good deal more than he'd ever made from petty crime.

His friendship with his landlady, Lilly, developed and a close bond grew between them. She recalled, 'He was a deeply lonely man and wanted me to go everywhere with him; even if he just wanted to take his car to the garage to fill it up, I had to go with him. It seemed he couldn't bear to do anything alone. If he was working late on the building site I would take his tea over to him, and then he would insist on me staying there until he had finished his work.'

Mrs Lilian Perry was a plain-looking woman, eleven years older than Roberts, but with her quiet Bristol accent, even temperament and down-to-earth common sense she provided the solidity, understanding and home comforts that he craved. In return she won his loyalty, trust and support. 'He used to come home from work, throw his pay packet on the table and say, "Have what you want and save the rest." There was often more than £40 in the packet.'

But there was a key element missing in the relationship between Harry Roberts and Lilly Perry, a lack that was more surprising. 'He was happy with me, I think. There was no sex between us. I'm sexless and Robbie didn't like it either.'

He could afford things for the first time and bought a black second-hand 1956 Daimler car for £650. When Perry's daughter Jean got married to her fiancé Lorne Richardson, Roberts drove her to the church; the Daimler was decorated with white ribbon and Roberts wore a borrowed chauffeur's cap.

Jean's recollections of him are at odds with the dark side of Harry Roberts, the one given to grim moods and sudden violence. 'I got on very well with him. There was no reason to dislike him.' She said he was quiet and liked to watch television a lot. Her husband Lorne added, 'He also liked making Airfix kits, model aeroplanes and boats and things like that . . . he was very good at it, actually. A number of them he sent to a children's place to be raffled.'

People who knew Roberts at that time talk of his kindness, thoughtfulness and generosity, an impression confirmed by his neighbour Frederick Holland who recalled: 'Roberts was a good neighbour when he lived next door. I lent him my car when his own broke down. He returned it to me each weekend with the tank full to the brim. When his own car came back he wanted to pay me hire money. I refused so he ran it down to a local garage and had two new tyres fitted.'

At work Roberts had ideas and ambitions. For the first time he was looking further ahead. In March 1965 he left his job with Wimpey, bought a yellow Ford Escort van, and set up as a subcontractor for Wimpey under the name Western Contractors Ltd, employing half a dozen men. The men who worked for him later said that Harry Roberts was a good boss and again the word generous was used. He'd never send the men home unpaid even if there wasn't enough work for all of them. He worked hard, harder than any of his men, and spent freely too.

Roberts's small business was prospering. On one job he cleared over £1,800 profit in six months – over £25,000 in today's money. He and Lilly Perry would eat out in expensive restaurants and go on weekend trips. They went to John O'Groats and back over one Bank Holiday, and Roberts was back in good time to start work on Tuesday.

However, while Roberts's business was doing well there were problems brewing in the wider British economy. Government measures to limit borrowing, popularly referred to as the 'credit squeeze', a wage freeze, and problems with the balance of payments all contributed to the creation of uncertain economic times that were to prove decisive in the fortunes of Harry Roberts and his bid to go straight and run his modest legitimate business.

Towards the end of 1965 the poorly performing economy was making things increasingly difficult for British business and for working people. Through lack of experience and foresight, poor management and failure to focus, Roberts and his subcontracting bricklaying business began to run into financial difficulties. The men whom Roberts employed noticed he was going on unexplained trips to London. There was still work to be found but the business was being neglected. Now Roberts wasn't making money, he was losing it.

Finally, in March 1966 he disappeared from Bristol, taking Lilly Perry with him and leaving behind several hire-purchase debts as well as a sizeable overdraft at a Bristol bank.

Harry Roberts and Lilly Perry turned up in his prized Daimler at the home of his only long-time friends, Colin and June Howard, who had a rented two-bedroom flat in leafy Maida Vale. In exchange for lodgings Lilly said she'd help look after the Howards' three children, Samantha, Barry and Paul. With June recently out of Springfield mental-health hospital where she'd been treated for a nervous breakdown and Colin Howard in prison at Wormwood Scrubs, Roberts offered to provide some much-needed income and do some odd jobs around the flat.

With Lilly Perry busy, Roberts went out and about in search of work. But he hadn't only abandoned his debts and subcontracting business in Bristol. Despite his early success, he had also given up the idea of making a living from bricklaying and the building trade. By day he hung around the pubs of the Portobello Road area and met up with an old acquaintance, thirty-six-year-old Jack Witney. And Roberts began to imagine that with a gun in his pocket he could make an easier living from the proceeds of crime.

'He just said he was fed up with work,' Lilly Perry said. 'He said he'd had enough, there's no prospects in it and he had no more interest in it.'

Despite no real lack of opportunity or ability, Roberts had fallen victim to the age-old mindset of most criminals. Things had conspired against him, life was unfair and if he couldn't earn what he wanted honestly, he'd take it at the expense of others.

Roberts went to Soho, to old haunts and bad company, trying to dream up some kind of a plan. He bought three guns and some ammunition in Shaftesbury Avenue for £90 from a thirty-year-old Greek Cypriot called Christos Costas. But the guns didn't enhance his reputation or his prospects of a criminal career.

In a 1966 ITN interview an anonymous member of the London underworld who claimed to have met Roberts expressed his opinion of him at that time. 'He was always boasting about guns because of his army career and that. Well, he was an on-and-off sort of chap.' The interviewee went on to say that one minute Roberts would be laughing and joking and the next he would become ambivalent and shut himself up. 'Not a person you could really take to, or trust.'

'What was Roberts's reputation as a criminal?' the interviewer asks.

'As a criminal? None, I shouldn't think,' was the curt reply.

These observations are in marked contrast to those of others who'd known Harry Roberts in Bristol after his release from Horfield prison and when everything was going so well.

In London Roberts attempted to get recruited to a gang who were planning a bullion raid. When they met in a café south of the river in the Elephant and Castle area, Roberts was dismissed as a 'nutcase' because of his enthusiasm for guns.

He met another South London criminal in a club in Regent Street who went by the name of Frank. Roberts told him of a robbery he had in mind, of a Securicor van outside a bank in Whiteladies Road, Bristol. The prize would be worth many thousands of pounds, Roberts assured him. But after driving to Bristol to look at where the raid was to take place and hearing Roberts's talk of firearms Frank was not sold on the idea and declined the invitation.

Lilly Perry had her own views about Roberts's reasons for buying guns. 'I think he felt he'd like to own some. Of course, he had them quite some time as you know before this happened. But it was just a thing, like boys liking cars. He did say once, they may be a good frightener. If they don't believe us, or don't believe me that they're real, perhaps they'll think otherwise if perhaps there was a wild shot fired, I don't know. But I don't think he ever intended to use them at all.'

Chapter 6

In his search for some kind of criminal venture Roberts began associating more closely with Jack Witney. He held Witney in some regard as a villain although Witney's criminal exploits had never amounted to much and simply helped subsidise his modest earnings from honest employment. In the early part of 1966 Roberts's Daimler car was often parked outside Witney's in Fernhead Road, much to the dismay, of Witney's wife. Mrs Lillian Witney was not happy about the conversations she overheard and even threatened to leave her husband if he continued to hang around with Roberts. 'I began to fear those visits. I couldn't understand why Rob, if he had this good business down in Bristol, kept coming up to London to see Jack. I was frightened for Jack. Sometimes when Roberts's Daimler drew up I would pull the curtains across and tell him Jack wasn't home.'

But the fact was that Roberts and Witney got along well. Like Roberts's, Jack Witney's family life was fragmented: his childhood had been unrooted and itinerant. Step by step a pattern emerged of him lurching inadvertently from one thing to another with no long-term aim or ambition, a hand-to-mouth rhythm of failure and petty crime. However, unlike that of Harry Roberts, Witney's biography contains no darker undercurrents, hidden contradictions or history of violence. And that puts Witney at odds with the event that would ultimately define him and be indelibly etched in his epitaph.

Six years older than Roberts, Witney was born in Notting Hill on Wednesday, 14 May 1930. He was an only child and his parents separated when he was very young. His mother, for whom he claimed to have great affection, suffered prolonged periods of illness and Witney said that he was brought up largely by his maternal grandmother and maternal aunts. Between 1939-45 he lived 'somewhat unhappily' at various temporary foster homes as a result of the wartime evacuation of children from London. And then, just as the war was coming to an end in 1945 his mother, who had been suffering from pulmonary tuberculosis for many years, died, aged thirty-four.

At the time, fifteen-year-old Jack Witney was in a London County Council boarding school in Hertfordshire where he was a good scholar – he still had a nicely bound copy of *David Copperfield* that he had received as a prize. He sat for scholarships to a number of schools and was successful on each occasion although, by his own admission, he failed to take advantage of his opportunities.

Following his mother's death Witney drifted between the home of his father, with whom he had only a shallow relationship, and those of other relatives. After leaving school Witney did various jobs – the longest one lasted eighteen months – until he joined the army in November 1947.

Unlike Roberts, Private Jack Witney, number 21181345, of The Corps of Royal Electrical and Mechanical Engineers (REME), was not a natural or successful soldier. Witney's army service is peppered with offences. Eighteen months after he enlisted, Witney was Absent Without Leave after being charged for 'loss of kit by neglect to the value of £6.9s.8½d'. A month later he was declared illegally absent by a Court of Inquiry held at Bordon in Hampshire. Witney was finally apprehended by civil police on 4 August 1949 and after a Court Martial hearing at Aldershot he was sentenced to 84 days' detention and sent to Military Corrective Training at Colchester on 5 September 1949.

After Witney was released twenty-eight days later he immediately absconded again. Over the next two years his army service was like an Ealing Comedy. He kept getting caught and then escaping at the first opportunity. Finally either Witney's evasion technique became honed to perfection or the army simply gave up searching for him.

The next time Jack Witney was arrested was by West London police for 'possessing housebreaking implements by night'. After receiving two years' probation he stayed out of trouble until January 1957 when he was arrested for 'attempting to take and drive away a motor vehicle without consent'. The week after that Witney was in the dock again at Willesden Magistrates' Court for breaching his probation and was given the option of a forty-shilling fine or a month in prison. Being broke he had no choice but to opt for the latter.

The crunch point came twelve days later when Witney was in court again for a litany of petty thefts. The grand total of his sentences was two years and three months' imprisonment.

Witney was released after serving only sixteen months in May 1958 and later that year he married Lillian Florence, who seemed to have taken him in hand and kept him out of trouble, or at least out of prison

There is no discoverable explanation why it was that, despite having been arrested by the police and appearing four times in London courts between 1954 and 1957, listed under his full name, correct date of birth and including a known alias (Derek Kennedy), John Edward Witney's whereabouts remained a mystery to the army.

By the summer of 1966 Jack Witney had been on the run as a deserter for fifteen years.

Witney's wife, fifty-three-year-old Lillian, was seventeen years older than him. By the time they married in 1958 she'd been married twice before and had had four children, two by each of the previous marriages. In 1966 Jack and Lillian Witney's ground-floor flat at 10 Fernhead Road, London W9 was a ten-minute walk from Wymering

Mansions where Roberts and Lilly Perry were staying at the home of Colin and June Howard.

Witney had most recently been working as a lorry driver for Scudders of Western Avenue, but in late June 1966 he left the job. The reason for him leaving is unknown, although, as becomes significant later in the story, he had regularly been doing illicit deals off the back of his lorry. Witney had no other prospects of gainful employment and he hadn't told his wife that he was out of work. With a family to support, the loss of income should have been a worry but it seems Witney was earning, or hoped to earn, enough money from crime not to be worried about legitimate work.

Roberts later said that he and Witney were doing 'dozens of jobs'. Rent collectors were easy quarry. Bookmakers carried substantial amounts of cash, too. Post Office and bank raids were common and security was lax. Another popular target in the crime-ridden capital at the time was wage snatches. Many workers were paid in cash by their employers which meant that on paydays cash had to be collected from the bank and transported back to firms' cashiers to make up the weekly wage packets.

But the hauls from the sort of smash-and-grab crimes that Roberts and Witney planned – and it is debatable how many they actually pulled off – were never big, a few hundred, possibly approaching a thousand pounds or so at most. The takings were scarcely going to make them wealthy and they were both intelligent enough to know that. Then there was always the chance of being caught and if they assaulted their victims or were carrying guns the likely risks and penalties would not be worth the possible financial gains.

Splitting the relatively modest proceeds two ways made the income slim enough and so it is strange that Witney and Roberts decided to recruit another man. In a club called Le Monde, Roberts's friend and landlady, June Howard, introduced them to a Scotsman called John Duddy. Duddy later said that he had previously come across Witney in January 1966 when he'd been a driver for Scudders.

The steps in John Duddy's life that took him to Braybrook Street on the afternoon of 12 August 1966 are not marked by an unhappy family background, a disrupted childhood and various dysfunctional relationships. In many ways it's harder to see why he ended up taking the life of a police officer: he was himself the son of a policeman, was a married man with four children and had once been a valued soldier with achievements to his name. Nonetheless, he slipped into the abyss.

Duddy was born in the Gorbals district of Glasgow on Thursday, 27 December 1928, the sixth child in a family of eleven. His father had been a Glasgow city policeman and, by Duddy's account, a strict no-nonsense Catholic. He 'leathered' Duddy and his other sons if 'they did wrong'. John Duddy had six brothers and four sisters; one sister had died aged twenty-one from meningitis. From the age of five to fourteen he went to school in Glasgow where he was an average scholar and he claimed that he never liked school. In 1942, at the age of thirteen, Duddy appeared before a juvenile court for stealing a bicycle.

When Duddy left school with no qualifications he got a job as a porter in a Glasgow hotel, left six months later and was then apprenticed as a painter and decorator. Despite the punishment and disapprobation meted out by his father, three years after his first appearance John Duddy was in front of the juvenile court for a second time early in 1945 for breaking into a warehouse and this time he was sent to borstal for two years.

When he was released Duddy said that he'd been taught a lesson but six months later he stole again and was sent to prison for three months. It took two more appearances in court in May 1948 and two more prison sentences of another three months and six months before the lesson seems finally to have struck home. He remained out of trouble following his release later that year and had no further convictions over the next eighteen years until in 1966 when he was arrested for murder.

On 28 May 1949 Duddy married Teresa Ann at St Luke's Roman Catholic Church, Ballater Street, Glasgow. They then moved to London and lived in lodgings at Clarendon Crescent, Paddington. They were there for a year and shortly after their first child Linda was born the family returned to Scotland and lived with Teresa's mother at 279 Thistle Road, Glasgow. They had a second daughter, Bernadette.

In 1952 at the age of twenty-three Duddy enlisted in the army on a regular engagement. Like Harry Roberts the army suited him. Duddy now had security, purpose and a change of heart. He was posted to Malaya and after a year his wife and daughters joined him. The family lived in Malaya for two years and during that time had a third daughter, Maureen.

Duddy spent three and a half years of his service in Malaya where he saw some action before returning to the UK. After his mother died in 1955 at the age of fifty-six of coronary thrombosis, Duddy was posted to London. The family lived at 4 Wheatstone Road, London W10 until he left the army only to be recalled six months later during the Suez Crisis. He served a further seven months. In total Duddy served seven years as a regular soldier and a further five years in the reserve. He had a number of jobs in the London area as a driver before the family returned once again to Glasgow in 1961.

After a fourth daughter, Yvonne, was born, the family moved back to London in 1963 to a flat at the newly built Treverton Towers off Ladbroke Grove, London W10, a few yards south of the main railway line to Paddington. He was living there with his wife and daughters when he fell in with Roberts and Witney

Thirty-seven-year-old Duddy was 5ft 5in tall, slightly overweight, with a fresh complexion, light brown hair, blue eyes, a tattoo on his right forearm and scars on the top of his right forefinger and both knees. In June 1966 he had an accident while driving a lorry when the brakes failed. The impact threw him through the windscreen and he sustained a head injury that needed hospital treatment. Since recovering he had felt too nervous to drive again, had remained unemployed and had started to drink heavily.

Roberts and Duddy had their time spent in Malaya in common. With Duddy's extensive army service he was as familiar with guns as Roberts was. But with no real criminal experience he was less concerned than others had been about Roberts's talk of carrying illegal firearms to commit crime.

When June Howard found out that Roberts had acquired guns she warned him that he would get fifteen years if he was caught with them. The remark was no doubt meant to discourage Roberts from having his guns in her flat when there were children around. Roberts chose to ignore her at the time but her warning would stay with him, ticking away in the back of his mind like a time bomb, and a few weeks later it would trigger disaster.

Chapter 7

It was just another day in the life of the Wombwell family. Shortly after 7:15 a.m. on 12 August 1966 at Eastfield Court, East Acton Lane, London W3, twenty-five-year-old David Wombwell kissed his wife Gillian and their two young children – Daen and Melanie – and left home for work. He lived fifteen minutes' drive in his green VW Beetle from Shepherd's Bush Police Station.

After saying goodbye to his wife Marjory and their three children – Ann (17), Paul (16) and Mandy (2) – forty-one-year-old Geoffrey Fox left his home at 1 Radcliffe Way, Yeading Lane, Northholt, to drive for forty minutes to Shepherd's Bush through the Friday-morning rush hour.

Around 7:30 a.m., thirty-year-old bachelor Christopher Head left his police accommodation at Ravenscourt House, 3 Paddenswick Road, London W6 and began a routine twenty-minute walk to work, a distance of just over a mile.

At eight a.m. at Shepherd's Bush police station,

57

Detective Sergeant Chris Head, Temporary Detective Constable David Wombwell and Police Constable Geoff Fox reported for their shift. All three officers were in plain clothes and had been working together since the beginning of July. They were the first of two crews assigned to patrol the streets of 'F' Division that day in an unmarked blue Triumph 2000 whose radio call-sign was Foxtrot One-One. The early shift was from nine a.m. to five p.m. when a second crew took over and worked from six p.m. until two a.m. the following morning.

Jack Witney's alarm went off as usual at seven a.m. He made himself a cup of tea, called goodbye to his wife Lillian and left his ground-floor flat at 10 Fernhead Road, London W9 for work at around seven-thirty. Lillian was under the impression that her husband was working for the windscreen company Triplex. But the truth was that Witney had left his last job at the end of June and hadn't told his wife he was unemployed.

In Flat 41 on the eighth floor of Treverton Tower, off Ladbroke Grove, London W10, John Duddy's sixteen-year-old daughter Linda was getting ready for work when someone came to the front door a few minutes after eight a.m. Her mother had left the family home two and a half weeks earlier after a row with Linda's father. She'd taken Linda's younger sisters, thirteen-year-old Maureen and four-year-old Yvonne, with her. They hadn't heard from her since.

Linda heard a man's voice which she recognised as that of a friend of her father called Jack. As she was leaving home with her younger sister, fifteen-year-old Bernadette, at around 8:30 a.m, Linda heard her father talking to someone in the living room. She was late for work and the door was closed so she didn't go into the room or say goodbye. She somehow thought there were two men with her father, Jack and another man she knew as Rob, although she only heard her father's voice. Linda, who worked as a telex operator and Bernadette, who was a filing clerk, left the block of flats by the back entrance so they couldn't say whether the old blue car she'd seen Jack driving was parked outside or whether it was the black Daimler that belonged to Rob.

Harry Roberts had a cup of tea and some toast and left June Howard's flat where he was staying in Wymering Mansions, Maida Vale at around eight-thirty 8:30 a.m.

Roberts, Duddy and Witney's work for the day was to steal a car. Roberts later said they intended to steal three cars, two Jags and a Ford Executive. But if, as he recounted, the reason for stealing cars was for a robbery on an engineering works in Northolt that they were planning, it is curious why the three men should need three cars for the job. In the records there's no mention of additional accomplices and Duddy had become fearful of driving – he hadn't driven since the accident in a lorry two months earlier. The other known fact is that Witney had had only one set of false number plates made up.

They were found in his car later that day and he intended to use them to disguise the vehicle that they planned to steal.

This anomaly is an example of the kind of discrepancy that inevitably arises between what participants in a crime later say and what the verifiable evidence indicates. At the best of times human memory has a way of constructing unreliable narratives. When it comes to recollections and statements made by criminals about their past exploits their versions are further influenced by the need to tell a good story to enhance their reputation, downplay their mistakes and make their actions sound clever, glamorous or even admirable.

By whatever means Duddy, Witney and Roberts certainly ended up in Witney's scruffy blue 1954 Vanguard estate car, its exhaust pipe held on by a loop of wire, and set off in search of their quarry. It was not the most inconspicuous vehicle for three men to drive around London in during broad daylight, hoping to steal cars unnoticed. According to Roberts they went first to Regent's Park to cruise around the Outer Circle. They knew from previous experience that commuters left their cars parked there all day and wouldn't notice them missing until after five p.m.

At nine o'clock that morning David Wombwell made the first entry in pencil on the right-hand page of the Q-car's RT (radio transmission) logbook: *ET ON WATCH 09.00 hrs. Driver PC 107F Fox. Observer DS Head. Operator T/DC Wombwell,* and signed his name in the next column. The Q-car crew's first task of the day was to take their guv'nor, Detective Inspector Kenneth Coote, head of the CID at Shepherd's Bush, to Marylebone Magistrates Court. DI Coote was due to appear as a prosecution witness in the latest case in a spate of attempted and successful escapes from Wormwood Scrubs prison. Two months earlier in June, five men had scaled the high walls and in the boot of the Q-car Coote had the incriminating evidence, including ropes and steel grappling hooks that had been the means of their escape.

With PC Fox at the wheel, T/DC Wombwell in the passenger seat beside him and Detective Constable Head and DI Coote in the back seats, they pulled out of the yard at the rear of Shepherd's Bush police station into Stanlake Villas. And a few seconds later the occupants and their unmarked Triumph 2000 Q-car were indistinguishable in the busy traffic streaming along Uxbridge Road.

The term 'Q-car' used by the Metropolitan Police was adopted in 1934 from the code name for the 'Q' ships that operated during the First World War, tracking down German U-boats while disguised as innocent fishing smacks or merchant ships.

After dropping DI Coote at Marylebone Magistrates' Court the Q-car was free to patrol the area of 'F' Division. The territory included Hammersmith and Fulham as far south as the river Thames, Shepherd's Bush in the centre, up to the A404 (Harrow Road) in the north and Acton to the west. Their brief was simply to keep their eyes open and from their unmarked police car spot anyone or anything that looked suspicious and then intervene if necessary.

The morning was routine and uneventful as far as they were concerned, apart from one incident that for some reason was not recorded in the Q-car logbook but was later recalled by Police Constable Dick (Taff) Bowen. Bowen was driving police patrol car Foxtrot Two, covering the area of Hammersmith and West Kensington, when he heard an R/T from the Scotland Yard Information Room. The message broadcast was that Foxtrot One-One was requesting urgent assistance at a scrap-metal dealer's yard in Scrubs Lane NW10. According to Bowen, when he arrived Fox was emerging from the yard. He waved and called, 'It's OK now, Taff – thanks, mate.' Bowen resumed his patrol and never did discover what the problem was. And those few brief words and inconsequential encounter was the last time he spoke to or saw Geoffrey Fox.

After parking the Q-car in the rear yard of the police station the crew reported to the duty CID officer in charge to say they were going to lunch. Wombwell, Head and Fox then walked east along Uxbridge Road towards Shepherd's Bush Green and the Beaumont Arms pub on the corner of Wood Lane where they lunched most days when working the nine-to-five shift. They were greeted by landlord Fred Brounfield and his wife Joyce, gave their orders and sat down to discuss the important business of Chelsea football team's prospects in the League Division One away match against West Ham the following Saturday (which Chelsea won 2-1). Chris Head was a devoted Chelsea fan, remembered by his colleagues in a tribute that hangs on the walls of the Braybrook Suite at Hammersmith police station: *a thick and thin supporter . . . Whenever his duties would spare him he followed Chelsea come fine weather or foul, not only to the four corners of this country but also abroad.*

Down the side of Marylebone station at Hills Patents Ltd, at around 12:30 p.m., twenty-one-year-old Christine Swanston attended to a customer who came to the first-floor enquiries office. She spoke to the man through a small hatch and he handed her a piece of paper with *Brook Green Motors, 47 Blythe Road, W14*, stamped on it. It was an order that had been taken over the telephone at 4:55 p.m. the previous day to supply a set of car number plates, registration JJJ 285D.

Ms Swanston asked the man if he was paying cash and he simply replied, 'Yes.'

She attached the order to a pre-prepared invoice and made out a receipt for £1.14s.9d.

The false number plates that Jack Witney had had

made up and had then collected from Hills Patents Ltd were a clone of the registration number of a dark blue 1966 Ford Corsair.

Shortly after one p.m. Duddy, Witney and Roberts finally spotted the type of Ford they were after in Harrow, parked down a side street next to the Tube station. Roberts and Witney both got out of the Vanguard but Jack Witney was the one with the car-stealing skills. He inserted a piece of wire into the lock of the Ford and jiggled it around. Before his nimble fingers could trip the tumblers the wire broke off and stuck in the lock. Roberts was exasperated and stormed back to the Vanguard. Witney followed, got into the driver's seat and the three men decided to leave the car and go in search of another one. As Roberts recalled, 'The morning was gone and we had not done a thing. So we decided to go to the pub and have some lunch.'

After their lunch at the Beaumont Arms, Head, Wombwell and Fox walked back to Shepherd's Bush police station. Chris Head had a conversation with duty sergeant Ken Law and asked him to arrange Geoff Fox's duties so that he could remain with them for the next month. In addition to the nine-to-five Q-car shift, the officers had a growing list of admin and past cases requiring attention. There were messages to respond to, forms to fill, statements to be written, correspondence to be dealt with, telephone calls to be made and in the pre-mobile phone and pre-computer age of 1966 it all had to be done on a typewriter and from a landline at the police station.

Meanwhile, Roberts, Duddy and Witney were lunching at the Clay Pigeon public house on the corner of Whitby Road and Field End Road, Eastcote. (In the evenings during the 1960s the pub was a popular rock-music venue.)

Shortly before two o'clock the Q-car crew turned out of the police-station yard with Head in the radio operator's front passenger seat and Wombwell sitting in the back. At three minutes to two Head reported to the Scotland Yard Information Room that they were back on patrol. Geoff Fox pulled out into Uxbridge Road, heading east, and once again the blue Triumph 2000 Q-car merged anonymously into the traffic.

Fox turned the Q-car left along Wood Lane. A minute or so later they passed the BBC Television Centre and beyond it White City Stadium. In a few hours the area would come alive with greyhound-racing crowds that invariably included the kinds of men in whom the police took an interest. But by day the sixty-year-old stadium, built in 1908 for the Olympic Games, was more or less deserted, showing signs of age and lack of income.

After pints of bitter over lunch and a game of darts at the Clay Pigeon, Witney, Duddy and Roberts got back into the Vanguard. Still on the lookout for a Ford to steal they drove south-east down Harrow Road towards Central London. Duddy was in the back seat and between Witney and Roberts in the front was a brown canvas bag. It contained some overalls and three guns belonging to Roberts: a .38 Enfield revolver, a nickel-plated .38 Colt Special and a 9mm Luger P08.

Chapter 8

Harry Roberts's motley collection of old handguns had been picked up on the London black market so he'd had to take what he could find. But as it turned out it was an interesting selection with some vital distinctions when it came to using them in the course of a crime.

From a firearms expert's perspective the least glamorous was the .38 Enfield ex-British Army service revolver made in 1939. More exotic was the nickel-plated Colt .38 Special made sometime in the 1930s. The third gun was an iconic German weapon: the more powerful recoil-operated semi-automatic 9mm Luger P08 made by Mauser. First patented by Georg J. Luger in 1898 this design is more mechanically complex than that of a revolver (first patented by Samuel Colt in 1836) and therefore more prone to malfunction when its parts become worn or dirty. The Luger that Roberts purchased was made in 1918.

Whether or not Roberts knew anything about the guns he bought, there was another significant detail which he either didn't know about or chose to ignore. The .38 Colt

Special and .38 Enfield are revolvers. After each round is fired the empty cartridge case remains in its chamber in the cylinder. The Luger's ammunition, though, is fed into the firing chamber from an eight-round spring-loaded clip housed in the pistol grip. When a shot is fired the empty cartridge case is automatically ejected from the top of the chamber.

This crucial difference is of little importance on a battlefield and when the gun is used legitimately. However, if the Luger is used during a crime, unless the criminal has time to gather up all the expelled cartridge cases they will be left strewn around the crime scene, marking the spot where the gun was fired. It is therefore a simple matter for a forensics team to map out how many shots were fired from a Luger and where the shooter was positioned in relation to a victim, thus providing investigators with key movement details.

When two or more suspects are involved in a crime, firing more than one gun, empty cartridge cases from an automatic will not show only where the gun was fired but, when cross-referenced with other shots and witness statements, will also help to identify who pulled the trigger.

By three o'clock on the afternoon of 12 August 1966, Head, Fox and Wombwell have pulled over in their Q-car to question a man in East Acton who is pushing a bicycle along the pavement. While Head and Wombwell are out of the car Fox receives an R/T from Shepherd's

Bush police station asking them to telephone Detective Inspector Kenneth Coote at Marylebone Magistrates' Court. When Head returns Fox passes on the message from their guv'nor and at 3:10 p.m. Chris Head speaks to Coote from a phone box. Coote has finished at court for the day and Head says they will pick him up, along with several heavy bags of exhibits, within the next twenty to thirty minutes.

Back in familiar territory, Witney turns right off Harrow Road and heads south along the A4000 over the railway lines at Willesden Junction. All the time Roberts in the front passenger seat and Duddy in the back are scanning for the elusive Ford Corsair that they want to steal. The tatty old Vanguard, its exhaust pipe blowing and rattling over every bump, continues down Old Oak Lane and after crossing the Grand Union Canal turns left along Old Oak Common Lane.

In the balmy heat of the afternoon and after pints of ale at the Clay Pigeon pub the gang's wits are less sharp than they were before lunch. Since becoming unemployed Duddy has been drinking heavily. What with his wife having walked out of the family home three weeks earlier, stealing cars is not the most pressing thing on his mind despite the prospect of much-needed income. With less focus and with a diminishing sense of urgency, they head towards East Acton Underground station. There are still a few hours left in the working day before commuters return to their cars and that is enough time to steal one and hide it in Witney's rented garage before the owner notices it is missing. A mile down the road they turn along Erconwald Street with East Acton Underground station two hundred yards away on the left-hand side. With their attention fixed on looking for a car to steal, Duddy, Witney and Roberts don't notice that by the time they reach the bottom of the street they are being followed by a blue Triumph 2000.

Although it's an unmarked police vehicle, the Q-car is not entirely unidentifiable. On closer inspection anyone with an eye for detail could spot the unusually tall aerial on the nearside front wing. The three young men inside in suits could well have been policemen. (Roberts later claimed that they spotted the car following them and knew it was a police car. Witney and Duddy said they only noticed it after turning along Braybrook Street when it pulled alongside.)

Several theories have been suggested for why DS Head decided to stop the Vanguard. Perhaps Fox, with his photographic memory for faces, recognised the driver, Jack Witney. Maybe the close proximity to Wormwood Scrubs prison had something to do with it: their guv'nor was giving evidence that day at Marylebone Magistrates' Court in a case concerning the recent escape of five men who'd scaled the jail's walls aided by accomplices on the outside. In any case, three men in an old car that looked barely roadworthy would have invited suspicion.

But it is curious that only minutes earlier Head had agreed to pick up Coote from Marylebone. It was at least twenty minutes' drive away through the Friday-afternoon traffic and the court closed at four o'clock. So it was odd that the Q-car crew decided to divert down Erconwald Street to follow the Vanguard unless they thought that there was something untoward going on, or about to take place.

The explanation might be that next to East Acton station was a telephone box and a police phone box. Fifty years later police phone boxes are better known as the Tardis in *Dr Who*, but in the days before policemen had personal radios police boxes were a vital means of communication for officers on the beat. The public telephone box in Erconwald Street was out of order that day. But if Chris Head had been calling Coote from the police phone box via the switchboard at the police station, it could explain why the Q-car was there and how its the crew first noticed Witney's dilapidated car with three men inside passing by towards the prison and thought it demanded closer inspection. The theory is supported by the fact that the following evening Roberts said to Duddy in the presence of Lilly Perry, *'It would never have happened if Jack hadn't gone down that turning.'*

Groups of children are playing on the browning grass of Wormwood Scrubs Park as Witney turns left at the T-junction into Braybrook Street. A hundred yards behind are the thirty-foot-high brick walls of Wormwood Scrubs Prison and the looming cell blocks of the imposing Victorian jail that was completed in 1891. To the left is a row of Arts and Crafts-style council houses, built as part of the 'Homes for Heroes' campaign when the Old Oak Estate was completed in the 1920s, with neatly clipped privet hedges and small front gardens overlooking the open expanse of parkland and the cooling towers, tall chimneys and factory roofs on the skyline to the north-east.

Residents of Braybrook Street are used to seeing cars and lorries come and go, their drivers stopping for a break to eat sandwiches, have a smoke and stretch their legs. A little way down the street Tom Dowdney and Alan Ayton are in their lorry, taking an afternoon nap. They have finished their deliveries for the Danish Bacon Company and are killing time before returning to the depot.

Geoff Fox accelerates and draws alongside the Vanguard. Chris Head winds down the front passenger window and waves his arm, signalling Witney to pull over. The Vanguard stops near the kerb outside 57 Braybrook Street. Geoffrey Fox positions the Q-car a hundred and thirty feet ahead, in the middle of the quiet road, and keeps the engine running.

The haze induced by the afternoon heat and lunchtime beer clears in an instant as Roberts, Duddy and Witney watch a young man in a dark suit get out of the rear door of the Triumph and walk back towards them.

As David Wombwell approaches the Vanguard he notices that there is no tax disc on the windscreen. Witney winds his window down. Wombwell bends his back, says he is a police officer and asks Witney why his car is not displaying a road fund licence. It's a routine question and not the kind of law enforcement for which the Q-car is deployed but it's a starting point from which to assess the car and its occupants.

Witney replies casually that he has no tax disc because the MOT on his car has run out. He says he was stopped the previous week for the same offence – which is true – but hasn't had time to sort it out. He appeals to Wombwell to give him a break.

Wombwell asks to see Witney's driving licence and insurance certificate. Witney reaches into the glove compartment and hands them over. Wombwell looks at them for a moment and then walks back to the Q-car. He's noticed that Witney's car insurance has run out three hours earlier at twelve noon that day.

While Wombwell discusses with DS Head, the senior officer, Witney's lack of MOT, insurance and tax disc and they decide what action to take, the time bomb in Harry Roberts's mind is ticking down. June Howard has warned him he will get fifteen years if he is caught with unlicensed firearms and in the canvas bag between him and Witney are his three loaded guns, beneath the overalls.

There are a number of choices open to Roberts in the few seconds that he has to think. He can try to conceal his guns surreptitiously and hope they won't be found if the car is searched. Removing them from the bag and concealing them somewhere less obvious might work. Roberts could surrender the guns if it comes to it and take his chances in court.

While Head and Wombwell are discussing what to do, Roberts reaches into the canvas bag and takes out the Luger P08. By the time Head and Wombwell are walking back to the Vanguard the Luger is concealed under Roberts's grey jacket. At the driver's window Wombwell leans down to speak to Witney. Head goes to the other side of the car and looks in. He tries to open Roberts's passenger door but it's locked. Roberts ignores him. Head asks Duddy to open the canvas bag that is still on the floor between the front seats. Duddy pulls out the overalls and shows them to him but Head says he wants to see what else is in the bag. On the other side of the car Witney's pleas are getting him nowhere. Wombwell looks into the car, eyeing each man in turn, and asks to see what's in the back.

In the front passenger seat, Harry Roberts pulls out the Luger from his jacket, extends his arm towards the open driver's-side window, shouts 'Fuck off!' and pulls the trigger, shooting DC Wombwell through the left eye and killing him instantly. Propelled by the force of the impact Wombwell's head flies back. His lifeless body goes down like a falling tree and he ends up lying flat on his back in the roadway, staring skywards and with his pencil still in his hand.

As the shot rings out and echoes across the adjacent parkland, nearby children stop and watch in disbelief. DS Head starts running back towards the Q-car shouting, 'No, no, no.' In one swift movement Roberts leaps from the Vanguard, aims his gun at DS Head and fires. The shot hits Head in the centre of his back and he goes down. Roberts runs over. Chris Head kicks out. Roberts grabs his legs, aims his weapon at the officer's face and pulls the trigger. There's a click but the gun doesn't fire. Roberts lets go of the detective's legs, takes a step back and ejects the jammed cartridge. With the chamber cleared Roberts tries to take hold of Chris Head's flailing legs and gets kicked in the face, the blow splitting his lip and making his nose bleed. Steadying himself, Roberts aims the gun again and pulls the trigger. There's another click and again the old Luger doesn't fire. Head scrambles to his feet, stumbles back towards the Q-car to take cover and collapses in front of the bonnet onto the road.

Realising that Roberts's gun has jammed Fox starts to reverse the Triumph at him in an attempt to run him down, backing away from Chris Head who is lying directly in front of the Q-car. Roberts turns to the Vanguard and shouts 'Come on!'

His brain still fogged by the lunchtime beer, Duddy takes the .38 Enfield service revolver from the bag and half-falls out of the nearside passenger door of the Vanguard. As he gets out Roberts screams, 'Get the driver!'

Duddy raises his hand and aims his weapon at the

Q-car. On the ring finger of his left hand is a knuckle-duster ring with an American Indian chief's head on it. On his right arm is a tattoo of a skull and the words *True to Death*. With his life now in tatters and alcohol fuzzing his mind Duddy pulls the trigger and the nearside rear window of the police car explodes, as does the driver's quarter light. The bullet narrowly misses Geoff Fox's chin. Suddenly realising that there's another gun Fox hits the brakes. The next round from Duddy's revolver also misses Fox and shatters the windscreen, leaving a gaping hole where it exits in front of Fox's face. Fox puts the automatic gearbox into forward drive. It takes a couple of seconds for the Triumph's automatic Borg-Warner gearbox to engage before the car starts pulling away. Duddy runs forward and fires again, at close range through the shattered nearside passenger window. The third shot hits Geoffrey Roger Fox in his left temple. As Fox is hit by Duddy's third round his foot jerks down on the accelerator and the police car lurches forward, driving over DS Head and wedging his abdomen and legs under the Triumph. The rear offside wheel of the car is half-lifted off the ground. The tyre squeals against the tarmac. There's a smell of burning rubber and smoke. The hot exhaust pipe sears through Head's dark suit and into the flesh of his critically injured body.

Meanwhile, Witney has grabbed his documents back from Wombwell who is lying dead on the road beside his car. The Vanguard is already moving backwards when

Duddy leaps in. For a moment Roberts thinks he's going to be left behind. He runs and dives into the front passenger seat.

Witney shouts, 'You must be fucking potty!'

'Drive, cunt, unless you want some of the same,' Roberts yells. 'Go! Go! Go!'

Chapter 9

Dozens of people, many of them children, witnessed the shootings and associated harrowing events in Braybrook Street that summer afternoon. Their first-hand accounts are immediate and compelling as each tells the story from a different viewpoint and perspective. Their narratives were given in their own words with the traumatic memory still vivid in their minds, while they were still trying to make sense of what they had seen that day.

Twenty-nine-year-old Bryan Deacon was driving to Wormwood Scrubs Park, his pregnant wife Pat sitting beside him in their car and their large boxer dog Buster in the back. They were stationary at the junction of Mellitus Street and Erconwald Street and about to turn right when Witney's Standard Vanguard came haring down the road backwards.

STATEMENT OF: Bryan Dennis DEACON
Age 29 years. Born 24.2.37.
14 Stokesley Street W12.

The Shepherd's Bush Murders

Occupation: Security Guard at Taylers Wharf, Church Street, Isleworth, Middlesex. Telephone: Isleworth 6324

On Friday, 12th August 1966 at about 3.30 p.m., as near as I can remember, I was driving my green Ford Prefect 226 UMX in Mellitus Street, W12, and in the passenger seat was my wife, Patricia, and my dog was in the back.

I was driving north from Stokesley Street towards the junction with Erconwald Street which runs across, East to West, Mellitus Street. It was my intention to turn into Erconwald Street up towards the Scrubs. I was then going to park my car and give the dog a run on the Scrubs.

I pulled up at this junction, still in Mellitus Street waiting to turn right and as I stopped a car reversed towards me in Erconwald Street from the direction of the Scrubs. What made me stop and notice it was that the car was screeching. The driver obviously had his foot down.

The car was an old blue Standard Vanguard Estate car, which unusually had no rear passenger doors but had windows in the side. It was light blue and it looked as though the paint was hand-painted. It appeared to be a flat finish and unpolished.

As the car backed and turned left into Mellitus Street, I could then see that the exhaust pipe was hanging down almost onto the ground. The car was then facing me across the other side of Erconwald Street. As they came towards me to pass me crossing the junction, the fellow in the back seat appeared to be either taking off or putting on a sports jacket, blue-grey in colour and about ¼" check. The man was leaning forward, seemed to have thickish, wavy, light-coloured hair and at a guess he may be about thirty years old. I don't think I would know this man again.

The driver I saw and I should think he was a bit older, about thirty-five or thirty-six years old, and he was thinner in the face with a pointed nose.

I then turned right into Erconwald Street towards Braybrook Street and I looked left and a woman from the corner house and a driver from a nearby lorry were facing me on the edge of the Scrubs and I called, 'What's happened?'

The lorry driver ran over, shouting 'Get the police! Get the police!'

I saw in the road a car with its back wheels spinning and blue smoke coming from it. It was almost in the middle of the road, facing north up Braybrook Street away from me. The offside rear wheel was off the ground and the engine was still going. I could see a man lying in the road about thirty yards from the corner. The car was twenty yards further on. I could see the head and shoulders of another man sticking out from under the offside rear wheel. His face was black but he seemed to be still moving. The back wheels of the car were bumping against his body. There were holes in the windows of the car on the nearside and the windscreen was shattered.

I turned round and went down Erconwald Street to telephone the police from a butcher's shop. I think the

index was PGT 276 or 726 but I wrote it down and later
I gave the number to the police.

Despite the shocking and extraordinary circumstances
Bryan Deacon's quick thinking and presence of mind in
noting the index number of the blue Standard Vanguard
was to prove the vital key in solving the case of the
Shepherd's Bush murders. His wife Pat's recollections
were much the same but her account gave a clearer
physical description of the driver of the Vanguard and
provided important additional details of the scene she saw
in Braybrook Street within minutes of the shootings. Of
course, at the time no one yet knew that the men who had
been shot were policemen since the Triumph 2000 Q-car
looked like a private vehicle and Wombwell, Head and
Fox were in plain clothes.

STATEMENT OF: Patricia Margaret DEACON
Age 26 years. Born 26.2.40.
14 Stokesley Street W12.
Occupation: Housewife.

We came to a crossing like my husband told you and saw
a blue car, like an estate car, coming towards us in the
street we were about to enter, screeching very loudly and
being driven fast. The car reversed into the road we were
in but across the junction. As it stopped and then started
forward it swerved and the exhaust pipe, which was

hanging down under the car, scraped the road causing sparks. It was actually the exhaust box not the pipe which scraped on the road. The scraping actually took place as the car was reversing. The exhaust pipe stuck in my mind because the pipe was sticking out of the side and not the back as usual.

The car was driven towards us and passed us on the side my husband was sitting. It was being driven very fast, away past us. I noticed there were three men in the car, two in the front and the other man in the centre of the back seat. The man at the back appeared to be bending forward and either putting on or taking off a coat.

The driver I saw clearly and he seemed to be about twenty-nine to thirty-four years old, but youngish-looking, with very dark hair, which was thick and pushed back and seemed to have a quiff in the front but had no parting. His face was longish with a pointed chin and a thinnish, medium-sized nose but with a bony ridge at the top of his nose. He wore a dark jacket and I don't know if he wore a tie but his shirt neck was done up. There's a good chance that I would recognise him again but not the others.

The man in the front passenger seat appeared to have brown hair, and seemed to be much shorter than the driver who I would say was about five foot eleven or six foot. The passenger I think would be about five foot four or five foot six. He had a full face and seemed younger than the driver, a sort of baby face. I would not recognise him again.

The Shepherd's Bush Murders

My husband turned right and came to another junction and we were going to turn right but we heard a commotion to my left and stopped against the kerb.

I saw a man lying in the road with his head nearly in the centre of the road and his feet towards the left kerb and I saw he was bleeding from the face.

Further up, about twenty or thirty feet, was a car, at an angle to the centre of the road. The back appeared to be up with the wheels spinning and smoke gushing from it. Just beyond the offside rear wheel I could see the head and shoulders of another man, who appeared to be alive because I saw him move his head.

I saw a man standing by this chap but I don't know who he was. The windscreen of the car was all shattered and there was a hole about a foot in diameter on the driver's side.

My husband then reversed our car and we drove away to find a telephone and my husband eventually phoned from a butcher's shop.

Along with invaluable descriptions of the assailants and their car, both Bryan and Pat Deacon's accounts agreed that when they got to Braybrook Street Chris Head was still alive and trapped under the Triumph Q-car.

Fifty-one-year-old Mrs Catherine Ryan was in her home at 41 Braybrook Street in the front room with her husband when they heard '*four loud bangs*'. Immediately, she looked out of the window and saw a blue car eighty yards away to her left and a man lying in the road with blood coming from his head. She ran to her phone in the hallway and dialled 999. Catherine Ryan's was the first of many 999 calls made that afternoon and hers was made when Roberts, Duddy and Witney were still in the street outside, just yards away from her home. While she was on the phone she could hear the sound of screeching brakes coming from the street outside. Seconds later she saw a blue-coloured vehicle flash past her open front door and she heard it accelerate away down the road.

Another Braybrook Street resident was just a few feet away from John Duddy when he fired his weapon. Edward Morey was also the first person to get to the men who had been shot.

STATEMENT OF: Edward Joseph MOREY
Age 34. Born 28.4.1932.
65 Braybrook Street W12.
Occupation: General Labourer.

On Friday 12th August, 1966, between 3 p.m. and 3.30 p.m., I was in bed in the front room of my house. I heard about six to eight bangs and woke up. I had no shoes on so I looked out of the window and saw a blue car stationary in the middle of the road, facing towards Old Oak Lane. I went to the front door and opened it. There was a man in a grey coat or suit standing upright with his right arm outstretched, firing what I thought was a revolver. After firing the shots, I think about three shots, the man turned, glancing at me as he did so, and ran away to the right.

I went out into the street and saw a lot of smoke coming from the rear wheels of the car and I saw a body lying about thirty feet behind, roughly in the middle of the road. I then went to the driver's side of the car and I could see a man slumped in the driver's seat. I looked down at the right-hand wheel and saw another man under the wheel of the car. The car engine was racing and the wheels were spinning against his hip. I tried to drag the man clear as another man in a shirt ran up. The other man said to me, 'Switch off the engine.' But then he switched off the ignition himself. When he stopped the car I tried again to pull the man from under the wheels. He was still moving about but he suddenly went mauve and died. He didn't say anything. I left him and I noticed the man in the driving seat had a hole in his head and was dead, so left him and went to the man lying in the roadway. There was a lot of blood coming from his mouth. He was also dead. I asked my wife to get a blanket and I put it over him. I did not see anybody else about at all, except for the man in the shirt and a lot of children.

The 'man in a shirt' who rushed to the scene to was Tom Dowdney. Moments before, Dowdney had been dozing in his Danish Bacon Company delivery lorry with driver Alan Ayton. Tom Dowdney woke first and shouted, 'They are shooting.'

Ayton was half-asleep and thought it was children playing with fireworks. He said, 'Do leave off.' He then looked through the windscreen and saw two cars, a Triumph and a Vanguard estate car, about a hundred yards away. There was a man running along the nearside of the Vanguard which had started to reverse. He couldn't describe the man he saw running but as the Vanguard came closer he got the impression there were three men in the car, which confirmed what others said. But he didn't get a good look at them.

As the Vanguard reversed into Erconwald Street Ayton noticed that the Triumph appeared to be on fire because smoke was coming from the rear. Dowdney jumped out of the lorry and ran over to the Triumph. Ayton said he was dumbfounded and remained where he was.

Fourteen-year-old Anna Dunleavy was looking out of the front window of 59 Braybrook Street at around 3:15 p.m. when she saw 'a pale green van' draw up before being overtaken by a blue car. Her memory of the shootings had a different sequence of events that was at odds with what others said, with the physical evidence, with the order in which the three policemen were shot and with where they were later found. Such is the nature of the recall of shocking events that take place over such a short time. However, Anna made a brilliant observation. She said the driver looked like Bobby Charlton. And at first glance Jack Witney did look uncannily like the England World Cup midfield player.

Many witnesses to the events in Braybrook Street were children who were no less observant than the adults despite the horror of what they saw. Fifteen-year-old Barbara Mary Spayne was in her bedroom at the front of number 53 when she heard 'two bangs' and thought it was a car backfiring. She looked out of the window and saw her neighbour Mrs Baker running along the pavement. She saw 'a dark-coloured van backing very quickly towards Erconwald Street . . . I saw several men – I'm not really sure how many – trying to get into the moving van. I heard Mrs Baker shout, "They killed him, they killed him." I saw the body of a young man lying in the road to the extreme left of the window. I remember staring at the body of the young man for quite some time and then I turned away as the blood I saw made me feel sick.'

Thirteen-year-old Colin Pell, who lived at 20 Braybrook Street, was standing at the corner of Erconwald Street and Wulfston Street with his friends Ronald Long, Malcolm Austin, Raymond Medland, Gary Collins and some other smaller children whose names he didn't know. He remembered a green van reversing quickly with three men inside, two in the front and one in the back. He said he didn't see the driver very well but he described the front-seat passenger. 'He had a white face and jet-black hair. He had a college-boy style of haircut, by this I mean smooth not long, it looked neat. He was wearing a light grey suit. The passenger in the back was larger. He had a plump face, I don't remember about his hair. He had a suit on but I don't know what colour. Five minutes later Raymond Medland, who had gone home, came down to us and told us there had been a shooting up the Scrubs. We all ran up there and round the corner I saw a body in the road with a sack or something over it and a bit further on, about fifteen yards, I saw a blue car all smashed up.'

Eight-year-old Danuta Palej who lived at 29 Braybrook Street told her story which is both poignant and surprisingly accurate. 'Today, about twenty minutes past three, I was playing in Braybrook Street with my brother Zabigniew, he's six, and a friend, Susan Coke, and she's twelve. I don't know her address, but her brother is friends with my brother, that's how I met Susan, so my brother may know the address.

'We were playing in the street near my house when I heard three or four bangs, like a gun firing. This made me look round and I saw a man holding a gun. He seemed to be firing the gun into a car that was almost in the middle of the road. The man with the gun was firing into the front part of the car, at the side of it. I think the man fired into the car two or three times. I saw the man with the gun walk quickly away, going towards the prison, away from where we were playing. I didn't see where he went because I looked at another man lying in the road. The car that was in the middle of the road moved forward and it ran right over the man lying in the road. The car seemed to stop with the man underneath it. Then I ran indoors and told my mum and a lot people came.'

Ten-year-old Gary Patrick Morey, whose parents had also witnessed the events, was in the front garden of 69 Braybrook Street, talking to his friend Paul Pickering. Their account only varied in the sequence of events. Gary gave a good description of the shooters and added a chilling detail. 'The man with the gun fired three or four shots at the other man who started to run back toward the blue car shouting, "No, no, no."' Gary Morey also said that the man who shot the policeman in the back yelled to the other men he was with in the blue car 'Come on!' and 'Get the driver!'

Nine-year-old Jimmy Newman lived at 115 Mellitus Street. 'After dinner time about 2:30 p.m. or 2:45 p.m. I was standing at the corner of Osmond Road and Braybrook Street. I was alone. Leslie Swarts and his brother were playing cricket on the Scrubs. It's the second square along. I think it's in Mellitus Street they live. It will be about halfway down.

'The first thing I saw was a man running out of a police car. I have seen it since and it has holes in the window. I saw a fat man coming out of a green van. It was a little bit bigger than a minivan. I think there were two other people in the van. I did not see their faces. The fat man had a gun in his hand about twelve inches long. He was nearly as tall as my Dad who is 5ft 11ins. He was quite big and had a beard – I think he had a beard. He was wearing a green jumper. I did not notice the colour of his trousers. He was not wearing a hat. I was not looking at him but at the gun.

'The man who came out of the police car was at the front of the van. The green van was behind the police car. I saw that the man who came from the police car was running backwards. I heard a shot and he fell. I saw another man shoot through the front window of the police car and the man who was the driver fell over. I then saw the police car move on top of the man who had fallen. I then saw the men with the guns get in the van and it drove backwards and went down Erconwald Street. I remember I saw two men get out the van but I did not see their faces. I don't know what age the fat man would be. I never saw him before.'

Jimmy Newman later told reporters, 'It was horrible. I was so scared I cried.'

There were many other children who witnessed the three murders in Braybrook Street that Friday and who saw Witney's Vanguard driving away erratically, including eight-year-old Mark Norman, thirteen-year-old Ronald Long, twelve-year-old Shirley Davies, nine-year-old Steven Davidson, nine-year-old Terrance Jackson, Kevin Dolan, who was only seven years old, and nine-year-old Paul Pickering and his mother Renee. She rushed out of her front door at 69 Braybrook Street when she heard her son screaming and saw a man standing by a blue car with his back to her and holding a gun.

Each of the witnesses, adults and children, spoke in their own way of details that others had also seen and added something of their own. From their unique vantage points and observations, a moment-by-moment mosaic of the murders of David Wombwell, Christopher Head and Geoffrey Fox, and the exit of their killers from the scene, comes together to convey the few terrible minutes of that fateful summer afternoon.

Chapter 10

In the Vanguard, Witney, Duddy and Roberts tore down Stokesley Street, turning left into Wulfstan Street then left again into Du Cane Road, driving east, parallel to the embankment of the Underground railway line and past the main gates of Wormwood Scrubs prison. According to Roberts a police motorbike came alongside them but quickly veered away and they lost sight of it.

Just a short distance away Foxtrot-Seven-Three was stationary in Sawley Road, W12. PC Daniel Owen was the observer with driver PC Keith Mordecai and radio operator TDC Howard, when they received an R/T from the Scotland Yard Information Room calling Foxtrot Three and Foxtrot One-One: '*Braybrook Street, near the prison. Serious GBH. Ambulance called. Vehicle concerned, a blue Vanguard with P and J in the index number, direction unknown. No further particulars.*' PC Howard acknowledged, saying they would assist since they were nearby. They raced off down Sawley Road, went left into Bloemfontein Road, left again and up to Savoy Circus, right into Old Oak Common Lane, right in Erconwald Street and turned along Braybrook Street about three minutes later.

The crew were not expecting the distressing sight that faced them. The radio message from the Scotland Yard Information Room had simply said 'serious GBH' but the unexpected grisly reality of a triple murder was immediately apparent. And on closer inspection the grim scene disclosed a further shocking revelation.

PC Daniel Owen was the first to identify the fallen men as police officers and colleagues whom he knew personally. 'On our arrival at the scene at approximately 15:22 I saw a body which was covered with a blanket about six feet from the south footway and outside number 57 Braybrook Street with the feet pointing south. There was a blue Triumph motor car index GGW 87C at the crown of the road about twenty yards north of number 57 and a body lying directly underneath with just the head protruding between the offside wheels.

'I identified the body as that of DS Head. I then looked into the car and saw the body of PC Fox still sitting in the driving seat and slumped over to the left with his forehead resting on the passenger seat. I could give no assistance to either DS Head or PC Fox so I returned to the body lying in the roadway and on lifting the blanket saw it was TDC Wombwell.

'PC Mordecai then went into a private house to telephone the inspector at the Information Room at

Scotland Yard. While PC Mordecai was telephoning I was given a scrap of paper with the index PGT 726 on, which it was alleged was the vehicle concerned and I radioed it to the Information Room for circulation.'

Faced with such a horrific scene PC Mordecai decided it would be better to telephone the Information Room rather than broadcast the grim details of the situation over the radio.

In 2015 I spoke to Keith Mordecai on the telephone after I'd been given his number by an ex-colleague. He was retired, elderly and in poor health. He said politely and wearily that he'd spent the last fifty years trying to forget that afternoon and he was very sorry but he didn't feel like talking about it.

PC Alan Mallet was the observer in patrol car Foxtrot-Three on 12 August 1966, PC William Buckley was the operator and PC Gerald Hunkin was the driver. They had started patrol at 15:00 hours and at 15:19 they had also heard the R/T from Scotland Yard Information Room calling their car and the ill-fated Foxtrot One-One. PC Alan Mallet acknowledged the call as they wove through heavy traffic to Braybrook Street.

'We approached the scene via Erconwald Street. I watched for any vehicle fitting the description of the car concerned but saw no trace. We turned into Braybrook Street at about 15:25 and I saw a blue Triumph 2000 motor car in the middle of the road. The windscreen was shattered, with a hole about six inches in diameter in front of the driver's seat. There was a similar hole in the rear nearside window. About 25 yards east of the car was a body covered with a quilt.'

The scene was horrific and it was hard to decide what to do but with Foxtrot Seven-Three and its crew already in attendance Mallet ran over to a meat lorry parked in Braybrook Street and asked the occupants, Thomas Dowdney and Alan Ayton, what had just happened.

PCs Peter Scott and Gordon Lang in patrol car Delta-Three based at Harrow Road police station were passing Westbourne Park Underground Station when they heard the radio message calling for urgent assistance at Braybrook Street. Although the 'serious GBH' was in a neighbouring Division the incident clearly needed all available backup and they were the third car to arrive within minutes of the shootings.

Foxtrot-Two then turned along the street and screeched to a halt. PC Hunkin was standing in the roadway and asked the driver to go to the junction of Braybrook Street and Osmund Street to close off that end of the road and Foxtrot-Two was positioned across the roadway on the far side of the crime scene to Foxtrot-Seven-Three.

By sheer chance Witney, Roberts and Duddy avoided being spotted by Foxtrot-Two, Foxtrot-Three, Foxtrot-Seven-Three, or Delta-Three as the four police cars and their crews rapidly converged on Braybrook Street. At the end of Du Cane Road Witney turned right and drove south along Wood Lane, passing White City Stadium and the BBC Television Centre, round Shepherd's Bush Green and on towards Hammersmith Broadway, passing Hammersmith police station on the Shepherd's Bush Road. They crossed the river over Hammersmith Bridge, then headed east to Putney and Wandsworth.

At Scotland Yard, former head of the Flying Squad, now Deputy Commander, fifty-five-year-old Ernest Millen had just been told of the shootings in Braybrook Street and was putting the phone down when Detective Superintendent Richard Chitty of the C1 Murder Squad walked past his office. Millen had the nickname 'Hooter', either because of his distinctive nose or because he didn't believe in internal phones or intercoms and had a habit of bellowing orders from his desk.

He called Chitty into his office overlooking the Thames, an office where every major criminal investigation in London had begun since the Metropolitan Police first took up residence there in 1890. The day before, Chitty had returned from Gloucester Assizes where he'd been giving evidence in a murder case he'd worked on around the clock for months. He'd recently moved to Kent and because he was so busy his wife had had to organise the move so he was hoping to spend more time at home over the next few weeks.

'Three policemen have been shot at Shepherd's Bush,'

Millen barked. 'I want you to go down there and take over.'

'But I'm not on call yet, Guv'nor,' Chitty replied. It took a moment for the implications of Millen's request to sink in. 'Are they injured?'

Millen was never a man to display emotion or to mince his words. 'They're dead,' he said. 'All three. Get down to the Bush as quickly as you can. I'll see you there.' Despite Millen's abrupt manner he knew Chitty was the best man for the job. Dick Chitty had worked in 'F' Division as a Detective Inspector at Hammersmith from June 1962 until the beginning of 1966 when he'd joined the C1 Murder Squad so he knew the area well.

And so it was that Dick Chitty, a veteran of fourteen murder investigations, steeled himself for his latest and most challenging case, one that was to place him in the full glare of media and public attention. He telephoned his wife, ordered a car and set off for his old patch in Shepherd's Bush, armed with only scant information.

Meanwhile Witney, Duddy and Roberts had ended up at Vauxhall where Witney had rented garage space in a railway arch off Tinworth Street. Witney dropped off Duddy and Roberts and then parked his car in the arch, leaned an old lorry tyre against the back to cover the number plate, padlocked the heavy wooden doors as he left and joined Roberts and Duddy down on the Albert Embankment.

Duddy was panicking. 'What the fuck we going to do?'

'We got to get some dough,' replied Jack.

Roberts said there was only one thing they could do. 'We will have to do a bank.'

'No way,' said Duddy. 'Fuck this – I'm off.' And with that he ran off down the street.

At Scotland Yard Ernie Millen contacted Detective Chief Inspector John 'Ginger' Hensley, second in command at Hounslow, who at that moment was at Chiswick police station. Millen appointed Hensley deputy to Chitty. In his usual dark suit and customary dapper bow tie Ginger Hensley set off for Shepherd's Bush accompanied by Detective Sergeant Begg, his colleague on many previous investigations.

Millen next said he wanted Doctor Donald Teare, the famous Home Office pathologist, at the crime scene and a call was put through to Teare's home. Also called in was John McCafferty, Senior Experimental Officer in the Ballistics Department of the Metropolitan Police Science Laboratory.

It is extraordinary how quickly and comprehensively the police at all levels responded, given their different locations and the limited means of communication available to them in those days. Thirteen minutes after the shootings Detective Sergeant Ronald Lawrence, Scenes of Crime Officer, No.1 District, arrived in Braybrook Street at around 15:30. 'On the footway, immediately next to the front garden of 57 Braybrook Street, approximately fourteen feet from the body of T/Detective Constable Wombwell I found a cartridge case. Nearby in the gutter, at right angles to a straight line, approximately twenty-two feet from the rear nearside of a police vehicle index number GGW 87C I found a live cartridge. On the kerb side, 7ft 3ins from that cartridge, I found another live cartridge. Under the body of T/Detective Constable Wombwell I found a cartridge case. I packed these items and later handed them to Mr McCafferty, Ballistics Department.'

At 15:45 Dr Roy Salole, the medical practitioner and Divisional Surgeon, arrived at Braybrook Street where there were already two ambulances and their crews at the scene. After a brief examination of Chris Head, David Wombwell and Geoff Fox – 'because of the necessary precautions for fingerprinting' – Dr Salole 'pronounced life extinct in all three officers.' By this time Braybrook Street was full of police officers from 'F' Division. They covered the bodies in the roadway, cordoned off the road and began erecting a makeshift screen from rolls of sacking.

At Shepherd's Bush police station, when twenty-five-year-old WPC Jean Cooper first heard of the shootings she was at the front desk dealing with a distraught young mother who had lost her twin children in Shepherd's Bush Market. Cooper was one of only two WPCs based at Shepherd's Bush in August 1966 and her female colleague,

Barbara Martin, was off duty that afternoon. Cooper was told to hand over the search for the missing children to Hammersmith police station when she was called to see her guv'nor, Chief Inspector (and acting Superintendent) Fred Rooke.

Ex-RAF, cool, upright, slim and athletic for his age, with thinning fair hair, Rooke asked Cooper to change into civilian clothes. He said he wanted her to accompany him to the homes of Marjory Fox and Gillian Wombwell to break the news.

Rooke and Cooper, driven by ex-heavyweight boxer Detective Constable Alistair Dent, nicknamed the 'Gentle Giant' by his colleagues, went first to the Foxes' home at 1 Radcliffe Way, Yeading Lane, Northolt. Marjory Fox was preparing tea for her two-year-old daughter. She had two other children: a son, Paul, aged sixteen, who was a laboratory worker interested in a career in colour photography, and a daughter, Ann, who was seventeen and worked as a secretary.

Marjory Fox knew what it was like to be orphaned. She had lost her mother when she was only fourteen, and had had to bring up a family of younger brothers and sisters. But nothing could have prepared her for suddenly becoming the widow of a murdered policeman that afternoon. Still in shock, she said later, 'I always knew my Geoff would get killed some day. But he always wanted to be a policeman and was proud of his job, and so was I – of his job and him.'

After leaving Marjory in the care of neighbours, Fred Rooke, DC Alistair Dent and WPC Cooper continued with their unenviable task and went to Eastfield Court. By the time they arrived at the Wombwells' front door, news of David's death had already reached his young wife Gillian. PC David Headland, who lived at the flats, had taken the initiative and gone to see her as soon as he'd heard the news.

Gillian's daughter Melanie's second birthday was three weeks away. Her son, Daen, aged three, had been playing with his sister and other children outside. When she first heard the knock on the door and saw David Headland's expression she thought something had happed to one of the children. Fifty years later Gillian said she doesn't recall much else about that day. She remembers sitting on a chair staring at the television and there being a lot of people around, coming and going.

David Wombwell's remarried mother, Daphne Scoot, was contacted by telephone. She and her second husband ran a picturesque country pub at Melbourn, Cambridgeshire. 'Ben, my husband, and I were choosing wallpaper for the kitchen when the phone rang that Friday afternoon. We argued, jokingly, about who should answer it, because we were so wrapped up in our decorating plans. In the end I went. A man asked for my husband and wouldn't say who he was. Then I heard my daughter-in-law, Gillian, trying to say something and crying. The man came back on again and asked for my husband. Ben took the phone and I listened in. It was the police and Gillian was with them, and they told us what had happened.'

Two hundred and sixty miles away in Torquay, Christopher Head's mother Phylia was having tea with a neighbour and listening to an orchestral concert on the radio. The music was interrupted by a newsflash announcing that three policemen had been shot in Shepherd's Bush. Phylia later said that she'd had a sudden, awful premonition that her son was involved. 'It was like a cold finger touching my heart,' she recalled. 'I tried to tell myself I was being silly. I tried to go on drinking my tea but the feeling persisted and I could no longer hear the music.'

She walked back across the street to her grey-painted terraced house and was playing with her two young grandchildren when the front door bell rang. On the doorstep was a uniformed police sergeant. 'From his face I knew what had happened,' she said. 'I suppose I had known from the time I heard the news on the radio.'

The torn-off piece of butcher's wrapping paper that was handed to PC Owen of Foxtrot Seven-Three had on it the car registration number PGT 726, written down hastily by Bryan Deacon. TDC Howard had radioed it immediately to the Information Room at Scotland Yard who put out a call to patrol cars all over London. In addition, telephone calls were made to the four London

County Council offices around the capital where vehicle records were kept.

In the pre-computer age of 1966 vehicle-owner records were not centralised and were still kept on index cards by local councils. As a result the Metropolitan Police held keys to the vehicle registration offices of local authorities so they could access vehicle records out of working hours. But with the weekend fast approaching, the job of finding the name and address of the registered owner of PGT 726 would be a lot quicker and easier with the assistance of LCC employees who were familiar with the records.

Detective Superintendent Dick Chitty arrived at Shepherd's Bush Police Station at 17:20. His first instruction was for an operations room to be set up on the first floor to coordinate things. The front line of the investigation was certainly going to need officers experienced in murder work. But Chitty knew from long experience that the men and women behind the scenes who would take telephone calls and collate statements and information and keep it all meticulously organised, cross-referenced and indexed, were going to be vital. And they would need more telephones.

After conferring briefly with local officers he set off ten minutes later for Braybrook Street with Detective Sergeant Ted Fosbury. Shortly after 5:30 p.m. they arrived at the scene and Chitty quickly got the detective work under way. With so many police officers on the scene it was vital that any evidence was preserved. 'All the necessary precautions were put into operation. I was present when photographs were taken. Instructions were given for the preparation of plans. Fingerprint officers attended and officers from the Metropolitan Police Laboratory.'

Home Office Pathologist Dr Donald Teare arrived on the scene shortly after Chitty. 'I went to Braybrook Street, W12, where I met Superintendent Chitty and other officers. Outside No. 57 I saw the body of an adult man lying on his back about two yards from the kerb. His feet were crossed right over left, the right hand extended by his side and a pencil lay between the fingers. There was a large quantity of blood about the head.

'In a car, registered index GGW 87C, almost in the middle of the road outside Nos. 61-63 facing roughly west, I saw the body of a man. He was sitting in the driving seat but slumped across to the left with his head on the passenger seat. The left rear window and the windscreen were shattered and there was a large quantity of blood about his head. Some brain tissue issued from a wound on the right forehead.

'I saw a third body under the car with the head protruding from the right side. The head and neck were extremely cyanosed [*having a bluish discolouration due to a deficiency of oxygen in the blood*] and some bloodstained mucus dribbled from the mouth. He appeared to be lying mainly on his left side.'

The number of CID officers in Braybrook Street was growing by the minute and included, Detective Chief

Inspector Harry Heavens who arrived with Detective Superintendent Bill Bailey of West End Central and the guv'nor of No. 1 District and Detective Sergeant Harry Clement from the Regional Crime Squad. Every man was acutely aware that nothing should be touched and everything was left exactly as it had been found. For the next two hours DCI Heavens and Detective Superintendent Squire of the Yard's Fingerprint Branch supervised the examination of the crime scene and the photographing of the Q-car and fallen men. They also organised the painstaking hunt in the roadway, gutters, hedges, front gardens and adjacent grass of Wormwood Scrubs Park for any less obvious physical evidence.

After examinations, photographs, sketched plans and measurements were taken, Chitty ordered that the bodies of David Wombwell, Chris Head and Geoff Fox should be carried to the grass at the edge of Wormwood Scrubs Park and covered to await transportation to Hammersmith Mortuary.

The Q-car was winched onto a trailer and was taken to the Yard's forensic laboratory at Theobalds Road, Holborn, WC1, so that the forensics team could examine it in minute detail.

Back at Shepherd's Bush police station Chitty was joined by Ernie Millen. In his 1970 memoir Millen wrote, '*I had gone to Shepherd's Bush in an advisory capacity only, for having put Chitty in over-all command of the investigation it was only right to let him get on with it without any interference.*' However, it's unlikely there was much distinction between Millen's advice and his orders, and to make it even less easy for Chitty 'to get on with it', another renowned senior officer turned up to advise, the Head of the Flying Squad, Detective Chief Superintendent Tommy Butler. Butler suggested that a valuable member of his Flying Squad team, Detective Inspector Jack Slipper, should join the investigation and that suggestion was to prove a masterstroke.

After a circuitous route back to West London by bus, Jack Witney and Harry Roberts arrived in Ladbroke Grove. John Duddy was peering anxiously out of the toilet window of his eighth-floor flat in Treverton Tower when Roberts and Witney approached. With his daughters still at work Duddy let them both in. They had a hasty discussion about what to do and it didn't take long to decide that they should split up.

Witney went back to his flat in Fernhead Road. As it was around the time he normally got home his wife would be none the wiser that he hadn't been at work all day. Roberts returned to Wymering Mansions. When he walked in Lilly Perry had the television on. She said, 'Have you heard the news? Three policemen are dead.'

Roberts said he replied, 'Have I heard? We fucking did it.'

Chapter 11

While the British nation read their Friday-evening papers, and heard and watched the news in stunned horror and disbelief, Metropolitan Policemen all over London were angry and eager to set off in pursuit of the three men who had gunned down their fellow officers in cold blood and shattered everyone's faith in the way things were supposed to be.

By early evening a mobile police-incident caravan had been set up in Braybrook Street. Some witnesses had been driven to Scotland Yard to look at photographic records of convicted criminals in the hope that someone would recognise the men they had seen shooting the three policemen before driving away in the blue car. It was a long shot and frustratingly none of the witnesses identified anyone from the mugshots.

As Dick Chitty walked around the scene of carnage that afternoon in Braybrook Street, accompanied by Home Office Pathologist Dr Donald Teare and the forensics team, his keen eye took in every detail of the task that lay before him. Despite the overwhelming turnout of uniformed officers and London's most eminent and experienced detectives, photographers, forensic, ballistics and fingerprint experts, the numerous witness statements that had been taken and the wealth of physical evidence, it all came down to just one clue.

In a few fleeting seconds Bryan Deacon had had the presence of mind to note the registration number of a blue estate car that he'd seen being driven recklessly. Several minutes later, when he saw the scene in Braybrook Street, he realised how vitally important that car number would be to the police. He scribbled down the number on a scrap of butcher's wrapping paper while making a 999 call, returned to the scene with his wife Pat now hysterical and sobbing and handed it to PC Owen. It was the only clue the police had that could lead them to the killers.

On the face of it, tracing the registered owner would be a straightforward task. But there was no guarantee that the car was actually owned by any of the men who had been seen in it after the shootings. All the police knew for certain was that by now the car would have been abandoned somewhere. Perhaps someone had noticed three men hastily leaving the distinctive Vanguard. The car might contain fingerprints and other evidence. And the trail was getting colder as the minutes ticked by so finding it was going to be a race against time.

The bodies of Chris Head, Geoff Fox and David Wombwell were taken to Hammersmith Mortuary. At

19:45, four and half hours after the shootings, Dr Donald Teare began the post-mortem. Also present were senior police photographer Brian Bellingham, Scenes of Crimes Officer Detective Sergeant Ronald Lawrence, John McCafferty, Senior Experimental Officer from the Forensic Science Laboratory in Holborn, and the man in charge of the investigation, Detective Superintendent Richard Chitty.

Dr Teare's report is disturbing to read and some readers may prefer not to. But the details are significant so it would be dishonest to censor or abridge what was recorded that evening.

POST-MORTEM EXAMINATION

At 7:45 pm the same evening at Hammersmith Mortuary Superintendent Chitty identified the bodies to me as being David Stanley Wombwell, aged 25 (No.1); Geoffrey Roger Fox, aged 41 (No.2); and Christopher Tippet Head, aged 30 (No.3).

1. David Stanley Wombwell.
The deceased proved to be a well-nourished adult man, 5'9½" in height.

The entrance wound of a bullet was seen on the left cheek immediately below the outer angle of the eye; its upper edge was ⅓" from the rim of the lower eyelid. The actual perforation was just over ¼" in diameter and the total area of bruising ³⁄₈" in diameter. There was no peppering or tattooing of the entrance wound.

A ragged exit wound was found in the right side of the back of the head, it was very irregular and rather star-shaped with a maximum width of ³⁄₄". The track of this bullet could be followed through the orbit and globe of the eye into the cranial cavity through the junction of the roof of the eye and the back of the roof of the nose. It pierced the mid-brain and the right occipitoparietal region of the brain to the corresponding area of the skull.

Fractures involved most of the right side of the skull over an area 5" long and 2" wide. Haemorrhage covered the surface of the brain.

Further examination revealed no natural disease in the body. Mr Wombwell was in other words a perfectly healthy young adult man, well-nourished and muscular.

The stomach contained a large undigested meal. The bladder was half full of clear urine. The heart weight 10oz; kidneys together 11oz; liver 3lbs 3oz; spleen 4oz.

I handed samples of blood to Sergeant Lawrence.

CAUSE OF DEATH:

Laceration of the brain due to a bullet wound.

2. Geoffrey Roger Fox.

The deceased proved to be a well-nourished, rather heavily built adult man, 5'9" in height.

The entrance wound of the bullet was seen on the left forehead 1½" above the outer angle of the left eyebrow; the hole was little more than ⅛" in diameter and the abrasions surrounding it made a maximum diameter of ⅜". There was no peppering or tattooing.

The exit wound was found on the right side of the head, just inside the hairline of the temple and 1¼" above and behind the outer angle of the right eyebrow, it was ⅞" long and very irregular.

The entrance wound in the left frontal bone of the skull was 5⁄16" in diameter and showed characteristic bevelling of the inner table. The exit wound in the skull was found in the right frontal bone at its junction with the temporal bone, it was ¾" long and ½" wide. Fractures ran between the entrance and exit wounds in the skull and from the entrance wound to the occipital region of the skull. The track of this bullet could be followed through both frontal lobes of the brain and haemorrhage covered its entire surface.

A quantity of blood was found in the air passages.

The stomach contained a large, partially digested meal. The bladder was half full of urine.

There was no natural disease in the body. The heart weighed 14oz; the kidneys together 14oz; liver 4lbs 8oz; spleen 6oz.

I handed blood samples to Sergeant Lawrence.

CAUSE OF DEATH:

Laceration of the brain due to a bullet wound.

3. Christopher Tippet Head.

The deceased was a rather heavily built adult man, 5'10½" in height.

The entrance wound of a bullet was seen in the back ½" to the left of the midline and 4' 3" from the heel. The entrance hole was ¼" in diameter, the area of bruising altogether nearly ½" in diameter. There was no peppering or tattooing of the wound.

The exit wound was in the middle of the side of the chest, 4'8" from the heel. It was irregular, its maximum dimensions being ½" by ⅓". The track of this wound could be followed through the 11th left rib 1" from its junction with the spine, through the lower lobe of the left lung, the front border of the upper lobe of the left lung and the left 7th rib in the midline of the side of the chest. The left chest contained more than two pints of fresh blood. There was a little vomit material and blood in the air passages.

Another series of injuries were found on the lower part of the body. These included an area of burning 3" wide which ran across both buttocks and was thought to coincide with some part of the exhaust system of the car under which he lay. In addition there was a lacerated wound 3½" long by 2" wide on the front of the left knee and upper shin, which was surrounded by grazes covering the whole of the upper part of the inner aspect of the calf and outer aspect of this knee. There were abrasions 7" long by 2" wide on the front of the right shin and knee and abrasion 4" by 3" on the front of the left upper thigh.

There were comminuted fractures of the upper third of the right thigh bone.

No natural disease was found in the body. All the organs were rather pale but otherwise healthy.

The stomach contained a large undigested meal.

The heart weighed 11½oz; liver 3lbs 13ozs; kidneys together 12oz; spleen 5oz.

I handed blood samples to Sergeant Lawrence.

CAUSE OF DEATH:

Haemorrhage from a bullet wound of the chest.

Dr Teare's report at post-mortem confirmed what was clear to anyone concerning the causes of the deaths of David Wombwell and Geoffrey Fox, both of whom had been shot at close range in the head. However, what is surprising is the absence in Teare's report of the contributory causes in the death of Christopher Head. It invites the question whether Dr Teare was asked to focus his medical findings on the gunshot wounds, as there would have been several good reasons for doing so.

First, if the Q-car running over Chris Head was viewed as contributing to his cause of death it complicated and blurred the murder charge against the man who shot him. Second, it might have been thought too gruesome and distressing to reveal publicly – and to the officers' families – that Head's death was in part due to, or had been hastened by, being run over by his colleague in the Q-car after Geoff Fox was shot at the wheel, thus inflicting additional injuries. Chris Head had been trapped under the vehicle with the weight of the car bearing down on his injured chest. And his critical condition had been exacerbated by witness Edward Morey's well-intentioned but ill-considered two attempts to drag the badly injured policeman out from under the car. It is possible that if Head had not been run over and had received prompt medical attention then his gunshot wound might not have proved fatal.

After frantic searches through local-authority vehicle records, by 8:30 p.m. the police had the name of the registered owner of the blue Vanguard PGT 726. With lightning efficiency Detective Sergeant James Pittendreight and a Detective Constable of 'S' Division based in Golders Green raced to 10 Stanhope Court, East End Road, London N3, half a mile south-west of Finchley Central Underground station. The detectives were joined by Dick Chitty and several vanloads of uniformed officers who surrounded the property.

Perplexed thirty-four-year-old insurance agent David John Richland answered the door. He confirmed to Chitty who he was but told him that he had sold the Vanguard some time ago. Chitty was in no mood to take his word for it and asked Richland if he possessed a firearm. Richland produced a .44 revolver from a trunk in the hallway. He explained that the revolver was an antique and over a hundred years old. During the subsequent search of the flat, three 9mm blank cartridges, a .45 bullet in an empty cartridge case and a holster were found. On a clothes hanger on a cupboard door in the sitting room was a police uniform. The items found did not prove Richland had taken any part in the shootings that afternoon but were enough to invite suspicion. Richland was asked to accompany the officers to Golders Green police station where after further questioning he agreed to make a written statement.

'In June or July 1964, I purchased a blue Standard Vanguard estate car from a man called Jim Willis, a member of the Flairavia Flying Club in Biggin Hill, Kent. I paid £100 cash for the car. I kept the car for just a little over a year and I advertised it for sale in the *Exchange and Mart*, I think in August or September, 1965. I had several replies to my advertisement and eventually I sold the vehicle for £25 to a mechanic employed by Wally Hainsby Ltd in Kilburn, who deal mainly in selling and repairing scooters, but I think they sometimes sell cars as I have seen them on the forecourt. I can't remember whether I notified the Council that I had disposed of the vehicle.

'I think about three months or so after I sold the car, I went to Hainsby's shop, hoping to sell some insurance. I saw the young Hainsby who had paid me the cheque. I asked him in conversation how the car was running and I believe he said it had been sold.'

Although Richland's explanation was plausible and he

appeared to be telling the truth there was still the matter of the gun and the police uniform found at his flat.

'With regard to the revolver and holster you found at my address today, this weapon I have had for about twenty years. I think I swapped something for it just after the war and it has been lying about ever since. Now and again I remember it and I take it out, look at it and oil it if I think it needs it. I have never fired anything from it and I wouldn't care to. The 9mm blanks and used .45 cartridge I have had for many years, in fact since I was a kid. I can't remember where I got them from; they have just always been there, actually.

'With regard to the police type uniform. This is in fact a film costume which I borrowed from Elvin Hood, a full-time film artist. I borrowed it for a part I got in a film called 'The Jokers' which I took part in last Saturday. I intended getting the shirt laundered and the trousers pressed before returning the costume.'

He gave a detailed account of his whereabouts and movements that day and eventually – bemused, shaken and much relieved – David Richland was released without charge.

Jack Slipper's account in his 1981 book *Slipper of the Yard* says: 'After one false start when officers picked up a previous owner of the car because the ownership records were not up to date, the registered owner of the Vanguard was traced.' However, that's not quite how it was. The job of tracing the current owner was a lot less straightforward than that and it came down to old-fashioned sleuthing and a bit of luck too.

Although Richland was clearly not one of the men responsible for the shootings in Braybrook Street that afternoon, there was at least some consolation and a glimmer of hope. He provided the name and address of the garage to which he'd sold the Vanguard and some additional details about the car. 'It was pale blue and fitted with a sun visor over the front windscreen and had a spotlight fitted to it on the front nearside just above the grille. It had a small, chrome, circular reversing light fitted above the number plate at the back on the nearside rear door; at least I think this was where it was. The car was fitted with a Triumph TR2 engine and gearbox. It had a four-speed floor change.'

Inspector Ron Steventon, Detective Sergeant Harvey and Detective Sergeant Burrows from West Hendon police station picked up the trail of the Vanguard owner. They questioned the man to whom David Richland said he had sold the car, Mr Wally Hainsby. Hainsby told the officers that as far as he could remember he'd sold the car to a man who lived in Kilburn for £55 pounds in October 1965. DI Steventon needed proof and details and asked for a name and address. Fortunately, Hainsby had kept a record of the transaction and eventually found it. He said that Derek Saar was the man and he lived close by in Tennyson Road.

When officers called at the address, just off the Kilburn

High Road, they were told by one of the occupants that Saar had moved to Canada two months ago, in June. But then, just when it was looking like the end of the trail, another occupant in the house recalled that Saar had relations who lived in Westbourne Park. It was another break, another slim chance and after further questioning Ron Steventon came away with another address.

A little over a mile and a half away the officers arrived at Leamington Road Villas, near Westbourne Park Underground station. All the while, only five minutes' walk away Jack Witney was at home in his flat in Fernhead Road. Because he had not taxed the Vanguard when he bought it or re-registered it in his name, and with the car now safely parked out of sight in the railway-arch garage in Vauxhall, Witney felt safe from detection, unaware that the determined efforts of the police meant they were now just one step away from connecting him to the old blue Standard Vanguard that had been seen driving away from the shootings in Braybrook Street five hours earlier.

Twenty-six-year-old Gerald O'Reilly, a painter by trade, answered the door of 30A Leamington Road Villas. He explained that he was Derek Saar's brother-in-law and told the officers what he knew about the car. He agreed to go to Harrow Road police station to make a written statement.

'My brother-in-law is Derek Saar who lived at 63 Tennyson Road, NW6. He owned a Standard Vanguard, index PGT 726. It was blue in colour and was a shooting brake. The bodywork and paint was bad but the engine was a Triumph 2 model and was in good condition. I am a learner driver and Derek was teaching me to drive on this car. The engine was very good and the car went well.

'My brother-in-law went to Canada in late June 1966 and asked my mother to sell the car for him and to use the money to send a trunk to Canada.

'Mum put a note on the car and parked it outside my house. She was asking £25 for it. She did not sell it and my step-brother, who lives at 10 Fernhead Road, found a customer who lives in the flat below him. I don't know this man's name. I'm not sure how much he paid Mum for the car, I think it was £25.

'It was about five weeks ago when Mum sold the car and I have seen it several times since, parked outside 10 Fernhead Road. I last saw the car yesterday at about 1 p.m.'

Chapter 12

At nine p.m. Detective Inspector Steventon, accompanied by Detective Sergeant Harvey and Detective Sergeant Burrows, rang the bell of the Witneys' ground-floor flat at 10 Fernhead Road, London W9.

As Lillian opened her front door the three officers entered and Jack Witney appeared from the back kitchen wearing a light blue T-shirt, blue trousers and slippers. He was carrying a towel and was drying his face.

Steventon said, 'We are police officers. Are you Mr Witney?'

'Yes, that's me – what do you want?' Witney replied,

'We are making enquiries concerning the owner of a blue Vanguard shooting brake, registration PGT 726, which we understand is yours.'

Racing through Witney's mind was how on Earth the police had traced the car to him and had done so in just five and half hours. With no time to think, Witney said, 'Oh no, not that.'

'What do you mean?' Steventon asked.

'We have just seen on the telly about the coppers being

shot,' Witney began. But before he could say any more Lillian interjected: 'They can't mean our car – where is it, dear?'

Witney said, 'I sold it today.'

'You didn't tell me,' Lillian protested. Witney must have been praying that she'd simply keep her mouth shut, but that was not his wife's way.

As far as DI Steventon and the other officers were concerned the story of the car being sold was by now a familiar one. Over the past few hours they and their colleagues from 'S' Division had been following the trail from the registered owner David Richland, via the dealer to whom he'd he sold it – Hainsby Ltd, West End Lane, London NW6 – to the address of Derek Saar, who had emigrated to Canada in June. They had questioned Saar's brother-in-law, Gerald O'Reilly, who had told them that his mother had sold the car to the downstairs neighbour of his step-brother at 10 Fernhead Road. But had Jack Witney really sold his car that day or were they now standing face to face with one of the murderers?

Witney was looking shifty.

'Who did you sell it to?' Steventon said.

'A man outside a pub in Eastcote,' Witney replied. 'He was in an Anglia,' he added for good measure.

While Steventon was trying to work out if Witney was lying and how best to trip him up, Detective Sergeant Harvey stepped in to keep up the pressure.

'Who is he?' Harvey asked.

Witney shrugged, 'I don't know. He came up to me in the car park and said, "How much for the old banger?" I said twenty pounds and he offered me fifteen and I agreed.'

Unconvinced, Harvey kept pressing, 'What happened then?'

'He jumped in the car, gave me a tenner, as that was all he had on him. Then he drove me to Hayes.'

Steventon came up with another idea. 'Didn't he test the car or look at it before he bought it?'

'He just left it there,' Witney said.

Harvey then asked, 'What's the name of this pub?'

'The Clay Pigeon,' Witney said. At least that had the benefit of being true. He knew as well as anyone that lies are often more convincing when they contain an element of truth.

Harvey said, 'How was he going to pay you the other five pounds?'

'He's calling round here in the morning to get the logbook for the car.'

The officers missed the next obvious move that would have tested Witney's story, which would have been to ask him to produce the logbook. Instead, Harvey said, 'Did you give him your name and address?'

'Yes.'

'Did he write it down?'

'No, he said he'd remember it.'

Steventon tried another tack. 'What were you doing in Eastcote, anyway?'

'I'd just gone for the ride and went into a pub about one o'clock. I just went there for a light ale.'

'What did you go to Hayes for?'

'Just wandering around,' Witney replied casually.

After hearing Jack's last answer Lillian couldn't contain herself any longer.

'You told me you'd been at work,' she protested. 'You didn't tell me you had sold the car. What's going on?'

In the circumstances Witney felt forced to tell the truth about something and he said, 'I haven't been to work for five weeks.' And then, to soften the blow and try to keep his wife on side, he added, 'I had to get some money for you.'

Lillian was not appeased but the fact that there were three determined-looking police officers in her flat questioning her husband about his possible connection with a triple murder still didn't seem to have struck home. She said, 'And you've let me get you up every morning and see you off, thinking you've gone to work.'

Now Witney was not only facing difficult questions from the police – there was also the wrath of his wife to contend with. It hadn't escaped Steventon and Harvey's attention that Witney was very agitated: he was trembling, perspiring freely, and he kept mopping his face with the towel he was holding.

Detective Sergeant Harvey said, 'What happened when you got to Hayes with this man?'

Although clearly off balance, Witney desperately tried

to keep his story on track. 'He dropped me and went off. I had a walk around, then I went to Acton, had a walk round there, looked in a betting shop, then caught a train home.'

Harvey said, 'What time did you get home?'

'Seven-thirty.'

Steventon had heard enough. 'I believe that men using your vehicle were concerned in the killing of police officers. I must ask you to come with us to Harrow Road police station for further enquiries.'

'I can't say any more,' Witney said. He'd said all he could think of to try and distance himself and he knew that his chances were slim.

He added that he needed to put on some shoes and get a coat but Steventon wasn't going to let Witney out of his sight. He stated later: 'We then went into his bedroom and Mrs Witney accompanied us. She was very upset and, embracing her husband, she said, "Please, darling, tell them the truth. What have you been doing, tell them who you were with." Witney replied, "I dare not say. Please get me a solicitor."

'We took Witney to Harrow Road police station where he said, "I had to sell the car to get Mum some money. I've been earning a living at the hoist."'

Steventon called the Shepherd's Bush operations room and at 11:45 p.m. Detective Chief Inspector Hensley arrived.

Hensley told Witney, 'I am taking you to Shepherd's

Bush police station where enquiries are being made into the deaths of three police officers who were shot earlier this afternoon.'

Witney made no reply.

The large crowd that had gathered outside Shepherd's Bush police station during the late afternoon and evening had gone home but there was still a posse of press reporters and photographers camped out who were eager for any news. None of them were aware that just under nine hours after the shootings the police now had a man in custody. Hensley and Witney arrived at the rear entrance of Shepherd's Bush police station shortly after midnight. Witney was smuggled in through the back door and was put into a cell.

At one a.m. Steventon returned to 10 Fernhead Road with Sergeants Harvey and Burrows and after searching the Witneys' flat took possession of various items of property:

One Dan Park showerproof coat.
One pair of Easiphit shoes.
Grey suit jacket.
Light beige woollen cardigan.
One pair of suede shoes.
One pair of check trousers.
Three darts.
One ballpoint pen.
Quantity of correspondence.

Whilst at the flat the detectives talked further to Mrs Witney who was understandably shaken and was very anxious about what had happened to her husband. Steventon told her that he'd been taken to Shepherd's Bush police station. Sensing an opportunity, he then asked Lillian if she knew the whereabouts of the car logbook. Without realising that she was contradicting her husband's story and incriminating him she said the logbook was always kept in the car. The officers returned with Witney's property to Harrow Road where it was handed to Detective Sergeant Lawrence.

At two-thirty a.m., two and a half hours after arriving at Shepherd's Bush and having had time to think things over, Witney was brought up from his cell to an interview room where Detective Chief Inspector Hensley and Detective Sergeant Begg spoke to him.

Hensley said, 'We are making enquiries into your explanation when you were first seen regarding your car. Have you anything to add to it?'

'No, what I told the officers is true,' Witney replied. He was returned to his cell.

Detective Superintendent Dick Chitty and Chief Superintendent Newman arrived at Shepherd's Bush and at 4:30 a.m. Witney was brought back to the interview room.

Chitty said, 'You know why you have been brought here?'

Witney replied, 'Yes.'

'I am told that the car concerned in the shooting was sold by you to a man outside a public house.'

'Yes, that's right.'

'To a man you had never met before in your life?'

'He asked me if I wanted to sell and how much and I told him twenty quid. He said he would give me fifteen pounds and I accepted. He offered me ten pounds and said he would bring the five pounds to my address tomorrow and get the logbook which was at home.'

Although DI Steventon had found no logbook at Witney's home and Lillian had told him that the logbook 'was always kept in the car', this crucial information had not been passed on to Chitty. No one had had much sleep and Dick Chitty had been got out of bed when Witney was brought in, which could explain why at half past four in the morning the normally sharp and shrewd Detective Superintendent did not challenge Witney's claim that the logbook was at his home.

Chitty said, 'What was this man like?'

'Just an ordinary bloke,' Witney replied. 'He was in a blue Anglia.'

'What time was this?'

'About two o'clock – before closing time, anyway.'

'Were you drinking with him in the public house?'

'No, I was on my own. He spoke to me as I was getting in the car.'

'As I understand it, he then left his own car at the public house and drove you in your car to Hayes.'

'That's right.'

'Where did this man live and where was he going with the car?'

'I don't know, he didn't say.'

'Why were you in the public house at all?'

'I went to meet a mate of mine who owes me five pounds.'

'You were going to see him in the public house?'

'No.'

'Where were you going to see him?'

'He lives that way.'

'Who is he?'

'John Crimmins.'

'Did you see him?'

'No.'

'So you went there for nothing really and just by chance someone buys your car and you say that the time was two o'clock?'

'Well, we came out of the pub before closing time.'

'We came out – who were "we"?'

'Well, *I* came out.'

'I'm afraid I cannot accept what you are saying about all this, but you will be given the opportunity to account for your movements in writing and you will remain here.'

At 6:30 a.m. Witney was brought up from his cell again and was seen by DCI Hensley and DS Begg. Hensley said, 'Do you wish to put in writing the details of your movements during yesterday?'

Witney replied, 'Yes, I've got nothing to hide.'

Witney then dictated his statement in the presence of DCI Hensley and DS Begg took it down. It took two hours and twenty minutes to record.

In his panic Witney had dug himself into a hole from which it was now impossible to escape. He had left home that morning with the intention of stealing a car in the company of Roberts and Duddy, little suspecting how that apparently ordinary day would turn out and determine the rest of his life. The decisions he made in Braybrook Street and what he later did and said from the time DI Steventon, DS Burrows and DS Harvey first arrived on his doorstep were pivotal in deciding his fate. After a sleepless night, at 6:30 a.m. on Saturday, 13 August 1966 Jack Witney was still struggling to come to terms with the inevitable and was desperately trying to make his story about selling his car sound more convincing.

STATEMENT OF: John Edward WITNEY
Age 36, Born 14.5.1930.
10 Fernhead Road, W9.
Unemployed.

About ten to eight yesterday morning I left home. I got into my car, a Standard Vanguard estate car, index PGT 726 which was parked opposite my house. I drove from my house up to Western Avenue through Great Western Road, right down Kensal Road, left at Ladbroke Grove, right at Barlby Road into North Pole Road, left into Scrubs Lane, right into Westway and on to the Western Avenue.

I went up Western Avenue as far as Northolt, pulled into a lay-by and went to sleep in the vehicle. I woke up about half past twelve and went, I don't know the name of the road but I turned right at the roundabout and went along and then turned off at Eastcote Lane.

I carried on up there to the Clay Pigeon public house. I turned left off the road into the car park and reversed so that my nose was parked facing the public house. There were about five or six vehicles in the car park but I cannot remember what they were. The nearest car to me was about three or four yards away or more.

I got out of my car, it would be about one o'clock, and I walked over to the saloon bar. It's on the front of the building and if you stand facing the building it is the left-hand door on the corner as you face it. I went into the bar; it is an 'L' shape and ordered a light ale and bitter. It was Courage's.

I sat down near the corner of the bar near the fireplace. I sipped my drink, had a smoke and overheard a cigar salesman talking. I think he was talking to someone who came from behind the bar. I heard the two men talking and it appertained to cigars. The salesman was telling the other man that these cigars appealed to cigarette smokers owing to their very mildness. They chatted for about fifteen minutes and the salesman just left and went out.

I stayed a few more minutes, finishing my drink, and got up and went into the toilet. It is on the left-hand side of the door, next to the fireplace. Then I left the bar by myself.

I didn't speak to anyone in the bar other than the man who served me with my beer. He was an Englishman, ordinary features, and I should say he was between forty-three and forty-eight years of age. From what I could see he would have been about 5'5" tall. I cannot remember anything more about the man.

The man who spoke to the cigar salesman was a very tall bloke and very heavily set. Judging by his complexion, very fresh and wearing horn-rimmed glasses, I would put him at 25. The cigar salesman was about 5'10", thickset and dark hair, wearing a dark suit.

As I said, I left the pub by myself, walked round to the car park. As I was about to get into my vehicle a man sitting in a small blue car, which I think was an Anglia, that was parked next to me leaned out of his window and called out, 'What will you take for the old banger?'

I thought he was joking but I said to him, 'Give me a score and you can take it away.'

He said to me, 'I'll give you fifteen.'

Being short of cash I accepted the offer. He got out of his car and said, 'Have you got the logbook?'

I said, 'No, not with me, it's at home.'

He said, 'Give me your address and I will pay you a tenner now and the other five when I pick up the logbook tomorrow.'

I accepted his offer by saying, 'All right, give me the tenner and I will give you the keys.'

He handed me two Bank of England five-pound notes. I then said to him, 'Which way are you heading?' and he said, 'I am going towards Hayes.'

I then said to him, 'If you drop me in the Uxbridge Road that will do fine.'

So we got into the Standard and he drove out of the car park and turned right down Eastcote Lane to the end, then we turned right through Northolt into Yeading Lane. We went right down the road to Uxbridge Road, Hayes. At Uxbridge Road we turned left and after about a hundred and fifty yards we pulled into the side and he said to me, 'Will this do you?'

I said, 'Yes, this will be fine.'

I got out and he said to me, 'I'll see you tomorrow at your place.'

I said, 'Yes, OK.'

DCI Hensley interrupted to ask Witney a few questions which are recorded in his statement.

'Did he tell you who he was?'

'No.'

'Did you ask him?'

'No.'

'When you gave him your address did he or you write it down?'

'No.'

'You did not mention giving your name and address in this statement.'

'I thought I did.'

'Do you want to put into this statement the matter regarding the exchange of your names and address between you and the buyer?'

'Go on, then. It was at the time of him asking if I had the logbook, when we came to the agreement that he should come to my place the following day, that was the time I gave him my name and address.'

'Do you know the area?'

'Oh, yes.'

'Shall we go back to your statement now?'

'Yes, sure. He drove off in the direction of Southall. I started walking down the road towards Southall. After a while I stopped at a bus stop and got onto a 207. I got off at Acton Vale and looked into a betting shop to pass the time. I don't know the name of the betting shop but it is almost opposite the King's Arms. I popped into it to see if I knew anyone. I didn't have a bet. I am not an inveterate gambler.'

Hensley asked, 'What time was it when you went into the betting shop?'

'About a quarter to three or three o'clock.'

'What race was on at the time?'

'I don't know. I didn't pay any interest.'

'How long did you stay in there?'

'I didn't really stay in there. I only looked in the door. I came out and turned down Uxbridge Road towards Shepherd's Bush. Then I went down Larden Road and I carried straight on the Goldhawk Road up to the Seven Stars, turned right along Paddenswick Road. I was going towards Hammersmith.'

Hensley asked, 'Why?'

'Just to kill time. I turned down Glenthorn Road towards Hammersmith and carried on through the Broadway and looked in some shops.'

'What shops?'

'Saqui and Lawrence.'

'Where did you go then?'

'Into the arcade and I hung around the Broadway for about three-quarters of an hour.'

'Why didn't you go home then?'

'Because my wife thought I was at work. I haven't been at work since June.'

'How have you been able to give her any money?'

'From various things and by thieving.'

'What kind of thieving?'

'Shoplifting, mainly.'

'Carry on with your statement.'

I walked through Shepherd's Bush by going down through the Grove. I turned into Goldhawk Road and wandered through the market. After looking about the market I walked up to Shepherd's Bush Green and sat down on the grass for half an hour. I then went to

Shepherd's Bush Station Metropolitan Line and caught a train to Westbourne Park. I got a paper when I came out at Westbourne Park and walked across the Harrow Road into Fernhead Road and I went indoors.

'Who was in when you got there?'

'My wife and two daughters.'

'The time was?'

'Just after seven.'

'During this long walk did you meet anyone you knew?'

'No.'

'You said you were looking for people in the betting shop. Do you know people in Shepherd's Bush?'

'Yes, I know a few people.'

'Describe the man who purchased your car.'

'He was very similar to your colleague (DS Begg) but his hair was parted the other side. He was aged 35, height 5'11" to 6'0", nose average, face just like yours (DS Begg) but darker just round the jaws, mouth smallish, good teeth, white shirt, blue tie with thin yellow stripes. Dark grey suit, single-breasted, wearing dark brown suede shoes. Thickset build. He would be 12½ to 13 stone in weight.'

Despite the wealth of detail about people that Witney had seen, the roads he'd driven along and walked down, the times and places, his alibi that he'd sold the car in the early afternoon the previous day was barely credible.

However, as far as the police were concerned they needed to prove that Witney wasn't where he said he'd been and hadn't sold the car in order for them to charge him and make that charge stand up in court.

Curiously, the key question of the location of the car logbook continued to be overlooked. There was no logbook found at Witney's flat and his wife Lillian had told DI Steventon that it was always kept in the car. But in all the lengthy questioning at Shepherd's Bush police station throughout the night of 12/13 August, Witney's interrogators never did establish that the logbook was not at Witney's home as he said it was. And the confirmation of this simple fact would have undermined the story that Witney gave to the police.

Nevertheless, there were a number of other details that would help discredit Witney's alibi. He said he had been to the Clay Pigeon pub and there would have been others drinking there that lunchtime who would remember him if that was true. He said he'd looked in at a betting shop in Acton Vale and that was another line of enquiry to follow. However, the focus of the investigation on that Saturday morning was on the blue Standard Vanguard and on trying to locate it. If by some slim chance Witney was telling the truth, the car could lead the detectives to the three men who had shot down their colleagues the previous afternoon. And if Witney was lying, finding the car would prove it.

Chapter 13

'That night was the longest night of my life. I couldn't eat, I couldn't sleep. Me and Lilly stuck to the telly and were watching the news when the newsreader announced that Jack had been arrested and taken to Harrow Road police station. The van registration number had been traced back to him. Shit! But at least they couldn't find the van,' Roberts recalled later in prison.

Shortly after dawn on Saturday, 13 August 1966, scores of police officers arrived in Braybrook Street to search the crime scene in even more detail. They crawled across the grass of Wormwood Scrubs Park on their hands and knees. The surface of the roadway and the gutters were re-examined inch by inch. Drain covers were lifted. The neat front gardens and privet hedges were searched meticulously for any small piece of evidence that might have been missed the evening before.

Among the search party was Detective Inspector Slipper from the Flying Squad, one of Tommy Butler's top men. The previous afternoon he'd been being driven through Acton when an urgent message had come over the radio calling all cars to contact the Yard following a serious GBH incident in Shepherd's Bush.

The following morning Slipper arrived in Braybrook Street at 6:30 a.m. and by 6:40 he was with DS Lovejoy when he found a piece of metal in the roadway, thirty feet from the footpath and a hundred and twenty feet behind where the Q-car had been. The fragment was handed to scenes-of-crime officer DS Lawrence. But it was later that Saturday that Slipper's involvement was to prove decisive and he later explained how that came about in his 1981 autobiography *Slipper of the Yard*.

It might seem odd to the public, but it wouldn't surprise another policeman to hear that nicking thirty-odd housewives for a washing-machine fiddle in the 1950s helped break the alibi of a murder suspect in one of the most violent crimes of the 1960s. The reputation and contacts you make at each stage of your career stay with you, and the name I'd acquired in Acton as a young Detective Constable helped put away the killers of the brutal Shepherd's Bush Murders in 1966.

The headline on the front page of Saturday's *Daily Mirror* was *MASSACRED IN THE LINE OF DUTY*. A large photograph took up half the page with the caption: *After the massacre . . . one detective lies dead in the road while a policeman pulls up a screen to hide the scene of the killings. In front of him is the Triumph 2000 Q-car under which can just be seen the head of another dead detective. The third detective was shot dead in the car.*

Under the photo was: *18,000 JOIN THE HUNT FOR*

KILLERS of 3 POLICEMEN. The opening sentence of the article below ended with a telling statement that four months later would be echoed by Mr Justice Glyn-Jones. *Two dead detectives lie in a street . . . still, silent symbols of the worst crime London has known this century.*

The report went on to say: *A wave of sympathy swept London last night as news spread of the massacre of three unarmed policemen* and that mystery shrouded the reason for the shootings. All of London's 18,000 policemen were searching for the killers, . . . *but humanly they felt just a little keener to run these particular killers to ground. In the hunt they gave London's underworld a shake-up it has never known before. Police cars criss-crossed the whole of London looking for the killer's getaway car – a blue Standard Vanguard which had the number PGT 726. But it was feared, by that time, that the car had been dumped.*

The reporting of how the murders had been committed was confused and inaccurate, but as far as the police were concerned all that mattered was the nationwide exposure of the make, model and index number of the car that they were desperate to track down. With the help of the press the police had at a stroke massively increased the number of those involved in the search beyond every police officer to millions of private citizens all over the country.

The urgency of the hunt for the killers was only matched by the feverish efforts of the press and TV reporters to discover exactly what had happened and what the police were doing about it. They wanted to give their readers and viewers every possible lurid detail. But for once even their customary hyperbole seemed inadequate.

On page two of the *Mirror* was the first of many items on a subject that was in the forefront of the minds of a lot of people: *The Police Federation last night called for the restoration of capital punishment for the murder of a policeman.* Mr Arthur Evans, the Federation secretary said, '*London and other large cities are in danger of being dominated by gangs of organised criminals.*'

It is understandable that the shootings should have been linked to the rise of criminal gangs in Britain's metropolitan areas at the time, particularly in London. It was hard for anyone to imagine that the horrific shooting dead of three policemen on a quiet London street in broad daylight was not somehow part of some wider, more sinister criminal enterprise. It was as tough to accept the reality: that instead the killers were criminal nonentities whose crimes up to that point had amounted to nothing more than acts of petty larceny for which they'd got nothing to show.

It was inevitable too that the murders should provoke intense feelings and reignite debate about the suspension of the death penalty that had passed into law just nine months earlier. It is central to understanding the shattering public impact of the 1966 Shepherd's Bush murders to comprehend how the penalty for murder stood in the opinions of the British people at the time.

In the Labour government's vision for a socialist Britain,

abolishing capital punishment was a priority when they came into office on 15 October 1964. The last executions in the country had been carried out simultaneously at eight a.m. on 13 August that year in Walton jail (HMP Liverpool) and Strangeways (HMP Manchester) when Peter Anthony Allen and Gwynne Owen Evans (real name: John Robson Walby) had been hanged for the murder of John West, a laundryman, whom they'd killed in the course of robbing him. In 1965, left-wing Labour MP Sydney Silverman, who had committed himself to the cause of abolition for more than twenty years, introduced a private member's bill to suspend the death penalty. The Bill was subsequently passed in the House of Commons by 200 votes to 98 and on 9 November 1965: the Abolition of Death Penalty Act suspended hanging for murder in the United Kingdom for an experimental period of five years.

However, the majority of citizens saw the death penalty as a vital cornerstone of British justice and the maintenance of law and order. For as long as anyone could remember, sentence of death had been the ultimate deterrent, an indispensable part of the process of crime and punishment. And the offences for which a convicted criminal could be put to death had in any case already been drastically reduced over the previous two centuries. During that time more than 200 crimes for which men, women and children could be hanged had been rescinded.

In April 1966 the disturbing trial of the Moors Murderers Myra Hindley and Ian Brady and the revelation of the depravity of their crimes had provided added ammunition for advocates of capital punishment. Four months later, after the callous murders of three police officers in Shepherd's Bush, the frightening conclusion was that suspending capital punishment had had destabilising consequences and, as critics had cautioned, would result in a significant increase in the number of unlawful killings.

During his career as an executioner for the state from 1932 to 1956 Albert Pierrepoint hanged more men and women sentenced to death than any other noose-man in British history, as far as is known. It is said that Pierrepoint executed at least 433 men and 17 women and was highly efficient – swift, and good at his job. It might be assumed that Pierrepoint was wholeheartedly in favour of capital punishment but in his 1974 autobiography *Executioner: Pierrepoint* he made a surprising comment.

It is said to be a deterrent. I cannot agree. There have been murders since the beginning of time, and we shall go on looking for deterrents until the end of time. If death were a deterrent, I might be expected to know. It is I who has faced them last, young men and girls, working men, grandmothers. I have been amazed to see the courage with which they take that walk into the unknown. It did not deter them then, and it had not deterred them when they committed what they were convicted for. All the men and women whom I have faced at that final moment convince me that in what I have done I have not prevented a single murder. Capital punishment, in my view, achieved nothing except revenge.

The Shepherd's Bush Murders

Although Albert Pierrepoint's view is persuasive, in the summer of 1966 fears and feelings were running high amongst policemen and everyday citizens alike who thought that the Braybrook Street shootings would never have happened if the death penalty had not been suspended.

Home Secretary Roy Jenkins, a man usually circumspect in his comments, said in a statement: 'The position is terrifying a lot of people and threatening the whole fabric of society.'

The public reaction was profound and widespread. People delivered flowers and donations of money to police stations all over the country for the widows and relatives of the victims.

On Saturday, 13 August Roy Jenkins broke off from his summer holiday and arrived at Shepherd's Bush police station where on the roof a Union flag was flying at half-mast.

After a meeting with Detective Superintendent Dick Chitty and his investigation team Jenkins came out of the main entrance and stopped to make an announcement to the large crowd of press and public that had gathered outside. There were angry shouts of 'Bring back the rope!' and the Home Secretary was only too well aware of the temperature of public feeling. 'Well, I can well understand the reaction and feeling of policemen at the present time. But it would be quite wrong for me to take a major policy decision in the shadow of one event, however horrible that may be.' Without further comment Jenkins climbed into his chauffeur-driven government car and set off for Braybrook Street to see the crime scene for himself.

Away from the public furore provoked by the shootings, Jack Witney sat quietly alone, in his cell, weighing up the odds. He couldn't be certain that the recently suspended death penalty would not be reinstated when it came to punishing the murderers of three police officers.

Although the story he'd given to the police about selling his car was improbable, the onus was on the police to prove that he'd lied if they were ever going to charge him successfully. While the search for the blue Standard Vanguard continued, officers went to the Clay Pigeon public house in Eastcote. John Cummins, the man Witney said he had intended to visit the previous day to collect a five-pound debt, was traced. And then there was the bookmaker's shop in Acton Vale that Witney said he had been into briefly on Friday afternoon.

Detective Inspector Slipper from the Flying Squad, 'Slipper of the Yard', had two things to offer on this aspect of Witney's alibi. First, the discouraging news that he knew that the manager of the bookie's premises was a cousin of Witney's, but second, that Slipper knew this man personally. He suggested that he should go and pay him a visit.

Chapter 14

Although he was a tall and imposing man who looked like he could take care of himself in a fight, forty-two-year-old Jack Slipper's method of getting what he wanted out of people was typically quiet and thoughtful, almost gentle at times. 'I planned to approach the betting-shop manager carefully. I knew that barging in with a heavy-handed, formal approach would be a mistake. The betting-shop manager wasn't a villain, but he was a useful sort of chap; a very experienced man who knew his way around and who was, unfortunately, very close to Witney's family, which meant a lot in a closely-knit community like Acton.'

While dozens of the murdered policemen's colleagues from 'F' Division were on their hands and knees searching for clues in Braybrook Street on Saturday morning, Harry Roberts went to Duddy's flat at Treverton Towers. Duddy told him that he felt trapped eight floors up so Roberts suggested they should go back to Wymering Mansions in Maida Vale. But Roberts's motive wasn't concern for the man he'd incited to shoot Geoff Fox the previous afternoon. It was simply self-preservation.

'Duddy collapsed on the couch. He was in a terrible mess. He couldn't eat or drink, at any little noise he leapt to his feet. I knew the only thing that could tie us in with the shooting was the van. I had to get rid of it. I had to find a way. I couldn't think straight – Duddy was making me uneasy. By the afternoon I just had to get out of the flat. I suggested that we all go to the park with June's kids.'

Hoping to disprove Witney's alibi about selling his car, Detective Inspector Donald and Detective Sergeant Harris Sergeant went to the Clay Pigeon pub. They spoke first to one of the regulars, Stanley Feathers, and asked if he remembered seeing a man fitting Witney's description drinking in the pub that Friday. In his statement Feathers was quite certain who had been in the pub at lunchtime that day. 'I am a regular at the Clay Pigeon Hotel, Field End Road, Eastcote. I have been using this house for 26 years, having a drink on some lunchtimes and evenings.

'At 12:45, Friday, 12 August, I entered the saloon bar where three of the regulars were at the bar. I spoke to them but did not join them. I stood alone at the bar. There were three people lunching at the corner of the bar near the fireplace. They came from G. Walker and Slater, builder of Field End Road. The three customers at the bar were Nobby Clark, Sid and another man in a blue-grey suit who I did not know.

'A regular named Bill came in later as did Jack Traynor and his son John. A customer named Stewart came in followed by Bob Rapson. That was the lot. I just remembered a man named Jock Davidson came in also. He is a transport driver and wears red overalls.

'I left dead on 2:30 p.m., but at no time did I see any man answering the description which you have told me about.'

Nineteen-year-old Hadyn Ingram, who had been left in charge of the Clay Pigeon while his parents were away on holiday, told more or less the same story. He said there were about a dozen people in the saloon bar that lunchtime and, like Feathers, he could not recall a man on his own who fitted Witney's description. As far as the police were concerned it all added weight to disproving Witney's alibi about going to the pub.

However, there are two details in Ingram's statement that were significant. He confirmed that 'at 1 p.m. a cigar salesman from Churchmans called at the premises and I spoke to him in the saloon bar.' And then there's a postscript at the end of the statement which echoes exactly something that Witney said in his. Ingram added, 'Further to my statement, the cigar salesman did say they were very mild cigars suitable to cigarette smokers.' In Witney's statement – which was riddled with many questionable details of his movements on Friday, 12 August – he had said, 'The salesman was telling the other man that these cigars appealed to cigarette smokers owing to their very mildness.' It wasn't decisive but it did add some credibility to Witney's account.

Fifty-three-year-old George Edwin Yates, who was

working behind the bar at the Clay Pigeon on that day, also recalled that a man from Churchmans was in the saloon bar at lunchtime. Yates's wife Phyllis said that she remembered seeing a blue Ford Anglia standing outside the public house after the lunchtime opening period. She thought the index number contained the figures 344 but did not notice the Vanguard or a man answering Witney's description.

Of course, unbeknown to the police and the people they questioned, the recollections of Feathers, Ingrams and others were skewed because Witney had not been alone in the pub that day but in the company of Duddy and Roberts.

Witney had mentioned that his reason for being in Eastcote was because he was hoping to see a friend of his, John Crimmins, who owed him five pounds. On Saturday afternoon Detective Sergeant Sugrue and Detective Constable Conroy went to the home of thirty-four-year-old John William Crimmins at 166 Southbourne Gardens, Eastcote. Crimmins confirmed that he knew Witney. 'Witney is related to my wife, in fact he is my wife's second cousin.'

It was not a promising start as the family connection made it doubtful that Crimmins would be prepared to say anything to contradict Witney and might even lie to try and help him. But, clearly nervous of being implicated, self-preservation was his overriding motive and Crimmins agreed to make a statement concerning his own movements on the day of the shootings and the origin of the £5 that he owed Witney. Fifty years later the details provide an insight into the everyday life of Jack Witney and his meagre ambitions and circumstances.

'The last time Witney visited my address was on Wednesday, 3 August 1966. He arrived at my address at 8:30 p.m. with his wife Lil. They arrived in a blue-grey old-type Standard Vanguard.

'During the course of the evening we decided to go for a drink and his wife decided to come with us. Before going for a drink he told me he had purchased the Vanguard from a man who had gone to Canada. He told me that he had bought the vehicle for £20. He also told me that he was going to dispose of his old car, a yellow and black Vauxhall Victor.

'We discussed what he was going to do with the Vauxhall and he said that he intended to break the vehicle up and sell the parts.

'During the conversation, he asked me if I was interested in buying the tyres from the Vauxhall car. I told him I only really wanted two of the tyres as I already had two good tyres on my own vehicle. He said that he wanted 30 shillings each for the tyres. The conversation took place in the presence of my wife and his wife in the sitting room at my address.

'At approximately 9:30 p.m. Witney, his wife and myself left my address in his Vanguard motor car and went to the Black Horse Public House at Eastcote. I do not know the exact address but I think it is in Eastcote Lane. Whilst drinking the topic of tyres did not come into the conversation. We left the public house at closing time, 10:30 p.m. and returned to my address. He did not come into the house and I made arrangements to visit his house on Friday, 5 August, in the early evening to pick up the tyres.

'I arrived at his address, 10 Fernhead Road, at approximately 7:30 p.m. He was at the house with his wife. We then both left his address and went round the corner in Kennet Road, where he had both his Vanguard motor vehicle and his Vauxhall car parked.

'We tried to get the tyres off the Vauxhall car but were unsuccessful. Whilst trying to get the tyres off I went to a taxi-cab garage which is in Fernhead Road and borrowed a tyre lever from the owner of the garage. As we were unable to remove the tyres I eventually returned to the taxi-cab garage. The owner then helped me and with his help we managed to remove the five tyres from the Vauxhall and put four of these tyres on my vehicle. Mr Witney was with us all the time.

'The owner of the garage charged me 50 shillings for fitting the tyres and the cost of new valves. I told Witney that I had paid £3 for the fitting and said I was only prepared to pay him £5 for the five tyres. I told Witney a lie about the price I had to pay for the fitting of the tyres. I did this because I was short of money and I thought I could get them cheaper.

'He agreed to this, but I said that I was unable to give him the money immediately and told him that I would see him on the Sunday lunchtime at his home, that would be 7 August.

'I never visited Witney on the Sunday and I haven't seen him, or been in contact with him, since and as far as I know I still owe him £5.'

There was the more pressing matter of whether Witney had actually gone to Eastcote the previous day to collect the unpaid debt. John Crimmins said, 'Witney had made no arrangements at all to visit me at my address or meet me at the Clay Pigeon Public House on Friday, 12 August. Witney is fully aware that I am employed as a painter and would normally be away from my address between 7 a.m. and 6 p.m. I should add that in the past he has called at my address when I have been out working and had a cup of tea with my wife.'

Crimmins gave an account of his movements the previous day. He had left home at 6:45 a.m. and driven to the District Hospital in Erith, Kent where his employers, Clean Walls Ltd of Blue Star House, Archway N19, had a contract to carry out some work. He picked up two workmates on the way and they were engaged in washing down the Out-patients Department until 4:15 p.m. and went without lunch. After finishing work Crimmins drove via Haverstock Hill NW3 and Greenford to drop off his workmates before finally returning home.

The statements taken from Feathers and Ingram at the

Clay Pigeon suggested that Witney had not been to the pub that lunchtime but the mention of the cigar salesman was an unlikely coincidence. The lengthy statement of Crimmins didn't prove that Witney had not intended to call at his house to ask his wife about the five pounds he was owed. From the start Witney's account of his movements and whereabouts on Friday, 12 August had seemed dubious but the police were still no closer to having concrete evidence that he was one of the three men who had shot dead three police officers in Braybrook Street the previous afternoon.

Meanwhile Jack Witney's wife Lillian was taken to Shepherd's Bush police station and agreed to make a statement. She said that she believed when her husband left home at his usual time on Friday morning he was going to work '. . . for the people who make windscreens. I believe it was Triplex.' She gave an account of how they had acquired the Standard Vanguard that fitted the facts already known. She came up with an additional detail that made the car more easy to identify. 'The car I would describe as being very old and may have in the past been converted from a van into a shooting brake.' Her observation explained the conflicting descriptions given by witnesses at the scene where some described it as an 'estate car' while others said it was a 'van'. Sharp-eyed Bryan Deacon had said that it was a Vanguard estate car but unusually had two doors, not four.

Lillian Witney continued with details of her and Jack's

domestic life and routines. When asked about John Crimmins and the five-pound debt her response was, 'I do not know of anyone owing my husband money and secondly Crimmins was a friend of my husband and he used to work with him years ago. It would have been last week, I believe, that my husband mentioned that we should go over to see Crimmins. I didn't want to go. I think Crimmins lives in Ruislip.'

It seems that overnight Lillian had reflected on her outbursts while her husband was being questioned by police officers when they had called at nine o'clock the previous evening. When DI Steventon had returned later to take possession of some of her husband's belongings, she told him that the logbook was always kept in the car. But in her interview at Shepherd's Bush police station the following day she said, 'The logbook was kept sometimes in the car or in the house. I cannot remember when I last saw it.'

Lillian Witney ended her written statement to the police with a curious remark that was a mixture of a disclaimer and an oblique indictment of her husband's associates: 'I do not know any of his friends. I do not allow any of them to come to my house and he never goes out in the evenings nor has he ever spent a night out.'

Detective Sergeant Bartlett of C10, the Stolen Motor Vehicle Investigation Branch, CID New Scotland Yard, was contacted by Deputy Commander Pollard. Pollard stated that a Standard Vanguard van conversion, similar to the vehicle described by Lillian Witney and by witnesses to the shootings in Braybrook Street, was urgently required for photographic purposes and asked Bartlett to assist. A suitable vehicle was traced to Mr A.V. Mundy of Mundy Motors, Bourneville Road, SE6, who agreed to loan his vehicle to the police.

By 5:30 p.m. Jack Slipper was in Acton Vale. He intercepted Charles Hughes as he was closing his betting shop for the day. Slipper told Hughes that he wanted to have a private conversation and took him to the King's Arms across the road where, in a quiet corner, Slipper explained the reason for his visit.

Despite the enormous pressure on the police to act swiftly and decisively Jack Slipper's account of the conversation is surprisingly matter-of-fact. 'I laid out the problem. When you want a written statement from a man like Charlie Hughes, the last thing you do is mention it. The line I took was that Charlie was the man in the middle and I was someone who might be able to save him some embarrassment. Charlie's attitude was that Witney was just a mug who couldn't possibly have been involved in a triple police murder.'

Hughes raised a good point: Witney did not have the kind of character or criminal profile to be one of the murderers. And with all the speculation about organised gangs and gangsters being responsible for the murders the hapless Witney certainly did seem out of place. But Slipper told Hughes that he and his colleagues were in no doubt that Witney was involved and the charges facing him were very serious. Hughes knew from past experience that Slipper was fair but determined and also that his offer to help him resolve the issue as painlessly as possible was genuine. As the conversation progressed Slipper gained Hughes's confidence and eventually Charlie Hughes relented and said that Witney hadn't been near the betting shop the previous day. 'I have every reason to be sure of that, even though I work in a back room. Witney often comes to the shop but he is always on the earhole. I was getting sick of it and if Witney had come in, the clerk in the front of my shop would have immediately warned me.'

The first step of Slipper's strategy had paid off but the point of his mission was to get Hughes to put it in a written statement.

'There's no way I can do it,' Hughes replied resolutely.

Slipper's softly-softly approach had reached the crunch point. Hughes was under no legal obligation to formally state that Witney had not been in his shop. He could easily fudge it if he chose to and say that he couldn't be certain one way or the other. Hughes said he'd have to talk it over with his family and despite the urgency Slipper had to bide his time. He said he'd visit Hughes at home the following morning.

Back at Shepherd's Bush police station his guv'nor, Dick Chitty, was not best pleased with Slipper's drawn-out approach. But he knew well enough from long experience that getting results often required stealth and patience. Still, with Witney in custody the pressure was mounting to produce the evidence with which to charge him – and the strength of feeling from the public, higher authorities and the government had been building throughout the day. As far as the police investigation was concerned, even with the enormous amount of manpower, resources and nationwide publicity devoted to the case, the simple fact remained that tangible progress had been limited during the twenty-four hours since David Wombwell, Chris Head and Geoff Fox had been murdered.

As the first frantic day of the investigation drew to a close, during which thousands of police officers all over London had been working tirelessly, the key to unlocking the triple murder finally came out of the blue when William Keeley and his wife Rebecca walked into Kennington police station shortly after 10 p.m.

Chapter 15

At 7:45 that Saturday evening, eighteen-year-old William Keeley backed his tipper lorry up to railway arch 102, where it was always garaged overnight, and got out to open the large wooden archway doors. He had been working for his father all day on a job in Sidcup repairing a house and demolishing an air-raid shelter. His father, William Keeley senior, rented railway arches 102 and 103 off Tinworth Street in Vauxhall. While securing the doors young William noticed through a gap in the doors of arch 103 a blue Standard Vanguard with a lorry wheel propped against the rear of the vehicle.

He had read in the newspaper that the police were looking for a Vanguard in connection with the recent murder of three policemen. 'I was suspicious and after putting my own truck away I went home to tell my mother.'

At 8:00 p.m. he returned to the nearby family flat where he lived with his parents and told his mother what he'd seen. 'She suffers with her nerves and she became alarmed. I was late for a date with my girl so I got changed as soon as possible and left home.'

William's mother, Rebecca, recalled, 'When he came in he said, "There's a funny bluish motor in the arch like the police are looking for." This is not the exact words but near enough what he actually said. I asked him if he had seen the number and he said no, there's a big tyre standing against the number plate preventing anyone seeing it.'

An hour later Rebecca's husband, forty-nine-year-old William senior, came home and she told him what their son had said about the blue Vanguard. William replied dismissively that he'd recently rented space in archway 103 to a man and the car probably belonged to him.

When the television news came on at ten o'clock the newsreader announced that the police were still searching for a blue Standard Vanguard, registration number PGT 726. Rebecca urged her husband to go and take a look at the car in the archway for himself but he said he had given the only key to the man who had rented the space. The man had said he'd get a spare key cut but had not yet done so. But Rebecca would not calm down. The nerves that her son referred to would not let her rest and eventually she persuaded her husband to go with her to Kennington police station.

In Harry Roberts's account he says that at around 10:00 p.m. he and Lilly Perry went to the railway arch. 'It was really quiet and nobody was around. I didn't like the look of it . . . The closer I got to the arch the more I was convinced it was an ambush.'

Shortly after midnight on Sunday, 14 August, Detective

Sergeant Bernard Harvey, in the company of Detective Constable William Hewetson from Paddington police station and other uniformed officers, arrived at Tinworth Street. Railway arch 103 was in darkness, the doors secured by a hasp and staple fastened by a padlock. The silence was interrupted only by the deep rumble of late-night trains passing overhead. With the aid of torches it was possible to see between gaps in the doors that a Standard Vanguard was parked inside on the right of the archway. But, as young William Keeley had told his mother, there was a large tyre resting against the rear of the vehicle so it was not possible to see the number plate.

DS Harvey ordered an officer to force the padlock but he was unable to do so. Ten minutes later a pair of bolt cutters was obtained from the nearby fire station on the Albert Embankment and the padlock was severed in two places. One door was eased open and torchlight flickered back and forth in the cavernous interior. The detectives entered cautiously, careful not to disturb anything, aware that there could be men concealed inside, behind a Ford Thames lorry parked against the back wall and an ex-army Austin Champ next to it. Two uniformed officers rolled away the large wheel at the rear of the Vanguard and in the light from Harvey's torch the index number of the car was revealed: PGT 726.

DS Harvey left the scene for assistance and later returned and was joined by Chief Superintendent Newman and the enigmatic ace detective, the 'Grey Fox' or 'One-Day Tommy', the Head of the Flying Squad, fifty-four-year-old Chief Superintendent Thomas Marius Joseph Butler. Harvey took possession of the severed padlock and handed it to Butler.

How the car seen driving away recklessly after the shootings in Braybrook Street had ended up in William Keeley's railway arch at Vauxhall and who had driven it there were still the overriding questions to be answered. But finding the vehicle was a major step forward. After thirty-three hours of intense activity now at least the police had something more to go on. And the car would doubtless hold more clues that would help solve why three colleagues had been gunned down and who were the men that killed them.

Roberts and Lilly Perry's independent accounts of going to the railway arches at Vauxhall that Saturday night to destroy the Vanguard suggest that they narrowly avoided bumping into the police. When he got there Roberts looked through the slats in the wooden doors but could not work out how to dispose of the car. And as the police officers discovered, it was impossible to even gain access to the archway without tools and Witney had the only key to the padlock. Roberts's plan was desperate and ill-thought-out. It would clearly not have been possible to destroy the car in situ without attracting attention. He could not have driven it elsewhere as the widely publicised vehicle and its registration number would have been quickly spotted. Anyway, Witney had the ignition key.

*

At eight o'clock on Sunday morning Detective Inspector Jack Slipper and Detective Sergeant George Garbut arrived at the home of Charlie Hughes in Roehampton. Slipper was about to find out if his tactful approach the previous day had paid off. The two detectives were invited inside. Slipper didn't need to remind Hughes and his wife how serious the situation was. 'We sat with Hughes and his wife during a very tense and gloomy breakfast.'

Slipper said, 'I'm sure you couldn't live with yourself if you lied to save him. You know that as well as I do, this isn't like covering up for someone who's been buying and selling a bit of gear.'

'I know it,' Charlie answered. 'I've talked to a couple of people and I know I've got to do it. I'll give you your statement.'

Charlie Hughes's statement was two and a half pages long. He didn't equivocate despite the fact that it would have been easy for him to do so. It was a credit to Slipper's skilful handling of the situation and playing it quietly despite the enormous pressure.

The central paragraph of Hughes's statement about his cousin Jack Witney helped to undermine the account that Witney had given to the police. 'I have been asked if Jack Witney had been into my shop on Friday, 12th August 1966. I must say with all honesty that he was not. Although I am in the back of the shop most of the time I continually go to the front counter to check the current bets prior to each race. I would have certainly seen him if he had only popped in because in this business you've got to keep your eyes open. Leonard Lay, my clerk, works on the front counter all the time and would have told me if Witney had shown himself. Last night I had a drink with Lay and mentioned the fact that Jack Witney had supposedly called at our shop on Friday afternoon and he confirmed that he had not seen him.'

Early on Sunday morning Duddy and Roberts went to Kenwood on Hampstead Heath to bury the guns. Duddy decided he would go to Scotland and lie low and he and Roberts parted company. Back at Wymering Mansions Roberts packed a suitcase and arranged to meet Lilly Perry under the clock at Paddington Station at three p.m.

At Shepherd's Bush police station Slipper showed his guv'nor, Dick Chitty, the statement that Charlie Hughes had made. It was a good start but it didn't provide nearly enough evidence to charge Witney. Now the car had been found they needed William Keeley to identify the man to whom he had rented space in railway arch 103. Keeley had been taken to Scotland Yard and had made a statement in the presence of the redoubtable Detective Chief Superintendent Tommy Butler.

'About Tuesday, 2nd August 1966 I was approached by a man who asked me if he could put his car in the arch. After discussing the matter he went away and returned again on 9th August. We again discussed the garage space and we agreed with him renting the arch for £1 per week. He gave me £4 for one month's rent. I mentioned to him there was only one key for the garage lock. I told him I wanted to get two keys made. The man said he would get a second key cut and took the only key.'

Keeley told Butler that his son had seen the car first and had told his mother and later on Saturday night he and his wife had decided to inform the police. However, Keeley said that he did not know the name or address of the man who rented the arch. He described him as about twenty-eight to thirty-five years old, around 5'9" tall, slim build, thin face, clean shaven, fair hair receding and combed back. 'If I saw this man again I would know him.'

In Vauxhall, fingerprint and forensics officers began the painstaking task of examining the Standard Vanguard. An initial inspection by Detective Superintendent Robert Peat, Fingerprint Branch, New Scotland Yard, found the following marks:

A palm mark on the outside rear offside body below the window.

A thumb mark on the outside of the glass of the revolution counter mounted on the nearside of the dashboard.

On the floor of the car, in front of the nearside seat he found a cardboard folder containing two number plates, index JJJ 285D. There were numerous other finger marks on the interior of the vehicle and it was decided they should be more thoroughly dusted and examined at the Metropolitan Police forensic laboratory at Theobalds Road.

Before the car was removed to Holborn by tow truck it was noted that the interior also contained a large collection of miscellaneous objects and general detritus. The most significant items were a spent cartridge case on the parcel shelf in the left-hand rear corner and a 9mm unspent bullet on the left-hand passenger seat between the back and the seat. On the nearside rear floor were three more spent cartridge cases. These, the most incriminating items, were handed over to the Scenes of Crimes Officer, Detective Sergeant Lawrence.

At neighbouring properties detectives went from door to door interviewing local residents, including twenty-six-year-old Elizabeth Pantlin who lived at 98 Tinworth Street and her neighbour, fifty-eight-year-old Helen King, who lived at number 99.

Helen King said that she'd been on her balcony on Friday afternoon talking to Elizabeth Pantlin when she saw a blue van drive into the entrance of the railway arches at the rear of their flats. 'The vehicle hit the side of the arch into which it was going and the driver, who I didn't see, reversed the van to get into the arch. I did not see any more because at that time I sat down on a chair on the balcony and the wall obstructs your vision. Betty, that is Mrs Pantlin, told me that one man came out of the arch and also that a man who has the arch next to the one into which the van went, thumped on the side of the van as if to say "Get in quick".'

Elizabeth Pantlin told the detectives, 'As we were talking, a blue van drove into the yard and the driver, although not driving fast, drove into the wall of the last railway arch, which is number 103. A man came from archway number 102 and banged on the side of the van. The driver of the van then drove into the other archway and out of our sight.

'About five minutes later I saw him walking out of the yard. I would describe the driver of the van as about 30-36 years of age, 5'10" tall, well-built and was wearing a white shirt and dark trousers. I stood talking to Mrs King on the balcony until five and twenty past four. I know it was about this time because I looked at my clock in order to get my husband's dinner on time when he came in.

'Thinking back I remember that the man who brought the van locked the gates to the arch where he put the van.

'I cannot help but be sure that the van I saw drive into that arch was the same as the one the newspapers said was used in the shooting at Braybrook Street, Shepherd's Bush because the index number PGT 726 was the same.'

Detective Inspector Slipper's next task was to collect William Keeley and take him to Shepherd's Bush police station. 'It should have been a routine assignment, but as soon as I picked up the garage owner at his flat, I knew it wouldn't be. On the way to the Bush the man assured me that he would be able to identify the Vanguard's owner, but I wasn't convinced. He was too nervous. His hands were sweating and his brow was damp. Inwardly he was shaking and there's nothing worse on an identity parade. When a witness is scared he doesn't look properly at the faces in the line. He just goes past in a daze.'

While Slipper was picking up Keeley, at Shepherd's

Bush police station Witney was brought up at three p.m. from his cell to the first-floor investigation office to see Chief Superintendent Newman and Detective Superintendent Chitty.

Chitty first cautioned Witney and then said, 'I have seen the statement you have made and I still think you are lying. Where is your car parked at night?'

Witney replied, 'It's always left in the street.'

'Have you ever put it in a garage or under cover anywhere?'

'No.'

'Have you ever rented a garage from anybody?'

'No.'

'Are you quite sure? Think very carefully – I have made a lot of enquiries since I last saw you.'

'What can I say?' Witney said. 'You don't think I would use my own car on a thing like this, do you?'

'The car has been found and I don't think I need tell you where.'

After a long pause Witney said, 'I've been lumbered, I can't say anything, I just can't.'

'What are you frightened of?'

There was another pause and finally Witney said, 'I'm not saying any more.'

'I believe you were in this car at Braybrook Street and that after the shootings you drove it to a certain pre-arranged garage. Many witnesses have been interviewed and I propose to put you on an identification parade.'

'Not here you don't,' Witney replied. 'I'll go on one at Brixton but not here.'

'You are refusing to go on an identification parade at this station, is that right?'

'Yes, I'll go on one at Brixton and then do something to get a solicitor.'

Witney was then taken from the office and returned to his cell.

When Slipper arrived with Keeley they went to the charge room and Witney was brought in at 5:55 p.m. Slipper's instincts about Keeley's nervousness were justified. 'From the looks the two exchanged, there was absolutely no doubt in my mind that we had the right man. Yet the garage owner wouldn't make the identification. He looked Witney up and down a couple of times then he said, nervously, "No. It isn't him. But it's so much like him, it's unbelievable." It was a bombshell. It broke the heart of the team of investigating detectives.'

Depressed but undeterred, Slipper took Keeley upstairs to a first-floor office to make a written statement.

At 6:30 p.m. Witney was brought back to the Charge Room and this time was confronted by fourteen-year-old Miss Anna Dunleavy, one of the witnesses at Braybrook Street. She lived at number 59 and had said in her statement the previous day that the driver of the blue car looked like Bobby Charlton.

Having seen Witney, Anna Dunleavy said, 'It's very much like him. I thought he had more hair at the front.'

She said later that she was too frightened to say that the man she saw face to face at Shepherd's Bush police station was the man she'd seen driving the car in Braybrook Street.

It was perhaps a policeman's instinct, but Slipper and his colleagues were convinced that Keeley was not telling the truth and for some reason had ducked out of identifying Witney. Before Keeley began his next statement Slipper said that with the capture of those responsible for the murder of three policemen at stake the investigation would be extremely thorough and it would be very much in Keeley's interests for him to be completely truthful. He advised Keeley that he should be careful about saying anything he would not be willing to repeat in court in what was going to be a very thorough, high-profile trial.

Keeley looked thoughtful but said nothing and began writing. Slipper played a waiting game. A few sentences into his statement Keeley suddenly looked up and said, 'I'd like to complete this statement later. I'd like to discuss it first with my wife and family.'

Harry Roberts had kept his rendezvous with Lilly Perry that afternoon to meet under the clock at Paddington Station at three o'clock. A few hours later they checked in for two nights at the Hotel Russell in Russell Square, Bloomsbury. Roberts gave the receptionist, twenty-two-year-old Inge Maria Ruf, their names and address – Mr and Mrs Crosbie, 47 Palermo Street, Springburn, Glasgow – and they were shown to room 749.

Chapter 16

The wily Jack Slipper knew that he was getting somewhere and took William Keeley back to his flat in Vauxhall. 'Keeley asked for two hours alone. I left him and shot across London to do another quite separate task, then went back to his flat.'

When Slipper returned he found an extraordinary scene. 'What looked like his whole family was gathered round, his wife, his children, some aunts and uncles, a cousin or two – the atmosphere was like a wake.'

Keeley took Slipper aside and said, 'I'd like to come back with you now and make a fresh statement. I wasn't telling the truth.'

Later in the evening of Sunday, 14 August at Shepherd's Bush police station William Keeley's second statement was to prove a tipping point in the murder investigation. Earlier that day he had begun the statement concerning the identification of Jack Witney in the presence of DI Slipper and several hours later he completed it.

'Further to my statement I made to police at 3 o'clock this morning. At 5:55 p.m. today, 14th August 1966 at

Shepherd's Bush police station, I was shown a man and asked by a uniform police sergeant if he was the person who had hired a garage space at one of my arches in Tinworth Street, SE11.

'Since I have been away I have talked this matter over with my family and have decided to tell you that I am now certain that the man I saw at Shepherd's Bush police station this afternoon was in fact the man that rented the garage space at my arch. I am absolutely certain that he was the person and will not change my mind in respect of this.'

What Keeley did not explain in his latest statement was the reason why he had not identified Witney when he'd seen him that afternoon. In reality, Keeley had known Witney for some time before he'd rented him garage space in the railway arch and he would only finally tell the whole story in a third statement the following day.

At 8:40 p.m. Witney was brought to the Charge Room where Detective Chief Inspector Hensley and Detective Superintendent Dick Chitty were waiting for him.

Chitty said, 'Shortly after three p.m. on Friday, 12 August, three police officers were killed in Braybrook Street. I was present later that day at a post-mortem examination on the bodies which revealed all three were shot dead. As a result of the enquiries I have made you will now be charged with being concerned with two others in killing the officers.'

Chitty cautioned Witney. Witney said nothing. He was

then formally charged that with others on Friday, 12 August 1966 at Braybrook Street he did murder Christopher Tippet Head, David Stanley Wombwell and Geoffrey Roger Fox.

Witney was asked if he had anything to say and he replied, 'No, sir.'

Hensley then took Witney to another room for fingerprinting and to get his other details where he was left with Detective Inspector Coote.

At 11:30 p.m. Hensley returned Witney to his cell. Witney said, 'I am worried about the wife and family. Will you give me five minutes to think things over and will you come back with Mr Chitty? Then I might have something to tell you.'

At 12.30 a.m. Hensley and Chitty went to Witney's cell. Chitty said, 'You want to see me?' and cautioned Witney before he replied.

'Are you sure my wife and family will be all right?' Witney said. 'I'm not scared for myself. I know I'm going away for a long time but I'm frightened for them.'

'You can come to my office,' Chitty said, 'and if you want to tell me anything it will be put in writing.'

The two detectives took Witney up to the investigation office on the first floor. He said, 'I honestly didn't shoot the coppers, guv'nor. I know you must have found out a lot and I'll tell the truth.'

'What you say will be put in writing,' Chitty reminded Witney. 'Will you write your own statement?'

Witney replied, 'Yes, I'll do it.'

Chitty wrote Witney's name at the top of the statement paper and handed it to him. He was given a copy of the Judges' Rules which he confirmed in writing at the start of his statement and signed it to show that he understood the implications of the confession he was about to make. '*I make this statement of my own free will. I have been told that I need not say anything unless I wish to do so and that whatever I say may be given in evidence.*' [*signed J. Witney*].

Finally, after all the lies, the ducking and diving, the hours of questioning and thinking alone in his cell it was time for Jack Witney to come clean.

'As God is my judge, I had absolutely nothing to do with the shooting of any one of the three police officers, as no doubt witnesses can testify.

I had just driven down Erconwald St and turned left into Braybrook St when a small car pulled alongside and flagged me down. I pulled into the side and two men got out and introduced themselves as police officers. They asked me if it was my car. I replied, "Yes." One of them said, "Where's your road-fund licence?" I replied that I didn't have one. The young one then asked me for my licence whilst the elder of the two walked to the other side of the car and said, "Let's have a look in here." Without anything further Roberts sitting at my side leaned across and shot the younger officer in the side of the face. The noise of the shot deafened and dazed me. The other officer ran towards his own car which had pulled in front of mine and Roberts leaped out of the side door followed by Duddy and gave chase. I saw the second officer stumble and fall to the ground and Roberts fired again. I don't know how many times. The third officer tried to pull away but Duddy raced alongside and shot through the window of the car. They then raced back to the car and jumped in and said to me, "Drive."

'I said, "You must be fucking potty," and Roberts said, "Drive, cunt, unless you want some of the same." I was petrified with fear and shock, but reversed back round the corner and drove away to Vauxhall and put the car in the garage where you found it. The garage owner just rented it to me in the normal course of business.'

Witney began his statement at just after 12:30 a.m. and completed it at 1:05 a.m. The sequence of events and the details that Witney described varied somewhat from what witnesses said but that was of little importance. Chitty asked about the men Witney said he was with – the men he said had done the shooting. Witney gave Chitty their names: Harry Roberts and John Duddy. Chitty asked where these men lived and Witney said he didn't know their addresses but agreed to go with Chitty and show him.

An unmarked police car was ordered to race out of the rear yard to distract the press camped outside Shepherd's Bush police station. Meanwhile, at a side door, Witney was put into a Flying Squad taxi, which looked like any other London cab, and Hensley drove slowly and quietly away with Chitty sitting in the back and Witney under a blanket on the floor.

Once they were clear of the police station Witney directed his captors first to Wymering Mansions and then to Treverton Tower, pointing out the flats where Roberts and Duddy lived. After a brief glimpse of the world outside Witney was smuggled back into Shepherd's Bush police station where reporters remained unaware of what had just happened.

By the time Witney was returned to his cell he had sealed his fate and given the police the means to move the murder enquiry forward. As he lay in his cell, fearful and exhausted, he had at least done what he could to save himself by his second statement and by showing the detectives where Roberts and Duddy lived. Along with the fact that he had shot no one Witney was hoping it would all be taken into account and work in his favour when the case was finally brought before the courts.

A few hours later, at five a.m. on Monday, 15 August, Wymering Road was cordoned off while residents slumbered. Detective Superintendent Dick Chitty, Chief Inspector John 'Ginger' Hensley and Detective Chief Inspector Tommy Butler led a team of Flying Squad men armed with guns and tear gas, plus several uniformed officers and four dogs with their handlers down the quiet street.

The Shepherd's Bush Murders

With Wymering Mansions surrounded, a raiding party led by Chitty burst into the Howards' flat on the ground floor of the building. In a bedroom they found a startled June Howard and her three frightened children, Samantha, Barry and Paul. While officers searched the other rooms Howard was questioned briefly but it was clear that Harry Roberts was not there.

Chitty did not have any time to waste. He told June Howard to remain in her flat and left officers to guard her to make sure that she did. The dawn raiders then moved swiftly on to Treverton Street a mile away to the west. With the Treverton Tower block cordoned off, Chitty ordered officers to shoulder open the door of Flat 41 on the eighth floor. But at John Duddy's home the heavy-handed approach and accompanying noise weren't necessary. As the door flew back the policemen could see there was a latch key dangling on a piece of string inside the letter box.

Sixteen-year-old Linda and fifteen-year-old Bernadette Duddy screamed as police officers poured into their home and it took some time to calm them down. The girls, still frightened and tearful, eventually explained that they were in the flat alone. Their mother had left home some weeks before and they hadn't seen their father since Saturday.

Harry Roberts and Lilly Perry left the Hotel Russell at around ten a.m. on Monday morning, unaware of the dawn raids on Duddy's flat and their own lodgings at June Howard's home in Wymering Mansions. At about a quarter past ten Roberts entered Victor Lawrence Merchants in Hampstead Road, London NW1, a shop specialising in outdoor clothes and equipment.

He approached salesman John Bennett and said, 'Can I have a look at a combat jacket?' Bennett offered him a size 40 and Roberts decided on that. He looked next at a green rucksack and asked to see their range of sleeping bags. Bennett took him upstairs and Roberts picked out a blue Easton nylon-backed 'Kipwell' priced at forty-five shillings. Roberts then chose a pair of khaki trousers, a pair of white socks and a pair of full-length green suede, rubber-soled lace-up boots, size eight. He selected two dark-green-and-brown check shirts, two 6ft x 3ft dark green groundsheets and a hiker's eating-utensils set consisting of two saucepans with detachable handles, an aluminium canteen and a tin mug. The grand total was £14.19s.6d. Roberts paid with three fivers, told Bennett he would call back for the equipment later that morning and left the shop.

At the Metropolitan Police forensic laboratory in Holborn, Senior Experimental Officer John McCafferty took a closer look at the Q-car, Foxtrot One-One. 'After examining the evidence I found that the two front-door windows of the police car were fully wound down. The rear nearside-door window, the windscreen and the driver's quarter light were broken. Each of these showed evidence of one bullet hole.'

McCafferty was able to determine that one bullet had

passed through the rear-door window from the outside and that the other two had passed through the windscreen and quarter light respectively from the inside. 'I sat in the driver's seat and found that the bullet hole was roughly at the level of my forehead and slightly to the left, or nearside. The hole in the quarter light was slightly under the level of my chin. The bullet hole in the rear window was about three inches lower than the one in the windscreen.'

Later that Monday, William Keeley was interviewed again, this time at Scotland Yard, by Chief Superintendent Newman and Detective Chief Superintendent Butler. Butler was always thorough, a man with an eye for every detail. He knew that Keeley's statement about identifying Witney was not the whole story and when it came to the courtroom and the scrutiny of defence counsel nothing less than that whole story would do.

Keeley had wrestled with his conscience and after the consultation with his family he had tried to minimise and gloss over his part in the events. But now he had no alternative but to tell the truth about how he had come to know Jack Witney. 'The man whose name I now know to be John Edward Witney used to be employed as a driver by Miles Druce Ltd, and during 1965 he made several deliveries of metal to arch 103, Tinworth Street and from time to time he dropped some metals over the side. It had obviously been stolen from his employers and I was tempted and fell because my business was in a perilous state. After Witney left Miles Druce I did not see him until about a fortnight ago. He turned up at my place alone one morning and said he would like to put a car in my arch.' William Keeley went on to repeat the nature of the deal.

He then moved on to what he'd been doing on the afternoon of 12 August and it would have been easy to miss that his account concealed an inconsistency. 'I finished work for the day between 5:30 p.m. and 6 p.m., locked up and went home. I did not see anybody close to arch 103 whilst I was there but it would have been possible for a car to have been put in, whilst I was working behind the closed doors of arch 102 or when I went away during the afternoon for tea at a local café.'

Keeley was unaware that Helen King and her neighbour Elizabeth Pantlin had been chatting on their balconies that overlooked the archways, had seen Witney drive in and that Elizabeth Pantlin had said, 'A man came from archway number 102 and banged on the side of the van. The driver of the van then drove into the arch and out of our sight.'

There were therefore still a few questions hanging over Keeley and the account he'd given. Had he seen Witney put his car into railway arch 103? Had he knowingly not informed the police initially that he knew where the much sought-after and publicised Standard Vanguard was hidden? And was it only because his son later spotted the car and under pressure from his nervous wife Rebecca that William Keeley finally came forward?

However, without the Keeley family's help the police would still have been searching for the car. Witney could not have been charged, would not have made his confession and would not have given Chitty the names of the two men he'd been with in Braybrook Street, the men who had murdered Wombwell, Head and Fox in cold blood. As far Tommy Butler was concerned, he decided that there were more urgent matters to attend to than pursuing Keeley any further about what he had known and had done or not done. Keeley never knew how close he'd come to being caught out.

Bernard Duddy was working in the Territorial Army Hall garage at 90 Hotspur Street, Maryhill, Glasgow where he was employed as a part-time driver and caretaker. He was a widower with two children – a girl aged eight and a boy of six and a half years. At about 10:30 a.m. that Monday he was in the garage when his sister-in-law Chrissie, who cleaned the premises, walked in. Immediately behind her was Bernard Duddy's younger brother, John.

Chapter 17

Bernard had not seen his younger brother for two years. John had put on weight and looked tired, anxious and dishevelled. He told Bernard that he was fed up and was looking for his wife who had left him. They chatted for about half an hour and then Bernard asked John to go with him to Nethercairn Street, Paisley, to collect his car which had broken down the previous day.

The Duddy brothers got a lift from Bernard's boss and clerk at the depot, Mr Cremore, and with his help they towed Bernard's troublesome Triumph Herald to get it going. They drove back to the Territorial Drill Hall and at around one p.m. they left to go to an aunt's house where Bernard had left his two young children.

As they were driving down Sauchiehall Street, John suddenly asked to be dropped off. Bernard asked him if he would like to go and get some dinner with him but John said that he had eaten a couple of pies earlier and was feeling sick. He got out of the car and it was not until the following evening that Bernard Duddy read in the paper that the police were looking for his brother in connection with the shooting of three policemen in London.

Back in London at Wymering Mansions June Howard was interviewed by Detective Constable David Stephenson. Howard began by saying that she would not make a written statement because she alleged that her husband had been 'verballed' by police on previous occasions.

Before the 1982 Police and Criminal Evidence Act (PACE) the practice of 'verballing' was common and could involve the invention of incriminating remarks or confessions alleged to have been made in the back of a police car or some other place and not during a formal interview under caution. When presented as evidence in court, judges could admit or overrule these verbal reports at their discretion.

June Howard told DC Stephenson that her husband, Colin Charles Howard, was serving a prison sentence at Wormwood Scrubs Prison and that he was due for release in about five weeks. While Howard was talking, DC Stephenson made a note of what she said:

'She has a woman staying at her flat called Lilly Perry. Perry sleeps with a man called Harry Roberts who will be about 30 years old. Roberts is a friend of her husband and has served prison sentences for robbery.

'Mrs Howard and her husband have known Roberts

for about ten years and were present eight years ago when he married Margaret Rose Crooks from whom he is now separated. She has never known Roberts to have any form of employment.

'Roberts has a friend called Jack who used to call at the flat for him several times a week. She last saw Jack some day last week. He is aged about 40 to 45 years, give or take ten years, tall, thin with a long nose, pointed features and fair to gingerish hair, receding. He has an old blue car similar to the one photographed in the newspapers as that used by the killers of the Police Officers. The letters PGT she remembers because they are her brother-in-law's initials.

'She last remembers seeing Roberts towards the end of last week. She says that Perry left with him then and she has not seen either of them since.

'She thought the description of the suspects in the newspapers matched that of Jack and assumed he was the man detained by police because he owned a blue car. She did not report it to police because she does not think Roberts or Jack have the nerve to shoot anybody.'

DC Stephenson added a footnote: 'NB: This woman is slightly neurotic. She has had a nervous breakdown in the past and suffers from nerves now but on the surface it appears that she *might* be telling the truth. Her mother, who appears a sensible woman, was present at the very end of the interview and stated that she did not think her daughter was lying. Mrs Howard has three children and appears to have little control over them.'

All the news reports and newspaper front pages headlined the discovery of the Standard Vanguard. On the front page of the *Daily Mirror* was an announcement that the newspaper was setting up a fund. *The deaths of three policemen, in a few seconds of appalling savagery in a London street, have sickened the nation . . . In order to help channel the public's expression of its feeling the* Mirror *is launching a nationwide fund for the dependants of the three dead policemen. The* Daily Mirror *is contributing £1,000 to this fund. Its companion newspaper the* Sunday Mirror *has already announced a similar contribution . . . The* Mirror *fund is being established to enable ordinary citizens to express their outrage at the Braybrook Street shootings.*

PC Kenneth Price of Hertfordshire Constabulary contacted Shepherd's Bush police station with some useful information about Witney and his car. On Sunday, 31 July at about 7:30 p.m. he was on traffic duty with his colleague PC Hymers. They were stationary on the A41 just north of Watford at Garaton when a blue/grey Standard Vanguard in shabby condition passed them. The officers noticed that the vehicle was not displaying a road-fund licence so decided to stop it and question the driver.

The suspect car was intercepted at the top of the M1 approach road on the motorway bridge. The driver was asked for his licence and gave his name and address as John Witney, 10 Fernhead Road, W9. He admitted he had not yet obtained a road-fund licence, explaining that he had only recently bought the car, on the previous Monday. Witney had no MOT or insurance documents with him and elected to present them at Harrow Road police station.

PC William Blewitt at Harrow Road confirmed that he was the Station Duty Officer when Witney called on Friday, 5 August. Witney produced an insurance cover note for a motor vehicle, registration PGT 726 from The National Insurance & Guarantee Corporation dated 12 July 1966 and valid for 30 days. But when Blewitt asked him for the MOT Witney could not provide it. He told PC Blewitt he would be seeing the previous owner over the weekend and would get the certificate from him and present it on the following Monday evening, 8 August. He never did return.

By the time the information from PCs Price and Blewitt reached the murder-inquiry operations room the Standard Vanguard had already been traced to Witney. Although the car was not registered in his name these additional details provided independent proof of his ownership and possession of the vehicle.

At 12:30 p.m. Roberts returned with Lilly Perry to Victor Lawrence, the surplus store in Hampstead Road, where he began packing all the things he had purchased earlier into the rucksack. He found it was too small and exchanged it for an 'expedition rucksack' in grey. Sales assistant John Bennett wrapped the sleeping bag in brown paper and Roberts and Perry promptly left the shop.

They went next to a food shop where Roberts bought a loaf of bread, three tins of baked beans, Oxo cubes, a packet of tea, some dried milk, Old Holborn tobacco and green Rizla cigarette papers. With his supplies stuffed into his rucksack Roberts and Perry walked north towards Camden Town where they caught a 718 Greenline bus.

Following other lines of inquiry the police traced the number plates found in Witney's car from an invoice that was still in the cardboard wrapping. Detective Sergeants Brown and Darlington spoke to Rona Jennings at Hills Patents Ltd, and she told them that one of her duties was to take orders for number plates and other components over the telephone. On Thursday, 11 August at 4:55 p.m. she took an order from Brook Green Motors, Blythe Road, London W14 'for two oblong plates on black bevelled-edge background.' The man who ordered the plates asked for white digits and quoted the number JJY 285 D. 'Almost immediately he changed the number to JJJ 285 D.' The man said he would pay cash when he collected the order but did not say when that would be. Another employee, Christine Swanston, said that a man had come to collect the number plates at around 12:30 p.m. on Friday, 12 August.

Meanwhile the number on the plates found in Witney's car had been checked against vehicle registration records. It was traced to thirty-four-year-old David John Renshaw in Beconsfield, Buckinghamshire. Renshaw told DS Warfield that his firm, Miehle Dexter Ltd, owned a dark blue Ford Corsair, registration number JJJ 285 D, and that he had been in possession of the car since its first registration in January 1966. It was often his routine to drive to East Acton Tube station and continue the rest of his journey to work by Underground. He said he usually parked in Erconwald Street near the junction with Fitzneal Street. During the last two weeks it had been parked at this location from 8:10 a.m. until 5:45 p.m., on all except two days. He said it was definitely parked there on 10, 11 and 12 August. Each day the car had been left locked and had contained samples and papers to do with his work. He had not noticed anything missing nor anything to suggest that the car had been tampered with. Renshaw confirmed that at no time had he ordered new number plates for his car or authorised anyone else to do so.

It was a curious feature of the case that the number plates found in Witney's car were copies of the registration number of Renshaw's Ford Corsair parked in Erconwald Street when Witney, Roberts and Duddy's objective was to steal a similar car and change the plates. Even fifty years later, with the benefit of hindsight and later statements and admissions from Roberts, Duddy and Witney, there is no obvious explanation why the three men chose to drive past Renshaw's car on the afternoon of Friday, 12 August just minutes before they were stopped by the Q-car.

Thirty-five-year-old John Harvey who lived in White City provided a helpful detail later in the day. He went to the front desk at Shepherd's Bush police station to say he'd read in the *Evening News* that the false number plates had been ordered by Brook Green Motors, Blythe Road, W14. However, he had been born in Blythe Road and had known the area all his life and was certain there had never been a garage of that name there.

It was another example of how releasing information to the press brought in a lot of unexpected data. The problem facing the staff working in the first-floor murder-operations room at Shepherd's Bush was not lack of information coming in from the public but the overwhelming volume of it. Sifting through it all for anything useful took an enormous amount of time and effort.

In the basement cells Witney had plenty of time on his hands and nothing else. He had never settled into life. His army career was a disaster. He'd been a deserter for fifteen years and had not stuck at anything apart from habitual thieving. He'd lied to his wife, ducked and dived, worked here and there for a time, all the while associating with other petty villains and scraping a living together where he could. But in the last forty-eight hours he had been catapulted into another dimension: he was now a man accused of the murder of three policemen and soon his name would be on every newspaper front page and in every television news report. He knew he'd be going to trial. He knew he'd go to prison. But he hadn't killed anybody and surely he would not be found guilty of something he hadn't done.

Harry Roberts and Lilly Perry got off the 718 Greenline bus at The Wake Arms public house, Epping Forest. Before its demolition in the 1980s, the pub was a local landmark. It had associations with highwayman Dick Turpin and had displayed various items of what was alieged to be Turpin's clothing for some years.

Roberts stepped off that bus into the unknown. With his newly acquired rucksack containing rudimentary camping equipment and scant provisions, and with a few pounds in his pocket he thought it might be possible to hide from justice in the sprawling 6,000 acres of beech, birch, oak and hornbeam of Epping Forest that had remained largely undisturbed for a very long time.

Roberts took his time changing his boots, with Lilly Perry standing beside him in her best coat and high-heeled shoes, trying not to let him see her cry. It was hard for her to comprehend how the man she had met in a Bristol pub and whom she had taken into her ordinary life had led her there. She had no idea how things might develop from here on. All she knew for certain was that for the past three years she had trusted him, provided support, stability, comfort, her loyalty and love and now suddenly everything had changed and it was time to say goodbye.

Chapter 18

When Lilly Perry returned to Wymering Mansions she found Detective Sergeant Wilmhurst of the Flying Squad in the living room. Wilmhurst explained why he was there and Perry agreed to make a statement.

She began by saying that for the past seven years she had been separated from her husband, Anthony Frederick Perry, who now lived with another woman. As a result of that relationship he'd had to resign from the Bristol police force and she had not seen him for a long time. Sometime in 1963 while living in Bristol she had met a man called Harry Roberts. At the time he was staying in Horfield Hostel as part of the process of acclimatisation to non-prison life as he completed his time inside. When he was finally released he came to lodge with her. A few months ago Roberts had asked her if she would like to come to London with him to stay with June Howard, whom she had met on a number of previous occasions during their visits to London. Howard had recently been ill and with her husband in prison Roberts suggested Perry could help look after her three children.

This much was true, although not the whole truth. It was at this point in Lilly Perry's first statement that she began to depart from the facts, omitting, editing, and fabricating in her account of what had happened since 12 August.

'Harry was staying at this address until Friday. When I got up at about seven a.m. he was still in bed. Later in the morning I went out shopping with the children and when I returned Harry was gone. It was usual for him to go off without saying when he will return. On Sunday lunchtime Harry called here. He did not tell me where he had been, he just said, "Get yourself ready, we are going out." I asked him where but he said, "Never mind. I'll take you out."

'He took me to a hotel, it was somewhere in London, I don't know where it was, what it was called or what name he booked into the hotel in. We had a meal about 5pm in a restaurant a short distance from the hotel. After the meal we walked around looking at shops, then we went back to the hotel and we didn't leave again until about ten a.m. today.

'When we left the hotel we walked around a bit, then Harry said, "You can go back to June's now and look after the kids." He didn't say where he was going. Whilst he was with me he didn't talk about anything in particular. I have not seen him since he left me outside the hotel this morning and he hasn't called me on the phone.'

In common with a number of the other witnesses in the Shepherd's Bush murder investigation, or 'Operation Shepherd' as the police investigation was dubbed by Dick Chitty, when Lilly Perry was first interviewed by the police her responses to questions and her subsequent statements were cautious, economic with the truth and sometimes downright lies. Some of those questioned were treading a fine line between loyalty to those that they knew, their own self-protection from prosecution and their awareness of the gravity of the crime in which they had unwittingly found themselves implicated.

Lilly Perry was taken to Shepherd's Bush police station where after further questioning she agreed to make a second statement with Woman Detective Inspector Harrison. Perry's next account amounted to ten pages. She expanded upon the facts given in her first account as well as providing additional information and correcting some of the incorrect details she had initially told, or not told, to Detective Sergeant Wilmhurst.

It was perhaps the presence of another woman that encouraged Perry to disclose the intimate details of her life with Harry Roberts. No doubt she had also begun to realise the enormity of the brutal murder of three police officers and was growing increasingly fearful of the repercussions of lying if she was later found out.

Lilly Perry began by recapping her own background. The details of her relationship with Roberts were on the one hand personal and disarmingly honest and on the other hand contradictory.

'After Rob was released in November 1963 he asked me if I could put him up and I did and without my daughter's knowledge we became intimate although he had his own room. We have remained like that ever since and I wouldn't like my daughter to know. I have no love for him but he has been good to me. We only have sexual intercourse about once in two or three months.'

Perry was asked if she knew any of the men Roberts associated with and in particular Jack Witney and John Duddy.

'I can't remember many of the men Rob knew in London. I think the only two he was in contact with were Jack and a Scotsman. I haven't met the Scotsman but once or twice Rob has said, "I'm going out with Jock." I've looked out the window and seen a man waiting near the car. He is about 47, biggish, dark hair going grey. I've seen him go off with Rob. Once Jock came to the house during the morning about two weeks ago and talked with Rob and Rob went out with him but he's been outside the house more than once.

'When I met Jack first, eighteen months to two years ago, he had a yellow and black car. I met him outside his house in Fernhead Road, I was sat in a car outside. Rob said he was seeing a mate and as he got out of the car this Jack came to the gate. Rob introduced us. I still stayed in the car and Rob went inside with him. On other occasions I've been with Rob when he's seen him in the street and waved and often I've sat outside whilst Rob's been inside Jack's house. I think they have known each other a long time.

'I have been inside Jack Witney's house on three or four occasions and I've met his wife. On many occasions when Rob's been up in London he's taken me round there in the evening. Rob and Jack often went out to get a drink and bring it back but all I've seen them do is watch television. They've never conversed in front of me. Sometimes when I've been with June, Rob has said, "I'm going out. I might see Jack."

'Jack came two or three times to June's to see Rob. They went out together but I don't know where they went. I have never seen Jack driving a blue van. They mostly used our car or walked away from the house. The last time I saw Jack was either Wednesday or Thursday, 10 or 11 August. He arrived at 9 a.m. or 10 a.m. He sat and had a cup of tea with us and they both went out. Rob got back about 5 p.m., I think but I'm not sure. He didn't say where he'd been. He never did and I dared not ask because he got annoyed when anyone pried into his business. He was never out later until this last weekend.

'I've seen Rob, Jack and Jock together about four times in the last month. I've seen them all going by in Rob's car on about four occasions. They've never been in June's flat together. I've only seen them in the car. I've never seen them in Jack's car. I've never seen them with anyone else.

'On Friday, 12 August at about 9 a.m. Rob went out on his own. He didn't say where he was going or who with. I don't think he took the car. I was in when he came back at about 7:30 p.m. He seemed a bit tired. He sank into a chair and sighed. I asked him what was wrong and he said, "I feel tired and fed up and I've got a lousy head, give me some Beechams." June was in the kitchen and asked if he was all right and I said he had a terrible headache. He seemed exhausted.

'I didn't ask where he'd been and he never told me. He never went out for the rest of the evening. In the afternoon, before he arrived home, I was in a shop and heard people talking about a newsflash about the murdered men. When Rob came in I told him that three policemen had been killed and he said, "Oh my gosh, three? I wonder if it was anything to do with the Scrubs. Was it policemen or warders?" I said I didn't know.

'When later the number of the van came up on television I was just walking in and he said, "Shh shh, that number is like the number of Jack's van. I've been riding round in that van. It looks something like Jack's number. I hope to God it's not his. If it is I've been riding round in the van and my hands were all over it. I even repaired it for him and my fingerprints are all over it. I am frightened it might be him involved. If he don't phone me I am terribly afraid and worried it might be. He honestly hasn't told me he's involved. He never said nothing about that day."

'I went to bed at about 10:30 p.m. Rob still had a headache. We got up and he went out on his own between 10 a.m. to 11 a.m. He seemed all right but he never came home all night. He never phoned. It didn't register with me anything was wrong. I thought friends had put him up and was too busy with the children as they're a handful.

'Rob eventually came home at 2 p.m. on Sunday. He never said where he'd been. He just told me to put some stuff in his case and washing stuff and I asked if we were going away for the weekend. I packed some socks, underwear, a single-breasted dark grey suit, a black low-neck pullover and a dark navy 'V'-neck pullover. He had a midnight-blue tie with stars or spots on, a black tie, another black one with cream stripes and a red and brown silk tie. He also had shoe polish. I never packed any shirts. He wore a single-breasted grey suit with turn-ups on the trousers, white shirt, the blue tie with spots and brown suede shoes like Hush Puppies. The case is brown leather, three feet long and about two feet high with cream piping round it.

'He doesn't wear rings and wears a watch, I think it's silver. This is not the clothes he wore when I last saw him. In the hotel he changed to the dark grey suit, the same white shirt, tie and shoes. He did not have a raincoat or overcoat.

'We went by taxi on Sunday afternoon to the Hotel Russell where we stayed in a room on the 7th floor.'

Lilly Perry had previously said that they left the hotel at ten o'clock, but here she changed her story and mentioned additional details that she had not spoken of before. Most significantly she now admitted that she had not left Roberts outside the hotel that morning but had stayed with him until much later in the day.

'As we came out of the hotel we turned right and went that way. He wanted to go to the toilet and left me. I didn't see where he went. When he came back he had no suitcase but I didn't notice it at the time. I might be able to point out where he left me. I did see a station which had scaffolding round it and that's near where he went to the toilet.

'We went on walking then but never had lunch and at about midday we arrived at Camden Town. We waited for a Greenline coach and got on it. We went a long way but at the time I didn't know how much fare he paid. We passed some men fishing at a reservoir and after quite a distance the coach stopped at a pub by a green. There was a refreshment van serving tea by the bus shelter.

'When we got off the Greenline, Rob said, "I'm going somewhere. You'd better get back to June. She'll be worried." He told me to get a 718 Greenline back to Camden Town and then get a 31 bus to the Chippenham

Hotel in Shirland Avenue, Maida Vale. He took me across the road and waited with me until the Greenline came and I got on. He stayed at the stop. I didn't see him move. I wonder if he came back on another bus. He left me at about 2 p.m. – 3 p.m. and I went back to June's.

'I haven't heard from Rob since then. If he wanted to get in touch he could phone upstairs. He has given me no number to phone or address to write. While we were in the hotel and coach he never discussed the murders at all.'

And this was where Lilly Perry let matters rest. Some of the information she provided in her two statements on Monday, 15 August was useful to the murder-investigation team in building a picture of the life she had with Harry Roberts and his movements on and since Friday, 12 August. But some of what Perry said was misleading and untrue and it would be another forty-eight hours until she was interviewed again. This time it was by Detective Inspector Jack Slipper – and the tall, quiet, imposing and softly spoken 'Slipper of the Yard' had a knack of getting to the truth.

Chapter 19

After watching Lilly Perry drive away on a Greenline bus back to central London on Monday afternoon Harry Roberts had at first disappeared into Epping Forest. However, after having weighed up the possibilities he decided not to take refuge there. As far as he knew he had not yet been connected to the Braybrook Street shootings but several people knew of his association with Witney and that could lead to Perry being interviewed. If she told the police where she had been over the last twenty-four hours Epping Forest would be the first place where they would come looking for him. Instead Roberts made his way north up the A11 at the edge of the forest. 'I knew exactly where I was heading – Thorley Wood near Bishop's Stortford. I knew the woods like the back of my hand as my mother used to take me there regularly when I was a kid. And I also knew that the only person in the world who would know where I was was my mum and that was comforting to me.'

At 9:35 a.m. on Tuesday, 16 August at Glasgow City Police HQ fifty-year-old Detective Chief Inspector Robert

Brown received an express message to all Districts from the Commissioner of the Metropolitan Police. Since Witney had first named his accomplices shortly after midnight on Monday morning, criminal records had been cross-checked and verified with statements and descriptions from witnesses. The profile and backgrounds of the two men who had narrowly eluded capture and were wanted by the police for questioning were growing ever more detailed, sharper and focused.

Reference Murder of three police officers at Shepherd's Bush, London.

John Edward Witney file name Derek Kennedy CRO 39725/45. Arrested and charged with offence on 15.8.66. It is now desired to trace the following two men for interview.

1. *Harry Maurice Roberts CRO 33943/54. Born Wanstead, London 21.7.36. Height 5 feet 10 inches; fresh complexion; brown hair; blue eyes. Half-inch scar below left eye and small scar on left eyelid also small scar on base of left thumb. Last known to be wearing grey suit, white shirt, dark tie, brown suede shoes. Is in possession of driving licences in names of Ronald Ernest Hall of 44 Brownlow Road, NW10 and John O'Brien of 263 or 293 Norwood Road, Southhall. Special Enquiries are requested to all establishments hiring motor vehicles to trace. Believed to have connections in Bristol.*
2. *John Duddy CRO 39353/45. Height 5 feet 5½ inches. Born Glasgow 27.12.28. Medium build, corpulent; fresh complexion;*

hair light brown; blue eyes. Scars on tip of right forefinger, both knees and top of left buttock. Tattoo on right forearm – piece skull and heart 'True to Death'. Last known to be wearing dark trousers and dark pattern pullover. Convictions in Glasgow and Perth. May visit these places.

Photographs of both men will be published in Police Gazette as soon as possible. Both these men are dangerous, are known to be armed and may well shoot on sight. Extreme caution to be exercised if traced. If traced detain. Do not interrogate and inform Det. Supt. Chitty, Murder Squad, Shepherd's Bush Police Station, London, at once.

Because of Duddy's connection with Glasgow and his father having once been a Glasgow policeman, DCI Brown immediately began enquiries, aiming to trace John Duddy's relatives and interview them.

In Hammersmith the inquest was opened into the murders by Dr Cyril Barton, Coroner for the western district of Greater London. He addressed his opening remarks to Chief Superintendent Chitty. 'I am sure the public are deeply grateful to you and other officers who are investigating this case for what I am sure have been very long hours and the tireless effort you have all put into it.'

Rather embarrassed by the public praise Chitty's reply was characteristically brief and modest. 'Thank you, sir. We have only done what was expected of us.'

The Coroner adjourned the inquest 'sine die' (without

a day) and concluded, 'I have preliminary pathological reports in all cases that the cause of death in each case was bullet wounds. These are appalling and dreadful crimes and have resulted in the deaths of three courageous police officers – officers who have been killed in the execution of their duty. They were officers whom the police could ill afford to lose.'

Later that morning Witney was taken from the cells at Shepherd's Bush police station to West London Magistrates' Court. Before he arrived a team of police officers carried out a security check of the building and uniformed officers were posted at all the entrances. In the narrow street of terraced houses behind the court a large crowd was gathered. Reporters, press photographers, television-news camera crews jostled with members of the public; there were anxious faces in neighbouring windows and at every possible vantage point overlooking the courthouse yard, all hoping to see for themselves the evil, nationally reviled criminal who had been arrested for the murder of three police officers. Twenty-five minutes before the court convened Witney arrived in a police van that was led by two police motorbikes and a car and was followed by two further police cars carrying detectives. There was a brief glimpse of a figure being led into the court's rear entrance with his head covered by a blanket.

At 10:20 a.m. John Edward Witney appeared in the dock, handcuffed between two plain-clothes officers. His wife Lillian, who had been photographed by the press leaving home that morning, sat in the public gallery, looking pale and with a fixed expression on her face. Witney was wearing a green checked jacket, blue open-neck shirt and grey flannel trousers, and his eyes were red-rimmed as he stood slightly stooped throughout the hearing and answered quietly but audibly the questions put to him.

A brief summary of the identification and arrest of Witney was given by Detective Inspector Kenneth Coote. Chitty told the magistrate that further inquiries needed to be made and that two other men were being sought. He requested that Witney be remanded in custody while the police investigation continued.

The magistrate turned to Witney and said, 'There is obviously an objection to you being allowed out on bail. I therefore propose to remand you until 23 August in custody, subject to anything you have to say. Have you anything you want to say to me about such a remand?'

Witney, looking straight at the magistrate, shook his head slightly and replied, 'Nothing to say.'

The magistrate asked, 'Are you in a position to instruct a solicitor?'

Witney said, 'No, sir.'

'Very well, then, I will grant the necessary certificate. Is there anything further you want to say to me?'

'No.'

Without further ado Witney was remanded in custody

until the following Tuesday and was led from the dock. A woman from the public gallery shouted out and was ordered to remain silent by the court bailiff. The hearing had lasted a little over two minutes. By 10:30 a.m. Witney was back in the police van and returned to Shepherd's Bush escorted by a convoy of police vehicles.

At 2:45 p.m. on Tuesday, Detective Inspector Jack Slipper and Woman Detective Inspector Harrison went with Lilly Perry to the left-luggage office at Euston Railway Station. Perry identified the suitcase that Roberts had deposited there the previous morning after they had left the Hotel Russell. The suitcase was taken away by the detectives and later handed over to the Scenes of Crimes Officer, Detective Sergeant Lawrence.

Later that afternoon – four days since the shootings and the day after armed police had raided their home at dawn – Linda and Bernadette Duddy were taken to Shepherd's Bush police station. They were asked to look at a collection of police photographs to see if they could identify the men they knew as Jack and Rob. Both girls picked out photos of Harry Maurice Roberts and John Edward Witney and afterwards they agreed to make written statements.

Since their father had become unemployed, sixteen-year-old Linda and fifteen-year-old Bernadette had become the family breadwinners. Their mother had left the family home with their two younger sisters two and a half weeks earlier: they had been left to fend for themselves and they had no idea where she was. And now their dissolute and abusive father had been arrested for murder.

Linda's statement was direct. 'My dad drinks a lot and he's always fighting. Most of his mates are in the pub. Mum left three weeks ago today after a row with Dad and she took my younger sisters Yvonne and Maureen with her. Someone said today they'd seen her down the Isle of Sheppey. Dad never knew where she was as she hasn't contacted us. That has left Bernadette and me at home alone with Dad.'

Linda explained that after her father's accident about two months ago while driving a lorry for Scudders of Western Avenue he had suffered from concussion and hadn't worked. Since her father had become unemployed the two men she'd identified from police photographs had started coming to the flat. 'Usually Mum has been there but the kids and Mum usually went out of the room and the men stayed in the living room.' She described the cars they drove: 'an old blue car and a black Daimler.' She recalled a man coming to the flat early on Friday morning, 12 August. She didn't see him but thought it was Jack and she hadn't seen her father since that Friday.

Threaded through the statements of both the Duddy girls are poignant insights into their young, precarious lives and their fractured family. They too were now caught in the wider web of misfortune and loss, their future overshadowed by those few horrifying minutes in

Braybrook Street. As with that of her older sister Linda, Bernadette's account provided details central to the police's murder investigation.

After spending Monday night sleeping rough Harry Roberts finally arrived at his destination just as it was getting dark on Tuesday evening. He was too exhausted to construct any kind of shelter and after brewing a cup of tea with water taken from a cattle trough he bedded down in the undergrowth at the edge of Thorley Wood.

Chapter 20

The *Daily Express* front-page headline on Wednesday, 17 August 1966 was: *YARD WARNS: DON'T HAVE A GO: Find these men but be careful.*

Every police force in Britain was mobilised last night to find Harry Maurice Roberts and John Duddy, wanted for questioning about the shooting of three policemen.

In the biggest such operation ever staged, raids were made by armed detectives in London, Bristol and Glasgow, road blocks ringed London and close watch was kept at seaports and airports.

In Glasgow, Vincent, Bernard, Charles and Betty Duddy were all brought into the Central Police station on the corner of Turnbull Street and St Andrew's Street for questioning by Detective Chief Inspector Robert Brown.

Bernard told DCI Brown that he had seen his brother on Monday, 15 August and had dropped him off in Sauchiehall Street at around one p.m. 'At five o'clock on Tuesday night after coming out of the pictures, I read a newspaper and learned that John was named as being a person suspected of shooting three policemen in London. I saw it later on television.'

Vincent Duddy said that he had last visited his brother John about two years ago in London and had not seen him since, until Monday, 15 August. 'That particular morning John arrived at my home quite unexpectedly. I asked him why he was in Glasgow and he told me that he had quarrelled with this wife, Teresa, and had left her.'

'I next met John completely by chance at about 2:30 p.m. on Tuesday in New City Road. He told me that he was on his way to visit our sister Betty who lives in Rose Street. I had just come from home, where I had learned on television that John and another man, Roberts, were wanted by the police in London in connection with the murder of three police officers. I told John what I had heard on television and he immediately said, "Look, I don't know what it is."

'I told him he had better tell the truth and John said, "I was in the car on the Wednesday before the shooting and also on a number of other occasions. My fingerprints must be all over it. I know the guy well who owns the car. The guys who did the shooting are well away."

'I asked John what the men responsible for these murders had done with the guns. John told me that they were probably in the Thames.

'When John told me that he was connected with the car, and also with the men responsible for this crime, I asked him what he was going to do. He told me that he did not know but pleaded with me to get him out of the road for a time, as he thought if the police traced him they would kill him. At this stage I didn't know what to do or where to take John. In order to get a little time to think things over I told him to go into the Cambridge Cinema, which is in New City Road, a short distance from where we were talking. He did as I requested.'

And then Vincent Duddy came to the crunch point. During the conversation with John, his brother told him that he knew Jack Witney but he denied knowing Roberts. On the way to the house where John was now hiding John suggested that if things got too bad Vincent should tell the police and turn him in. It was a difficult decision to make but Vincent really had little choice. He was facing the prospect of being charged with harbouring his brother if he didn't tell the police what he knew. Vincent concluded that the chase was over. All he could do now was to try and ensure that his brother John came to no harm.

DCI Brown was acutely aware of the sensitivity of the situation. 'Vincent Duddy, with great reluctance, eventually told me that he knew where his brother was but would not tell me the address as he was afraid if I went there with other officers his brother would be harmed and probably shot. I gave him an assurance that his brother would not be hurt and he said that he would take me to the house. He would go in first and I should follow him.

'At 1:20 p.m. along with Vincent Duddy, Detective Chief Inspector Robertson, Detective Inspector Binnie and Detective Sergeant Linklater, I went to the home of William Crummer, a tenement property at 261 Stevenson Street. Crummer was unaware that the man he'd agreed to put up was Vincent's brother and that he was wanted for questioning in connection with the shootings in London. The apartment was situated on the first floor with windows overlooking the street.

'As arranged, Vincent Duddy knocked on the door and called through the letter box, "John, it's me, Vinnie."

'The door was opened by Mrs Crummer and Vincent Duddy immediately walked in. I followed immediately after, followed by the other officers. John Duddy was lying on a single bed. He was fully clothed with the exception of his jacket, shoes and tie.

'I cautioned Duddy and told him I was taking him to the Central Police Office where he would be detained in connection with the murder of three police officers in London on Friday 12 August 1966.

'He said, "It's all right. It's all right." '

DCI Brown led Duddy quietly out of the tenement to the car. While en route to the Central Police Office Duddy said, 'I was in that car but didn't do the shooting.' Brown cautioned him and told him that he would be well advised not to say anything about the incident but Duddy replied, 'I know my prints will be on the car. I was in it a number of times.'

After arriving at the Central Police Office Duddy was charged with having: 'On the 12 August 1966 in

Braybrook Street, London, while acting along with others, assaulted three police officers and discharged at them loaded firearms whereby they were so severely injured that they died and did thus murder them.'

When cautioned again Duddy replied, 'I've got nothing to say.'

On the way to the cells Duddy said, 'I was there but didn't do the shooting. Roberts told me when the number of the car was shown on the television that he and I would have to run and that he was going to Bristol.'

Again Brown told Duddy that he would be well advised to say no more. Duddy replied, 'I would like to see my father as he is the only one I can tell the truth to.'

Back in Maida Vale, London, Detective Sergeant John Quarrie supervised the loading of Roberts's black Daimler onto a lorry. It was taken for examination where it was handed over to Detective Superintendent Barnett of the Metropolitan Police Science Laboratory.

At Shepherd's Bush police station Detective Inspector Jack Slipper had been talking to Lilly Perry. She had already made two statements but the general feeling amongst the investigation team who had read them was that she knew more than she was saying. Once again Slipper's skills proved decisive. 'I spent a lot of time riding around London with Roberts's girlfriend and a woman Detective Inspector [Detective Inspector Harrison] checking on the stories she had told about Roberts's supposed departure from London. The girlfriend was a very odd sort of woman to be the lover of a man like Roberts. She was a very plain suburban housewife. She didn't talk or live flashily and although she seemed to have no wish to protect Roberts, now it was known he was a police killer, I was convinced the stories she was telling us were part of a false trail laid by Roberts. I was wrong, as it happened, but at the time it was frustrating to have to go through her story, step by step, when I didn't think it was going to lead anywhere.'

However, although Slipper felt there was little to be gained by going over the story yet again with Lilly Perry, thanks to his knack of getting the truth out of people – and with her conscience by now weighing heavily on her – she eventually agreed to make a third and vital statement.

She admitted to being with Roberts when he acquired the guns and the descriptions she gave would later fit the forensic profile of the murder weapons. 'Robbie went to a place called Moulin Rouge. I had to wait in the car while he went in and bought three guns. He got some ammunition at the same time. He told me he paid £90 for them. Two of the guns had round chambers, as Robbie called them, the other one was smaller with a long handle.'

She next said that she knew Roberts and Witney were engaged in various robberies. 'Robbie has told me about jobs they have done together, by that I mean snatching money from rent collectors and that sort of thing. One job was a betting shop and they snatched only £17.'

Perry then came to the crux of the matter – the events of 12-15 August – and her account couldn't have been plainer.

'Seven o'clock that Friday evening when he came home I noticed he was very upset and worried. I told him there had been a newsflash that three policemen had been shot dead near Wormwood Scrubs Prison. Robbie did not answer but when June Howard left the room he said to me, "It was us." We didn't talk any more about it until we went to bed, then Robbie told me exactly what had happened. They had driven down the road when the police car pulled them up. He said one of the policemen got out the car and started questioning them about the tax licence, then another policeman, who was a sergeant, got out of the police car and said, "We are going to search the van." Robbie told me he realised they were going to be caught with loaded guns on them and he would get anything up to fourteen years so he had to shoot them. He didn't say which police officers he shot but he did say bullets were flying everywhere. Robbie told me that he and Jock had got out of the van when the shooting started. He said one policeman went down near the front wheel of the police car and one was still sitting at the wheel of the police car when Jock went over and shot him.

'The next morning Jock arrived about 9.30 or 10 a.m. Robbie said to Jock in my presence, "What a mess we made of that yesterday." Jock replied, "Yes, I wish it had never happened." They both discussed getting rid of the guns and after a while both agreed that they should do so. Jock had taken the guns home with him after the shooting and had brought them back on Saturday morning. I saw both of them pushing what were obviously guns into the tops of their trousers. They both went out and returned about two hours later.

'Jock asked Robbie for some money as he was going up to Scotland to get out of the way. Robbie gave him two five-pound notes and he went. He did not have any luggage with him. Robbie did not tell me where he got rid of the guns.

'We stayed in all Saturday. Robbie went out early on Sunday morning on his own. He came back about two o'clock and told me to get a cab to Paddington Railway Station and meet him there as he was taking me out. He told me to bring something to wash with and I realised we were going to stop out for the night.'

It was clear that Perry was telling the truth. Her recollection of what Roberts had told her described the sequence of events at the murder scene, which she otherwise could not have known.

She next came to the burning issue of where Roberts was now.

'We eventually got off the bus and crossed the road and I caught the next bus back. I went back to the flat and you know the rest. I told you lies at first because he told me that if anyone grassed on him he would shoot them and I know he means it. He has often said he would not go back to prison again without putting up a fight. If he knows I have told you the truth I'm afraid he will do something to me. I still think a lot of him and am only telling you this because of the terrible crime he has committed. He has always looked after me very well and I cannot say anything against him.'

It had taken several days, three statements and the supreme skills of Jack Slipper for Lilly Perry finally to tell what she knew. Until her latest disclosure about Roberts buying camping equipment before heading north out of London on the Greenline bus, the only hope that Dick Chitty and his murder-investigation team had of finding Roberts was that sooner or later he might be spotted somewhere by a member of the public. From Lilly Perry's description of her journey with Roberts on Monday afternoon it did not take any great powers of deduction to work out that the place where she and Roberts had got off the bus was at the edge of Epping Forest.

It would take a small army of police officers to search the 6,000 acres of Essex woodland and there was the real and ever-present danger that ex-soldier and marksman Harry Roberts was armed. He had already killed without hesitation to avoid capture. But now, at least, the police had a specific area in which to hunt him down and bring him to justice. And this time they too would be carrying guns.

Chapter 21

By Wednesday, 17 August the Home Office had received more than 1,000 letters and £5,000 in cash for a new fund set up for police officers who were killed or injured in the line of duty. London's 18,500 policemen pledged to donate a day's pay. Among other gifts, the widow of Detective Sergeant Raymond Purdy – shot dead by Gunther Podola in 1959 – donated £10. Ten-year-old Nigel Morte held a jumble sale at his home in Peterborough and when his takings fell just short of his target of thirty shillings he sold the shirt off his back.

On Wednesday evening Detective Inspector Jack Slipper and Detective Chief Inspector Hensley arrived at Glasgow Central Police Station, having flown up from London.

Hensley told Duddy who they were and said to him, 'We are going to take you back to Shepherd's Bush police station where you are wanted for questioning in respect of the murder of three police officers on the twelfth of August.' Hensley cautioned Duddy who replied, 'Yes, sir, I understand.'

Duddy was sandwiched between Slipper and Hensley

in the back seat of a black Ford Zephyr police car. With DCI Brown in the front passenger seat they were escorted by a police van out of the gates of Glasgow Central police station, passing the large crowd that had assembled outside, and drove off at high speed down Turnbull Street towards the airport at Abbotsinch. All the while Duddy's head was kept covered with a fawn raincoat to hide him from press photographers who followed in hot pursuit throughout the journey.

The police convoy arrived at the airport shortly before 8:30 p.m. and swept straight onto the tarmac, pulling up at the foot of the steps of a BEA aircraft. With his head still covered and with one wrist handcuffed to Slipper, Duddy was hustled up the gangway. Twenty-two-year-old stewardess Patricia Docherty showed the detectives and their captive to their seats in the aircraft.

Once Captain Harry Lea had the scheduled flight BEA 5065 to London airborne, Slipper removed the handcuffs from Duddy's wrist and the raincoat from over his head. The two detectives and the murderer were the only people flying First Class. The other sixty-five passengers on board were the other side of a dividing curtain with Ginger Hensley standing guard, his pipe in his mouth. 'You couldn't buy a seat in here for £100,' he told one curious man.

As Patricia Docherty served her unusual passengers an incongruous light supper of smoked salmon, brown bread, cucumber, lettuce and egg, Duddy suddenly said, 'I must tell you what happened.'

It could have been an opening remark in a dinner-party conversation. Perhaps, after all the tension and danger of the last few days, John Duddy had been lulled momentarily into a false sense of security.

Slipper reminded Duddy that he was still under caution. 'I don't care,' Duddy replied. 'It was Roberts who started the shooting. He shot the two who got out of the car and shouted at me to shoot. I just grabbed a gun, ran to the police car and shot the driver through the window. I must have been mad. I wish you could hang me now.'

After writing down what Duddy said in his notebook Slipper called Hensley over and read it out to him. Hensley said, 'Is that right?' and Duddy replied, 'Yes, sir.'

As the flight was coming into land at London Airport a resourceful *Daily Express* photographer who had managed to get a seat on the flight got a quick snap of Duddy, who was now back under the raincoat with Slipper next to him.

After landing, the aircraft taxied to Stand 60 and before the propellers stopped turning four cars, a dog van, a Black Maria and a motorcycle escort moved to the plane's tail. The rear door was opened and two plain-clothes detectives ran up the gangway and into the plane. On the tarmac thirty uniformed officers formed two lines from the foot of the steps to the Black Maria.

A few minutes later Duddy appeared in the aircraft doorway with the fawn raincoat still draped over his head. Ginger Hensley walked backwards to steady Duddy who felt for each step with his foot as he descended while handcuffed to Jack Slipper. Duddy was guided into the back of the Black Maria, its blue light flashing. Once Duddy had been secured inside, the convoy was led away by the motorcycle escort.

By the time the police convoy turned off Uxbridge Road at 10:16 p.m., a crowd of over 600 members of the public had gathered outside Shepherd's Bush police station. Held back by uniformed police, people started shouting the moment the vehicles came into view. The gates of the yard were swung shut as soon as all the vehicles were inside but some of the crowd broke through the cordon and tried to climb the wall and had to be restrained.

Duddy was taken up to the first floor investigation office where at 10:25 p.m. he was interviewed by Chitty with Slipper and Chief Superintendent Newman present.

With the late-night traffic thinning out along Uxbridge Road, photographers and pressmen had camped on the pavement and the large crowd was still gathered outside Shepherd's Bush police station. Up on the first floor behind the Venetian blinds that had been permanently closed since the murder investigation began, Chitty faced the latest man who had been brought in for questioning. 'You have been brought here in connection with the killing of three police officers at Braybrook Street on Friday the twelfth of August.'

'I'll not give you any trouble, sir,' Duddy said quietly. 'I'll tell you all you want to know.'

First photograph of the crime scene by Anthony O'Connor, 43 Braybrook St.

Braybrook Street on the afternoon of Friday 12 August 1966.

Geoffrey Fox

David Wombwell

Christopher Head

The crime scene.

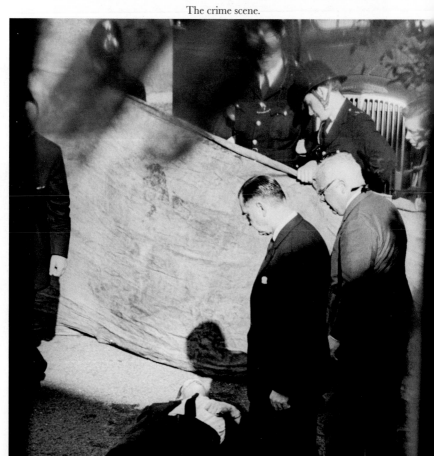

Harry Roberts after his arrest.

Right: Jack Witney

Far right: John Duddy

Funeral cortege in the Uxbridge Road on the morning of Thursday 1 September 1966.

Detective Chief Inspector 'Ginger' Hensley (left) and Detective Inspector Jack Slipper (right) at London Airport on their way to collect Duddy from Glasgow.

METROPOLITAN POLICE

£1,000 REWARD

MURDER

A reward or rewards up to a total of £1,000 will be paid for information leading to the arrest of **HARRY MAURICE ROBERTS**, b. Wanstead, Essex, on 21-7-36, 5ft. 10in., photo. above, wanted for questioning in connection with the murder of three police officers on the 12th August, 1966, at Braybrook Street, Shepherds Bush.

Information to be given to New Scotland Yard, S.W.1, or at any police station.

The amount of any payment will be in the discretion of the Commissioner of Police for the Metropolis.

J. SIMPSON,
Commissioner of Police.

Head of 'Operation Shepherd',
Detective Superintendent
Richard Chitty.

Harry Roberts's hideout
in Thorley Wood.

Daily Mirror

4d. Thursday, August 18, 1966 • No. 19,487

Midnight—Yard issue picture

THIS IS
HARRY ROBERTS

IF YOU SEE HIM TELL THE POLICE

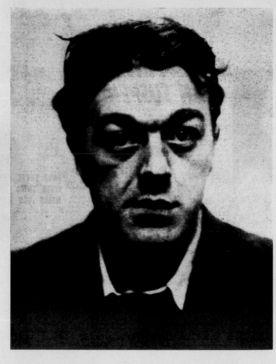

By EDWARD VALE and HAROLD WHITTALL

THIS is the man every policeman in Britain is looking for

His name: Harry Maurice Roberts— alias Ronald Hall, alias John O'Brien.

He is the man wanted by police investigating the shooting of three London policemen.

Warning

Scotland Yard issued this picture of Roberts at midnight. And they repeated this warning to the public:

"If you see a man answering Roberts's description, ring the nearest police station—but don't go near him."

Roberts is armed and he is dangerous.

Roberts is thirty years old, five feet ten inches tall, with a fresh complexion, brown hair and blue eyes.

He has a half-inch scar below the left eye, a small scar on the left eyelid, and another on the base of his left thumb.

Police believe that Roberts has bought a change of clothing and is now wearing a check shirt and a dark-green Army combat jacket.

Earlier, a massive police

Continued on Back Page

HE IS ARMED
HE IS DANGEROUS

'I want to know everything. What were you doing in the car at Braybrook Street that afternoon?'

Duddy gave his account of the shootings which deviated slightly from the accounts some witnesses had given but confirmed that Roberts had first shot Wombwell, then had chased Head and shot him in the back. Duddy recalled someone shouting at him, telling him to shoot the driver – which he had.

'And what happened after that?'

'We all got back into the van and drove back to the garage at Vauxhall.'

'What about this garage? Tell me what you know about that.'

'Witney arranged it. We got it to put the stolen cars in. We were looking for a car and we were going to sit on the grass and fix up to do a rent collector.'

'You were going to switch the number plates with the ones found in the Vanguard?'

'Yes, sir.'

'Who arranged to have these plates done?'

'We were all in it. I think it was Roberts who collected them; he used to organise things. We didn't do a job that day, just looking around and we were going to work things out on the grass to pass the time as Jack's wife thought he was working and he couldn't get home before five.'

'Had you been with these two men all day?'

'Yes, Roberts picked me up at home about eight o'clock in the Daimler. Jack drove up in the Vanguard and we all got into his car. We drove around, went to a pub at Eastcote and then came back looking for a car to do the job.'

Chitty said, 'Will you put what you say in writing?'

'Yes, sir.'

'Will you write it yourself or do you want me to write it?'

'You write it, sir.'

Duddy's admission to having shot Geoffrey Fox confirmed what Witney and other witnesses had said. In his statement Duddy expressed remorse and it appeared genuine. 'I didn't mean to kill him. I wanted money the easy way. I am a fool. I used to work as a driver up to six weeks ago but Roberts and Witney used to organise the raids we went on and it was easy.'

There were important new facts concerning the guns. Roberts had used a Luger, Duddy a revolver and they'd had not two but three guns with them in the car that day. The murder weapons could be verified with forensic and ballistic reports and would cement the case for the prosecution of the murderers and would confirm the part that each man played in the killings.

Chitty interrupted Duddy to ask, 'What kind of gun did you use?'

'It looked like an army revolver.'

'What type of gun did Roberts have?'

'A Luger, sir.'

'What happened to the guns?'

'Roberts took them from us.'

'What do you mean, "took them from us"?'

'We all three had guns but I don't know if Witney used his or not. I believe he did.'

Duddy's final remark raised another new question. It had previously seemed that Witney had been caught up inadvertently in the shootings rather than actively participating in them. Roberts had threatened him to make him drive the three of them away from the scene but Duddy's last comment suggested that Witney was not as innocent as he had said.

By midnight on the fifth day of the police investigation into the murders of David Wombwell, Chris Head and Geoff Fox two of the three men seen fleeing from Braybrook Street in an old blue car had been traced and apprehended, had admitted their participation and were now locked up.

Chitty had good reason to feel some sense of satisfaction that the murder enquiry he had been appointed to lead was delivering swift justice. The level of determination and cooperation between Metropolitan police divisions across London and the thousands of police officers around the country who had also responded swiftly in following possible leads – most of which proved fruitless, however – had been exemplary. It had been without precedent in the history of British policing. But Operation Shepherd was far from over. There remained the task of hunting down and arresting Harry Roberts. By all accounts he was both the instigator and the key man in the shootings and he had killed twice.

When his mother Dorothy was interviewed she said

that she had only learned about the murders from the press reports. Her son had not contacted her since the shootings and she appeared distraught to learn that he was involved. Witney and Duddy had been relatively easy to trace but Roberts was not only the most dangerous but also the most resourceful of the three.

Late on Wednesday night the police decided to release a photo to the press of the third man they wanted for questioning. This black and white photograph of Harry Roberts would appear on the front page of every newspaper and would headline television news reports throughout the late summer and autumn of 1966. Fifty years later it still remains the most enduring image of the Shepherd's Bush Murders.

While Duddy was being apprehended in Scotland, a force of three hundred police officers from all over the East London area assembled at the edge of Epping Forest. As daylight was fading, roadblocks were erected and motorists were stopped for questioning. Portable floodlights were set up at rallying points at the Robin Hood and Wake Arms roundabouts.

By torchlight unarmed officers and dogs began to comb the woodland bordering the A11 Newmarket trunk road. Armed men were stationed on the perimeter, ready for their quarry to be flushed out. But after several fruitless hours, at midnight Chief Superintendent Wynn Evans – in charge of 'J' Division – returned to the search headquarters at Loughton and called off his men until dawn.

Chapter 22

Uniformed officers and patrol cars were stationed at intervals around the Epping Forest borders to stand guard. Throughout the night the police roadblocks set up the previous evening remained in place. At first light on Thursday, 18 August 1966, 600 police officers of every rank gathered at the edge of Epping Forest armed with guns and tear gas, truncheons and clubs and any other self-defence items that they could lay their hands on.

Lines of uniformed and plain-clothes officers, mounted police, police dogs and their handlers fanned out to begin a systematic sweep of the sprawling acres of woodland and dense undergrowth, while overhead a light aircraft buzzed back and forth across the clear blue morning sky. On perimeter roads patrol cars were positioned at junctions. And as the morning progressed traffic officers tried to marshal the mass of vehicles and people who had come to watch it all.

In dappled sunlight the search party beat their way diligently through glades, bracken and tangled thickets, conscious that at any moment and without warning they might come under fire. All the while Harry Roberts was sixteen miles north of the hunt in Thorley Wood, Hertfordshire, busy constructing his hideout.

With the two groundsheets he'd bought at the Victor Lawrence surplus store and some discarded fertiliser bags he'd found nearby, plus branches and sticks from the surrounding woodland to create a supporting structure, he managed to erect a makeshift tent. He covered it with leaves and green foliage until it blended seamlessly into the surrounding habitat. There was a stream nearby for water and he had a methylated-spirit stove, tea, powdered milk, some basic provisions, a few pounds in his pocket and his army training and ingenuity. With his two battery-powered transistor radios he would have some idea of what was going on in the outside world and would perhaps know something of what the men who were hunting him were doing. His skilfully camouflaged encampment would do for now but how long could he stay concealed before necessity forced him to break cover and venture out of the wood?

The unfolding story of the Shepherd's Bush Murders continued to dominate newspaper front pages and the radio and TV news. *The Times* had a photo of John Duddy being led by Jack Slipper up the rear steps of BEA flight 5065 in Glasgow. Under the headline *Police Fly Duddy to London* was *250 go to Epping Forest in search for Roberts*. The report gave a brief summary of Duddy's arrest and journey to London and the start of the hunt in Epping Forest the previous evening. However, although the article mentioned

'A photograph of Roberts was made available earlier today' the picture of Harry Roberts had clearly not reached *The Times* news desk in time to be included on their front page.

The *Daily Mirror* must have been put to bed later as the headline was: *Midnight – Yard issue picture: THIS IS HARRY ROBERTS*. Two-thirds of the front page was taken up by the now unmistakable image of Roberts: the slight squint, almost a smirk, the thick George Robey eyebrows and that expression with its look of simmering resentment. There was a detailed physical description of Roberts that ended: *'Police believe that he has bought a change of clothes and is now wearing a check shirt and a dark green Army combat jacket.'* And just for good measure the *Mirror* finished with: *HE IS ARMED HE IS DANGEROUS*, all underlined and with the word 'dangerous' enlarged in case any of its readers had missed the point.

On the back page was a photograph of John Duddy with his head covered being led down the aircraft steps by Ginger Hensley at London Airport. Keen to report every available detail, the *Mirror* article said that Duddy's brother Vincent had taken police to a Glasgow tenement and called through the letter box to John seconds before detectives burst in. It is remarkable that the crime desk at the *Mirror* had found out so much about the raid from police insiders. But without an explanation of how and why Vincent Duddy had helped the police, readers were left to draw their own conclusions about Vincent's apparent betrayal of his younger brother, albeit in extenuating circumstances.

On the Isle of Sheppey in Kent, John Duddy's wife was traced to Harts Holiday Camp in Leysdown and was taken to Sheerness police station. Thirty-six-year-old Teresa Ann Duddy was interviewed by Detective Constable T. Thorpe of 'G' Division and agreed to make a statement. She began with some simple background facts from which it was hard to see how any of it had led the ordinary and straightforward John Duddy to becoming a cold-blooded killer. But then, as her statement progressed, there were revealing insights into her husband, his moods and ways, how he had changed during the life she had shared with him.

Teresa Duddy said she had been married to John for seventeen years. After they were married in Glasgow they moved to London in May 1949 and took lodgings at Clarendon Crescent, W2 where they lived for about a year. After their first daughter Linda was born they returned to Scotland and stayed with her mother. Shortly after their second child was born her husband joined the army and was later posted to Malaya. John had been stationed in the Far East for a year before she joined him, together with their two daughters Linda and Bernadette. The family lived in Malaya for a further two years. Their third daughter, Maureen, was born there.

They returned to Scotland in 1955 and initially lived with John's parents until moving back to London where John was posted next. They lived in a flat off the north end of Portobello Road. While they were there John was demobbed but shortly afterwards he was recalled owing to the 1956 Suez Crisis. In total John Duddy completed seven years as a regular soldier and a further five years as a reserve. After finally leaving the army John Duddy took his family back to Scotland in 1961 where they occupied a council house in Glasgow for two years and Duddy had a number of jobs as a driver.

It was at this point that Teresa touched on the events and reasons that had led to her husband becoming unemployed and getting involved with Witney and Roberts, and to her leaving the family home sixteen days earlier.

'I noticed that my husband changed considerably in character when he left the Army. He had a number of civilian employments as a driver in Glasgow and started to go out drinking on his own and when he came home he would beat me for no reason at all. He always had a quick temper but things worsened as time went by. He would often shout at the children and me for no apparent reason.

'In 1963 we moved into our present council flat at 41 Treverton Towers. My husband worked fairly regularly until about three months ago when he told me that he was not going to work any more at all. I pleaded with him to work so that we should have money for the children but he refused.

'Since he stopped working he has been regularly

associating with two men who he called Bob and Jack. I believe it was Jack who called to pick up my husband one night about two months ago. He had a black Daimler car. He boasted to me that he carried a gun but said that it wasn't loaded and that he had it to scare people. He told me that the other men carried guns as well. I never saw any guns at our flat. He told me once that they intended to rob a betting shop, but he didn't say which one.

'About a fortnight before I finally left my husband, he produced fifteen pounds which he gave me. At other times he gave me small amounts which he told me came from Bob. He said it was expenses. It was obvious that he was getting money from somewhere as he was always drinking.

'At the start of this year things finally got so bad that I couldn't stand it any more and on the advice of my doctor I left home with my youngest daughter Yvonne and went to stay with a friend at Clapham Common for about ten days. My husband didn't know of this address or where I was. He contacted the Probation Officer at Marylebone Magistrates' Court and apparently threatened to commit suicide if I didn't return home. I didn't really believe it but for the sake of the children I decided to go back to him.

'Everything went all right for about two months and then he started staying out every night after he left work, sometimes he stayed out until two a.m. When I questioned him about this he told me that he had been talking business with Bob and Jack.

'On Tuesday the 2nd of August, my husband arrived

home at three a.m. and then went to bed without saying anything. I got up in the morning and made his breakfast and he got up at ten a.m. He didn't eat the meal I had prepared and didn't speak to me. He left the building and I decided that this was the last straw. I packed some clothing and took my two youngest daughters, Maureen and Yvonne. I didn't really mind where I went as long as I could get away from him for a while.'

However, there was another aspect to Teresa Duddy's leaving her husband that she did not disclose. When Roberts and Witney came to her home there was talk of easy money, big money, about 'having a bank over', doing rent collectors and raiding betting shops. Teresa finally reached breaking point and walked out on her husband a second time, hoping to bring him to his senses.

'Eventually I caught a coach from Victoria to Leysdown on the Isle of Sheppey. Since then I have been living in a caravan at Harts Holiday Camp in Leysdown. I have been working at a café there and my daughter Maureen has been looking after the baby. I have not seen my husband since the 2nd of August and he does not know where I'm staying.

'I think my husband has been suffering from some form of mental strain as he has changed a lot since I first married him. For the last eight years or so my husband has often struck me, causing bruises etc. This has affected my nerves and I have been under the Doctor for the past nine months. My husband has become bitter towards the world generally and has said that he has worked all his life for nothing. He spoke a lot about crime and having big money and how easy it would be to achieve it by criminal means rather than working.'

Teresa Duddy's account of her husband's casual violence and domestic abuse helped to create a clearer picture of the man he had become by the summer of 1966. It seems that his Army experiences had changed him and left him suffering from 'mental strain'. His two older daughters talked of the accident he'd had when driving a lorry that had resulted in a head injury that had given him concussion and had led to him discharging himself from hospital. He had become directionless and despondent. John Duddy had been reduced to a wife beater, a layabout, a brawling drunk, a thief and most recently a murderer. These were the faltering and fatal steps that took him to Braybrook Street. With no job or belief in himself, abandoned by his wife and probably groggy after the lunchtime drinking at the Clay Pigeon pub, when Roberts ordered Duddy to 'shoot the driver' he did what he was told, picked out a revolver from the bag, got out of the car and fired three shots at Geoffrey Fox, finally killing him at close range.

Chapter 23

Inevitably – with the widely publicised appeal to members of the public to report any sighting of Harry Roberts to them – the police received an overwhelming number of telephone calls.

While hundreds of policemen continued the search in Epping Forest in sweltering heat, fifty officers raced to London Airport following a reported sighting of Roberts. The alarm was raised after a BEA coach driver reported that a man who used to share lodgings with Roberts and now worked at the West London Terminal said he had seen Roberts there. The buildings were searched and staff and passengers questioned. But after four hours there was no sign of Harry Roberts and it appeared to be yet another false alarm.

Similar operations were carried out following reported sightings of Roberts across the country including at Barry, Glamorgan, where he'd supposedly been seen boarding a ship; at Slough, near the film studios; Tilbury, in an old fort; Gosforth, Cumberland and at Stirling, hiking; at

Dunton, Essex, breaking into a house; at Bristol – a total of 35 times; at Great Yarmouth, walking on the prom; in Knightsbridge, entering Harrods department store wearing a pinstripe suit and bowler hat. All were followed up. All drew a blank.

At Birmingham Airport, twenty-two-year-old stewardess Wilma Grainger reported seeing a man who fitted Roberts's description sitting next to a clergyman on her London to Birmingham flight, BEA 4314. When the passengers had disembarked forensic officers made an inch-by-inch search of the aircraft and took fingerprints from the seat belt where the man had been sitting. Finally the clergyman was traced. He turned out to be a Roman Catholic priest who said the man sitting next to him had been Persian, he thought.

In the late afternoon of Thursday, 18 August Detective Superintendent Dick Chitty had John Duddy brought up from the cells at Shepherd's Bush police station.

'At 4:46 p.m. on 18 August 1966 I saw Duddy in the charge room, and said to him, "In connection with the killings of the three police officers at Braybrook Street on Friday, 12 August and the causes of deaths established at the post-mortem examination on the bodies, as a result of the enquiries I have made and what you have told me, you will now be charged with being concerned with others with the murder of these men." I cautioned him and he made no reply. He was then formally charged and cautioned and he said, "I don't know what to say, sir." '

The following day, on Friday, 19 August the front page of the *Daily Mirror* had a dramatic photo taking up most of the front page of a lone plain-clothes detective looking like a Wild West gunslinger with a revolver held in his right hand as he stalked through Epping Forest. The emotive banner headline was: *THE HUNTER AND THE HUNTED*. *The day-long search for Roberts was in vain but just before it was called off for the night there was an alarm. Detectives spotted smoke rising deep in the forest. At the spot they found signs of a hurried retreat, scattered ashes, a gas lighter and a squirrel was cooking in an old saucepan.*

On Friday morning a large crowd outside West London Magistrates' Court booed the arrival of John Duddy. The escorting police van that had brought him from Shepherd's Bush police station drove straight into the yard behind the courthouse and Duddy was taken out swiftly with his head covered in a blanket.

Handcuffed between two police officers, John Duddy was led into court and stood in the same dock where Jack Witney had stood three days before, on Tuesday. Duddy replied with no more than a whisper and a shake of the head when the presiding magistrate Mr E.R. Guest asked him if he had anything to say. From the witness box Chitty told the court, 'This is the second man to be arrested in connection with these charges. A third man is still being sought.' The magistrate remanded Duddy in custody for a week. In just a few minutes his court appearance was all over and Duddy was taken away.

In his hideout in Thorley Wood near Bishop's Stortford, Harry Roberts only used his transistor radio to hear the news in order to preserve the battery. When he switched it on that morning the last thing he expected to hear was his mother's voice. 'If you're listening, Robin, give yourself up. Don't kill anyone else. Please, Robin, listen to what I'm saying. I'll come with you if you give yourself up. We'll go together. This is your mum speaking. Everything will be all right, Robin.' Her voice was strained and anxious but Roberts convinced himself that his mother knew where he was and that her public appeal wasn't genuine. She'd been asked to do it by the police and for the sake of appearances she had agreed.

National newspapers reported that the trail of 'the third man' was growing cold after a grim two-day search of Epping Forest by hundreds of policemen had drawn a blank. There were numerous alleged sightings of Roberts from around the UK but despite all the reporting and searching, and despite most of Britain being on the lookout for him Harry Roberts had vanished into the blue.

The hunt had actually spread far beyond Britain, with

Roberts's photo and description distributed to Interpol and other police organisations in ninety-five countries.

All the while Roberts was hunkered down in his camouflaged hideout in Thorley Wood just sixteen miles from the search. So near yet so far from the biggest manhunt ever mounted by British police.

Margaret Roberts, now thirty-one, made a plea from her flat 'in a Northern City' where she had lived for the past six years while working as a striptease dancer. ' "Wherever you are, Harry, give yourself up . . . Please, please don't hurt anyone," ' she said to press reporters. She said he was, ' "good in many ways. He didn't drink or gamble overmuch and he used to tip up the wages. He was a lorry driver then. But we didn't hit it off. Then I lost our baby after a seven-and-a-half-month pregnancy and that finished us. I've never seen him since." '

Margaret was by now under police protection, 'frightened that a knock on the door might bring back into her life the man she left eight years ago.' ' "If he knew where I was, he might feel I was the only one he could turn to . . . I know from a friend that he was trying to find me two months ago, before all this happened." '

Understandably, she did not disclose to the press the real reason for the break-up of her marriage. Or that she feared that her husband trying to find her two months earlier was to seek revenge for her telling the police that he'd been responsible for the robbery and brutal attack on her elderly ex-landlord and friend William Gaylard. Having been shopped by her once it was not remotely likely that Harry Roberts would feel she was 'the only one he could turn to', or be expecting her sympathy and help. The more pressing concern for Margaret Roberts was that her whereabouts might now become publicly known and that was why she was desperate for police protection.

The next steps forward for the police investigation in building a more complete picture and understanding of the third man they were hunting in connection with the Shepherd's Bush Murders came on Sunday in statements from two people close to Harry Roberts, a man they each thought they had known well.

On Sunday, 21 August PC Patrick McEnvoy of the Somerset Constabulary interviewed forty-year-old Lewis Anderson at Weston-super-Mare.

Anderson was employed by George Wimpey as a builders' foreman. Since 1963 he had known Harry Roberts both as a work colleague and personally. He said Roberts worked on a number of Wimpey building sites at Bristol, Bridgwater, Radstock, Locking, Weston-super-Mare and also at Hutton near Weston-super-Mare.

Lewis Anderson explained that he first met Harry Roberts while Roberts was still serving a sentence at Horfield Prison and had come to work at the Wimpey site in Hedley Lane, Bristol on an 'Open Release' scheme. Roberts was placed under Anderson's supervision at the site from March 1963 until about August and by that time he had finished his sentence at Horfield.

Anderson recalled that Roberts was 'a good worker so we sent him to another site for about two months until our new site at Radstock opened up. He knew that when he moved to Radstock we were going to make him a chargehand over a five-man gang of bricklayers. He then worked at the Radstock site until around August 1964. It was during that time that he bought a Daimler car and I met his woman friend. She was called Lil and lived in Bristol with Roberts. Today in the *News of the World* I saw this woman's photograph in an article about Roberts. He used to bring her out to the site on the occasional Saturday morning. He mentioned about being very fond of her.'

In April 1966, while Anderson was working at a building site in Dolphin Square, Roberts turned up, seeking work. He said that he had heard that there was a hotel on the seafront that was being renovated and asked if Anderson could help him get on the job. Anderson wasn't able to help. The two men then went to the Three Queens pub for a drink and Roberts mentioned that he was worried because he was getting very little work. He said that unless things improved he intended to go back to London. Anderson said that was the last time he saw Harry Roberts. Lewis Anderson concluded his interview with PC Patrick McEnvoy by saying that in all the time he knew him Roberts never mentioned crime or criminals and never discussed guns.

As far as the police investigation was concerned, what was surprising about Lewis Anderson's view of Harry Roberts was that it didn't fit the profile of an unpredictable, violent and seasoned criminal, let alone a man capable of murder. The Harry Roberts that Anderson spoke of was an ordinary, honest, reliable, hard-working, rational man whose character was strangely at odds with that of the ruthless cold-blooded killer the police wanted for questioning in connection with the Shepherd's Bush Murders. And that made the task of predicting Roberts's next move and working out where he might be all the more difficult.

Chapter 24

June Howard knew more about Roberts than anyone. On Sunday, 21 August Detective Inspector Jack Slipper interviewed her at Shepherd's Bush police station and his remarkable ability for persuading people to talk openly proved decisive once again. Howard finally agreed to make a written statement. When she was first interviewed on Monday, 15 August by Detective Constable David Stephenson there had been concerns about her emotional stability and the truth of what she'd said. But, as is often the case with people who suffer from emotional disorders, June Howard's perception was astute and penetrating albeit driven by the need to distance herself from recent events.

Among her observations and background knowledge of Roberts and his movements around the 12 August were also many telling insights into her own character and life, along with admissions that her and her husband's ten-year friendship with Harry Roberts was not without its darker side.

'I first met Rob, by that I mean Harry Maurice Roberts who you are looking for, about ten years ago in a club called Colonnade in Mead Street, London W1. I was living with Colin at the time but was not married to him. We used to drop Rob off at night at Kendall House where he was living with his mother.

'About twelve months after meeting Rob he was sentenced to seven years' imprisonment for robbery with violence. I saw him about six times between the end of 1963 and October 1964. Towards the end of 1964 he asked me on several occasions if I could get hold of three or four automatics. He said he wanted .38s. Each time I saw him I told him I would let him know when I got them.

'In October 1964 Colin and I were offered a flat in Chiswick Village, London W4, but we had to pay a quarter's rent in advance. This came to about £165. Colin and I decided to tell Rob that we could get three guns but needed the money beforehand. I telephoned him at Bristol and told him I could get hold of three guns for £65.

'Within two hours he sent a telegraph money-order to a post office in Kilburn High Road. I went the same day to the post office and got the money out. The order was made out in my name as I had to do all the business because Colin was on the run from the police. We then obtained the lease of the flat, the remaining £100 we got from pawning Colin's watch. I kept putting Rob off, saying the guns had not arrived.

'On 16 or 17 December 1964 Colin was arrested and

charged by police for conspiracy to defraud and on this particular day I asked Rob to call at Chiswick Village to see me. When he arrived I told him that I had left the guns in the boot of a stolen car Colin and I had been using. This, of course, was not true. I never did get the guns.

'The first time I knew Rob had obtained a gun was between December 1965 and February this year. I was up in Mrs Howarth's flat at 144 Wymering Mansions when Rob and Lil Perry came up. Rob and I went into the bedroom to use the telephone and he suddenly threw a small canvas bag over to me. I stepped back and it fell onto the floor. I said, "What the hell is that?" Rob said, "A shooter." I told him to get it out and I think he later put it in his car. He told me he had no money and thought he should go round to people who owed Colin money and frighten them into paying.

'I made a couple of phone calls pretending I was in agreement but the next day I saw Colin in prison and told him what had happened. Colin told me to drop him out.

'In June this year I had a feeling that something wrong was going on and looked in the pockets of Rob's jacket, which was in the children's bedroom. I found a long metal container which had bullets in it. I showed it to Mr Howarth and he told me that it was a magazine containing live ammunition for a Luger.

'A few days after 21 July, I returned home about midday and found Rob and another man who I knew as Jack, and have since found out it was Jack Witney, in my kitchen. Rob told me he wanted to see me in his car as I could make myself a few bob. I went out and got into the front passenger seat. Jack got into the back while Rob got into the driver's seat. Rob asked Jack to give me an envelope. I opened it and found it contained a Post Office Savings book, three orange paper slips and a large white slip.

'They asked me if I would go into a post office in Baker Street and draw out £47. That was the amount shown on the white slip. I asked where it had come from and Rob told me to mind my own business. Jack then asked me to pass him something from the compartment in the door where I was sitting. I pulled the flap open and saw there were two guns in there. I said, "Leave me out. I don't want to touch it." He said, "It's the small one, don't be silly."

'I took the smaller gun out and passed it back to Jack. Rob leant over me and took the other gun out and put it into the top of his trousers. I was afraid to get out of the car. I was not scared of Jack but Rob was a different kettle of fish. I was never sure of him, he had cold eyes.

'We then drove to Queensway where we met a man called John who I now know to be John Duddy who you have charged with the murders. After some discussion between the three men they decided to burn the white slip as the Post Office Savings book they had was not the right one for this particular slip. They then said I should go in and get £10 on each of three days.

'There was also three sickness-benefit slips, one of these Rob took in himself. That day I went into the big post office at Shepherd's Bush Green having already practised the signature of the owner of the book. One of the men suggested I bandaged my right hand to excuse the different writing should the counter assistant notice. Duddy waited behind the wheel of Rob's car, the black Daimler, which they parked a little way down the road. All three of us then entered the post office. I got a withdrawal form and made it out for £10. While I was doing this Rob got a driving-licence renewal form and Jack went to the telephone. I went back to the counter and while I waited for the £10 both Jack and Rob stood behind me. Although they had loaded guns they did not produce them. After I got the money we went back to the car and drove off.

'Rob took the £10 off of me and when I asked what I was going to get out of it he just laughed. I got very annoyed and said, "Why involve me when Lil gets the benefit of the money?"

'We then went to a post office near Wormwood Scrubs by a roundabout. The same three of us went in and I obtained £6 from one of the benefit slips. We then went to a post office in West Ealing and Rob cashed another benefit slip on his own.

'The next morning when I got up Jack and Rob were in my flat. The three of us went to a post office in Kensal Rise. Both of them had their guns with them. When we got back home Rob told me he would get my shopping and pay for it himself.

'I had read in the late edition of the *Evening Standard* that a postman had been held up in Walmer Road, North Kensington early on that Thursday morning and some property stolen. I showed this to Rob and he said, "So what?" But I felt sure this is where the savings book came from.

'I used to see Rob go out with a small light fawn zip bag, the one you have on the table now, and at other times he took my fawn-coloured plastic bag which is about 18" by 18" with two brown handles and a brown plastic strip along the top. He used to keep the bags on top of a water tank in my kitchen.

'One day Rob showed me a newspaper cutting about an armed robbery at a betting shop in Du Cane Road, Shepherd's Bush. He said to me, "We must be bright, we done that and got £13 between us." By that I realised he was going about armed.

'On the Friday when the three policemen were shot dead Rob came in just after seven p.m. He indicated that he had been in that area the time of the shooting but he did not admit to being responsible. About lunchtime the following day, Saturday, Rob came in with Duddy. I don't remember if they discussed the shooting or not. Rob and Lil went out with two of my children for a walk in the park. I stayed in with Duddy. About 3:30 p.m. Rob and Lil returned. I went out to the hairdresser at 3:45 and returned about 5:15 p.m. I left again about six p.m. and went to a friend's house in Brook Green.

'The following day, whilst at my friend's flat, I received a telephone call from Rob. He told me to go back home straight away as he and Lil had to go away immediately. I asked if Lil's daughter Jean was sick and Rob said, "Don't ask questions. If you don't get home soon we will have to leave the kids."

'I left straight away and got a taxi. When I arrived Lil was still there. She was white and looked very shaky. Lil had her new coat on and her best shoes, also a suitcase, which she said contained his clothes. That is the suitcase you have just shown me. I telephoned a taxi for her. Lil told me that she had to meet Rob but she did not say where.

'Lil came back the following day, Monday, 15 August, at about three p.m. She let herself in and sat on the sofa, burst into tears and said, "Oh, June, that car what was involved in the shooting was Jack's and it must have Rob's fingerprints all over it." She was crying and I asked her where he was and she said, "I don't know." I said, "What do you mean, I don't know?" She said, "You know I don't know London."

'Lil then told me that she had arranged to take a telephone call from him at the kiosk in Elgin Avenue. The next morning at one a.m. I woke her up and told her that Witney had been charged with the murders. She then asked me if I would take the telephone call at the Warwick Road kiosk as she may be followed.

'The police officers had already called at our flat but had gone away without learning very much. It was obvious they did not know when they called who was living there. I refused to make a statement.

'Lil made a statement which she later told me was lies. She also told me that Rob wanted her to drive his Daimler car to a spot in Carlton Hill, St John's Wood. She told me her licence was out of date and I took the ignition key from her.

'I have told my solicitor all about this and he has advised me to tell you the truth and that's what I've done.'

June Howard's six-hour-long interview included a ten-page statement taken down by Jack Slipper in the Inspector's Office at Shepherd's Bush police station that began at four p.m. on that summer Sunday afternoon and took until 7:10 p.m. The past criminal exploits of Roberts, Duddy and Witney all sounded rather inept but they provided some kind of understanding of why when they were stopped and questioned on the afternoon of Friday, 12 August they had panicked, overreacted and lost control.

Beyond the criminal confines of the police murder investigation Howard's statement is a vivid portrait of hand-to-mouth existence on the margins in mid-1960s London. In the 'swinging city' of 1966 children played unsupervised on numerous bomb sites overgrown with weeds, still commonplace all across the capital. Most of the urban population lived amid decaying grime and rising damp, in soot-stained run-down housing with primitive heating and sanitation. This was the world of Harry Roberts, Jack Witney and John Duddy, the context of their lives, hopes and aspirations in a post-war Britain still struggling to modernise and stay afloat, a time of change and confusion, paradox and disorientation.

June Howard's long friendship with Harry Roberts, such as it was, was threaded with deception and exploitation on both sides. Her detailed observations of and close association with Roberts were invaluable in constructing a profile of him, his recent movements and contradictory nature. Piece by piece the police investigation team were building a sharper picture of the elusive third man they were working night and day to track down.

Chapter 25

The *Daily Express* headline on Monday, 22 August was: *SOHO STRIP CLUBS RAIDED. Forty Murder Squad detectives raided four strip clubs last night. The raid followed a tip that Harry Roberts, wanted for questioning about the killing of three policemen, was hiding in a room above one of the clubs. Police cars drove up to the clubs before they were opened to the public. Girls rehearsing their strip routines were locked in their dressing rooms while the detectives – some of them armed – searched the premises.*

It was another false alarm but the possibility that Roberts was concealed in a London nightclub was more plausible than some other tip-offs, as would be shown later that Monday when antiques dealer Gerald Reynolds was interviewed at Shepherd's Bush police station.

Reynolds's account revealed a marginally more imaginative and ambitious side of Harry Roberts's criminal money-making schemes and his association with the fringes of London's nightlife and underworld.

'About three weeks before Whitsun of this year I was introduced to a man called Robbie by Mrs June Howard at the Antiques Supermarket on Barrett Street, W1. Mrs Howard told me that Robbie and herself wanted to get some money and did I think they could give cheques to get antiques. She explained that the cheques would be drawn on Robbie's account in Bristol but that there was no money in the account. I told them that they would be able to buy antiques with cheques because most of the business is done in that way. After this they came to the Antiques Supermarket where I work every day for about ten days. They brought stuff in to me; I sold it to dealers and afterwards gave the money to Robbie. Altogether I gave them a few hundred pounds.

'At first glance, I would not recognise Robbie from the photographs in the newspapers. The photo makes him look older than he actually appears. I would describe him as looking about 27 or 28 years. In the time that I knew him I didn't notice that scar on his cheek. He has got the gift of the gab. He has an obsession for suede shoes, although I told him to get a smart pair of shoes to help impress people when passing cheques. He had a light and a dark suit which were smart but he persisted in wearing thick-soled suede shoes. He looks as though he could grow a beard quickly. His hair was always well trimmed, light brown always swept back, but some fell over his forehead. He never wore grease on it. His face is long and pale, sunken cheeks, his brow never seemed wrinkled. He never wore white shirts, they were always coloured.

'I first heard of Robbie two years ago when Colin

Howard said he had received some money to buy guns for him, but he had pocketed the money and Robbie was now asking George Osborne, who owns the Le Monde club in Kings Road, Chelsea, to get them for him. Colin Howard did mention that Robbie also wanted to get a passport in a different name and that Howard was arranging this. When I met Robbie he mentioned that he wasn't worried about passports and I assumed that he already had one.

'In May or June this year I went out with both Roberts and June Howard on one occasion. We drove out into the country somewhere, I don't know where it was – Robbie was driving. We went to an antique dealer in a little village. Robbie said it was on the way to Bristol and he seemed to know that part of the country very well. They went in and bought some stuff, then we all came back to London and I showed them where the antiques supermarket was in the Kings Road, Chelsea. I waited in the car while they went in to buy a carriage clock on my recommendation [*where Roberts bought a clock for £55 using a cheque book for his Bristol bank account in which there were insufficient funds*]. After this we all went back to my Antiques Supermarket, where it was immediately sold.

'On the last occasion that I saw Robbie, which was the Friday before Whitsun, I was talking to June Howard in Robbie's car in Barrett Street and she told me that he had a Luger in the glove compartment. This frightened me off and I haven't seen him since.'

*

Reynolds went on to mention Roberts's associations with club owners Joe Rosenburg and George Osborne and with other London nightclubs and it was significant as it was part of the wider criminal web of mid-sixties London. It was no coincidence that Gerald Reynolds's illuminating statement was taken on the same day that police raided several London nightclubs in their search for Harry Roberts. During the 1950s and 1960s a new generation of London nightclubs sprung up in Soho and London's West End offering late-night drinking, music, dancing and cabaret. Some had striptease acts and hostesses to lure customers into buying overpriced drinks with the thinly veiled promise of sex to follow. The clubs attracted a potent mix of the rich and famous who rubbed shoulders with hardened influential criminals like the Kray twins, the Richardson brothers, Freddie Foreman, Frankie Fraser and Billy Hill, whose former wife Aggie ran The Modernaires in Old Compton Street and the Cabinet Club in Gerrard Street.

Although Harry Roberts lacked the necessary criminal ingenuity, drive, style and self-confidence to join this kind of fraternity, its image of gangster chic seduced him into thinking that a life of crime was something he could aspire to. And as far as the police were concerned it seemed increasingly likely that somewhere in this shadowy world of murky characters there could be an informant who with a bit of persuasion – and for the right price – would provide the vital lead to where Roberts was currently hiding.

*

On 23 August, Jack Witney appeared for a second time at the West London Magistrates' Court, having been remanded in custody for seven days the previous Tuesday. He was again remanded pending further enquiries. On his journey to and from the courthouse Witney was accompanied by Detective Constable George and Detective Sergeant Berry. Witney appeared keen to help the police track down Harry Roberts and DS Berry made a note of the conversation that took place between them.

'Excuse me, sir, any news of Roberts yet?'

'If you speak to me, you are doing so of your own free will, you understand that.'

'I know the score, sir. I only want to help find Roberts.'

'If you are making helpful suggestions I will listen to you and note them.'

'The photographs I have seen in the paper are not good of Roberts, you know.'

'They are the only ones we have. I don't think there are any more about.'

Berry then produced a copy of the photo of Roberts that had been released to the press.

Witney said, 'Roberts's face is not so fat as in this photo and he has not got a dimple in his chin or whatever you call it.'

'Do you mean "cleft"?'

'Yes that's right, a deep cleft.' Witney paused, thought it over and then said, 'You did not find him in Epping Forest, then?'

'No.'

'You might find him in Savernake Forest – it's in Wiltshire somewhere. He went there camping with Perry earlier this year when he was trying to avoid the CID in Bristol.'

'How long was he there?'

'I think about a week. I don't think Roberts can have a lot of money.'

'Why is that?'

'The last job where we got money I'm not proud of – we got about two hundred and eighty quid. Duddy and I got seventy or eighty quid each and Roberts kept the rest.'

'How long ago was that?'

'About a month ago at Notting Hill, a rent collector.'

'Roberts has got a few pounds, then?'

'Yes, but he did say he had to pay out expenses for that job.'

Since he'd been charged with the murder of three police officers and imprisoned on remand, Jack Witney had had time to reflect on his calamitous association with his friend and criminal partner, Harry Roberts. Without Witney's help the police investigation would not have been so swift and effective in identifying the other two men who'd been with him in his car on the afternoon of Friday, 12 August in Braybrook Street. Without Witney they would not have traced and arrested John Duddy. But if it wasn't for Roberts, Witney would not now be facing a triple murder charge for three killings in which he had taken no part and could not have foreseen until Roberts pulled the trigger of his old Luger pistol. If Witney could help the police further, perhaps be instrumental in the arrest of Harry Roberts, he might moderate his own plight and mitigate his impending punishment.

Since John Duddy's arrest his mind too had been ticking away. Now the chase was over for him he'd also had time to think it all through. Detective Constable George and Detective Sergeant Berry would accompany Duddy when his turn came to appear again at the West London Magistrates' Court that Friday. And during his journey to and from court Duddy would strike up a conversation with DS Berry in a desperate attempt to improve his own prospects.

Chapter 26

In Bristol, forty-one-year-old builders' labourer Kenneth Hacker was interviewed by Detective Sergeant Ryan. When Roberts started to subcontract for Wimpey at Patchway during March 1965 Hacker had begun working for him there. Hacker recalled that Roberts had had about twelve men – bricklayers and labourers – working for him at various times. After they'd completed the job at Patchway there'd been a shortage of work but although Hacker had not been working Roberts had still paid him £20 a week for about two weeks.

Like others who had worked for Roberts at the time, Hacker spoke of Roberts's generosity as an employer. He paid for Hacker to have driving lessons and Hacker then used the yellow Ford van that Roberts had purchased to convey men to different sites. Hacker's account differed from that of others in that he said that Roberts's subcontracting business had had a good flow of work, albeit with seasonal fluctuation during the winter of 1965/6. It was at this time that Roberts seemed to lose interest and motivation.

'Although Roberts had men working at Windmill and Hutton he spent less and less time on the jobs himself. And about April this year he faded right away and I made numerous visits to Filton Grove to see him without success. On one such visit I did see him and told him that various agents wished to contact him but he just laid on the bed and said, "I'm finished." I then discussed the position regarding the van which I had at home. He told me to look after it. I have not seen Roberts since April.'

Hacker's statement provided nothing substantially new to the police murder investigation but it did pose a new question. Why had the apparently reformed ex-prisoner Harry Roberts suddenly abandoned his promising prospects of an honest future in Bristol and gone to London in pursuit of the infinitely more precarious and financially uncertain life of a small-time criminal?

Setting aside the matter of any criminal ambitions he might have had, it would seem that Roberts's short-lived entrepreneurial subcontracting business failed more through his lack of ability to run it than any lack of opportunity to make it a success.

Three decades later Roberts told author Kate Kray when she visited him in prison that he never made any money from his subcontracting business, 'but it was a useful front'. However, if that were the case it was a bizarre arrangement to have a lucrative business as a front for petty criminal activities that yielded little financial gain. In reality no serious criminal in their right mind would shoot two police officers and risk spending the rest of their life behind bars when there was so little at stake.

This is the vexing question that persists in the story of Harry Maurice Roberts and the misery he unleashed in a few minutes in Braybrook Street on 12 August 1966. From what he's said subsequently, even fifty years later, it is only possible to conclude that, though articulate and by no means unintelligent in other ways, Roberts has never understood – or spoken about – his horrendous crimes with any perception, maturity or honesty. Nor has he expressed any genuine remorse and repentance.

Former Deputy Assistant Commissioner, New Scotland Yard and Commissioner of the CID Ernest Millen wrote in his 1970 autobiography: *They were thieves and robbers; they raided betting shops and robbed rent collectors; but compared with the armed gangsters of the underworld they were merely petty delinquents, and the murders they committed in Braybrook Street were not the result of planned and deliberate evil. They murdered in panic, in that hysterical panic to which men of low intelligence are prone.*

However, when set against the personal statements, viewpoints and opinions of those who knew Witney, Duddy and Roberts, people who shared their lives, hopes, fears and dreams with them, Millen's pithy statement seems inadequate and does not ring true.

But in late August 1966, the murder-investigation team were less concerned with the whys and wherefores. They were still hell bent on simply trying to find Roberts. After a week of false alarms, Detective Sergeant Maurice

Harding of West End Central spotted a man who looked like Roberts in Gerrard Street, Soho. Keen to avoid a gunfight in the middle of crowds of late-night shoppers he decided to follow the man and in Shaftesbury Avenue he saw him board a number 38 bus. Harding commandeered a taxi and tailed the bus into Charing Cross Road. The taxi had no radio so the driver called over to another cab and a message went out for urgent assistance.

The crowded 38 bus turned along New Oxford Street, on to Theobald's Road and into Rosebery Avenue. At the Angel Islington the suspect got off the bus and Harding leapt from his taxi. But the man vanished in a maze of small streets. Police cars and officers were quickly on the scene in a blur of flashing blue lights. A door-to-door search was made of the nearby Spa Green Council Estate. Other officers went to Dorothy Roberts's flat, just two miles from where the man was last seen, but were informed by a neighbour that she'd gone away. Lorries, buses and cars were stopped in St John Street and Rosebery Avenue and the search spread south as far as the Post Office Headquarters at Mount Pleasant.

At Sadler's Wells Theatre in Rosebery Avenue tenor Emile Belcourt was singing the title role in Offenbach's *Bluebeard* in a dress rehearsal when a posse of armed detectives suddenly burst in. While the policemen rushed up the aisles, clambered over seats and searched the cloakrooms, Belcourt continued with his *bravissimo* and the pianist played on. With theatrical zeal Belcourt later told a reporter from the *Daily Express*: 'You simply don't falter, even if the place falls around your ears.' But amid all the chaos, opera and melodrama, which at times bordered on French farce, Harry Roberts was nowhere to be found.

On Thursday, 25 August Chief Superintendent Newman travelled from London to Bristol. By now Lilly Perry had returned to her home and had agreed to make another statement. The murder investigation team were hoping that with further time to reflect she might provide some new detail that would give them the lead they so desperately needed.

Perry began by saying, 'I can only again apologise for the misleading information given in my earlier statements.' However, the honesty of her latest recollections further deepened the mystery of the man who had, in an instant, suddenly taken the lives of David Wombwell and Chris Head in such a barbaric and callous way and had then told Duddy to shoot Geoff Fox.

'We got off the bus, which pulled up just beyond the Wake Arms, then crossed over the road and stood about five yards from a police box. I remember there were some men working on the road nearby. There was a grey trailer near the police box which had a door one end and men sitting next to it drinking tea. We stood near the police box and I said to Robbie, "What happens now?" He said, "This is as far as we go together. I shall have to make my own way from here." Then Robbie started crying and said, "Go and get on your bus back to Camden Town before I get worse." He said, "When you get to Camden walk round the corner and get on a 31 bus to the Chippenham Hotel, then you know your own way from there."

'He walked away and stood back from the bus stop. I waited about five minutes and a double-decker Green Line marked Windsor came along. I could see Robbie from the bus but he didn't wave.

'When I left Robbie I thought it was his intention to sleep in the forest. He did not say he was going to do this but I presumed he would because of the equipment he had bought at the shop in King's Cross where I took the police officers. He had never said he could live rough and I can't imagine him doing this for long as he likes good meals and clean clothes.

'All the time Robbie lived with me he was very quiet. During the day he worked hard on building sites and he seldom went out at night except to phone his mother about once a week.

'His hobby was making plastic models of ships, aircraft and tanks. He was an avid TV viewer, apart from this his only other interest was his car, on which he spent a lot of time and money. Robbie seldom drank and when he did he drank gin and tonic and two was about his limit. I have never known him to be a regular at any pub.

'He smoked but not heavily and he usually smoked

king-size Rothmans. To my knowledge he never gambled at all, not even the football pools.'

When Roberts and Perry left Bristol and went to stay with June Howard in Maida Vale the quiet routine of Roberts' life remained much the same.

'In London he went out most days but in the evenings he was content to watch TV and make models and help me look after the children. He never told me where he went during the day although he mentioned on one or two occasions that he had been playing snooker.

'I can assure you I have no knowledge of Robbie's whereabouts. I have had no communication with him since I left him at the bus stop. If Robbie contacts me I will let you know at once or if I learn anything that will help you to locate him.'

Perry's account of Roberts's unremarkable routines, habits and nature, and how he behaved when they said goodbye, gave an intimate view of a quiet, reserved, rather inadequate man, who didn't gamble, drink, or smoke excessively, with no particular talent, ability, or ambition and whose chosen pastimes were watching the television and making plastic models. It wasn't the portrait of a violent criminal or a man who seemed given to sudden and murderous violence. But with every new fact the profile of the man behind the black and white photograph was being pieced together more completely and the chances of working out how he thought, what he might do and where he might be were increasing.

Later on Thursday, Harry Roberts's mother Dorothy collapsed while filming a television appeal for her son to give himself up. Mrs Roberts insisted on continuing. Her face in deep shadow to avoid identification, she appeared on BBC and ITV after asking police to let her plead with her son. With her voice near to breaking point she said, 'This is your mother speaking to you. I ask you from the bottom of my heart to come into the open and give yourself up. If you make an appointment with me I will come with you. The whole thing is killing me. And I'm sure I'm advising you correct. Please do as I ask you before there's any more bloodshed.'

After the filming was over Mrs Roberts said, 'He and I aren't very close. He is my only boy but I haven't seen him for eight or nine months.'

On Friday, 26 August John Duddy returned to West London Magistrates' Court and, as with Witney's second appearance three days earlier, Duddy was remanded for another week pending further police enquiries. During his journey to and from the court in a heavily escorted black prison van, he was accompanied by Detective Constable George and Detective Sergeant Berry and struck up a conversation.

Duddy: 'You have not found Roberts yet, sir?'

Berry: 'Bearing in mind you are in custody, anything you say will be noted by me.'

Duddy: 'I don't mind. I feel terrible about this. I wish I could help. I have not had much sleep still thinking about what happened.'

Berry: 'We haven't found him yet, but we want to get to him as quick as possible to avoid any further shootings.'

Duddy: 'Roberts will not come easy – he has still got the guns. He may have gone up to Glasgow. Witney sent a telegram there once to a Little Jimmy. I think he knows Roberts as well.'

Berry: 'I will see that is checked out.'

Duddy: 'I don't know, sir, but you may not know that Roberts is a big eater, he certainly likes his food. Witney, Roberts and myself went into the Glasshouse pub, opposite the Porchester Baths, the day before the shooting and the day before that, to have food.'

Berry: 'Did Roberts know anyone personally in there, like the governor or the manager?'

Duddy: 'I do not know that. Have you seen that fellow called Joe at Vauxhall? Witney knows him. I think this Joe used to use the garage at Vauxhall before for stolen cars. I believe I have heard Witney talk about a pub in Reading with a restaurant they used to go to, it's a big place before you get into Reading. Witney should know which one it is.'

Berry: 'Do you know where Roberts had his suits made?'

Duddy: 'I was only with them for about five weeks, I cannot help you there. Roberts was a smart dresser, though. I have just remembered another place where I went with Roberts and Witney, it's a metal dealers' place, Harlesden I think it is. I know we went down Tubbs Road after leaving Harrow. We went there about three times and Roberts spent an hour in the office.'

Berry: 'How long ago was this?'

Duddy: 'This was about a week or ten days before the shooting.'

John Duddy assisted in drawing a layout of the area he described when he was in the holding cell at West London Magistrates' Court. His conversation with DS Berry provided other useful new lines of investigation, too – places and people. On the face of it there was nothing decisive in what Duddy said: much of it was rather vague. Nevertheless, there was a possibility that one of the locations or individuals he mentioned could be the crucial link to where Roberts was hiding.

After drawing a blank in Epping Forest the investigation team was considering whether Roberts might have deliberately created a false trail by buying camping equipment and travelling with Perry to the forest only to put her on the next bus back home. But sooner or later it was likely that Roberts would need to contact someone he knew for money, or food, or shelter.

The Friday front pages of the *Daily Mirror* and *Daily Express* had photos and reports of an incident in South London the previous day involving criminals, guns and unarmed police officers. It began when a small boy saw men in a grey Wolseley car pulling on stocking masks in Deptford High Street. The sharp-eyed public-spirited boy called 999 from a nearby phone box.

Constables Anthony John Gledhill and Terence Frederick McFall, both twenty-eight years old and married with children, in patrol car Papa-One spotted the Wolseley and gave chase. The two cars screeched through back streets touching eighty miles an hour at Surrey Docks, weaving between lorries, going in the wrong direction at one point down a one-way street.

Thirteen-year-old Wayne Bradshaw saw the chase and later told reporters, 'They had guns in their hands. I heard shots and saw blue gun smoke.' A dozen or so shots were fired before the suspect car reached Southward Park and after passing under the railway bridge it swung into Galleyhill Road. Gledhill's skill got Papa-One round the corner without mishap but the driver of the bandit car misjudged it, skidded and crashed.

Five occupants leapt out. Three men ran one way, two in the other direction and several more shots were fired at the police car. Gledhill and McFall followed the three men into Raymouth Road where one man climbed up the arches and onto the railway line while a second man ran into a timber yard.

Harry Nelson saw Papa-One go after them. 'Suddenly the police car stopped. In front of the car was a man pointing a pistol shouting, "Get out – hands up!" The two policemen got out, then the man with the gun and his mate jumped into the police car and started reversing.'

The police car stopped and while the gunman momentarily looked away to engage first gear Gledhill flung himself at the driver and grabbed the gun. The car shot forward with Gledhill swinging on the open door, fighting for the wheel. The Wolseley snaked from side to side and veered across the street, a tyre burst against the kerb and Papa-One collided head-on with a parked Bedford van. The two bandits took off on foot again, into a builder's yard. The police officers yelled at passers-by coming to help, 'Get back, they have guns!'

One of the fleeing men vanished while the man with the gun attempted another shot but there was a tell-tale click signalling that he was out of ammunition. As he tried to run away he was brought down with a rugby tackle and McFall and Gledhill set about him with their truncheons. McFall later said to reporters, 'It was them or us.'

Meanwhile other officers had arrived on the scene. The man who had escaped over the railway tracks was spotted by Fred Barrett who was working on a nearby bridge. 'I saw a man with five policemen running behind shouting, "Stop him!" Me and my mates were ready to have a go, then he took a flying leap over the bridge.'

The fugitive landed almost on top of Alfred Pales who was working below. 'He looked really scared. A policeman jumped down and they disappeared along the tracks. A goods train was coming out of the yards and another was going in.'

The man was trapped in the middle and it was feared he had gone under one of the trains but when they had passed there was no sign of him.

With his left arm in a sling PC Anthony Geldhill was later asked by reporters outside Tower Bridge police station if he had been frightened. 'Anyone would be scared when you have a pistol pointed at your head,' Gledhill replied and added coolly, 'But with all this shooting going on there was only one thing to do: have a good go back at them.' Anthony Gledhill was later awarded the George Cross and Terence McFall was awarded the George Medal.

Two weeks after the Shepherd's Bush shootings this was a heroic and upbeat story in the relentless fight against violent crime in the London Metropolitan area. And for the exhausted officers involved in Operation Shepherd, as the second week of their murder investigation moved into the Bank Holiday weekend their determined searching and their interviews with witnesses, friends and associates meant that they had found out a great deal more about the contradictory, elusive and unpredictable Harry Roberts. But, frustratingly, they were still no closer to catching him.

Chapter 27

On Saturday, 27 August the *Daily Express* had a small column on the front page reporting an appeal made on ITV on Friday evening by thirty-one-year-old Margaret Roberts for her estranged husband to 'give himself up'. 'Don't hurt anyone,' she pleaded. She told reporters that she'd decided to make the appearance after seeing Dorothy Roberts on television the previous day.

In his hideout in Thorley Woods, Harry Roberts was unaware that his mother and Margaret had been on national television. He had heard his mother's appeal on his transistor radio a week earlier and it was unlikely that her latest pleas would have made the slightest difference. Living rough for twelve days in his skilfully concealed isolated hiding place it was easier to delude himself that his situation wasn't hopeless. He was still clinging to the idea that once the heat had died down he would somehow be able to return to some kind of normal life and never be apprehended.

On Saturday morning at Victor Lawrence Ltd, thirty-three-year-old John Bennett, who was employed as a sales assistant at the shop where Roberts had bought camping equipment, spoke to Temporary Detective Constable Donald Keil. Bennett confirmed the various items purchased by Roberts and explained why he hadn't come forward earlier. 'I did not associate this man with Roberts until I was shown the photograph by the police officer that came to the shop last Wednesday.' Bennett said that he was, 'absolutely certain that it was Roberts' whom he had served on the morning of Monday, 15 August. He also confirmed what Lilly Perry had said. 'I would like to add that when he [Roberts] came in he was accompanied by a woman. This woman was the one who later came with the two officers into the shop on the Wednesday afternoon.'

Manager of the shop Derek Boulton also identified the customer as Harry Roberts from a photograph he had seen in the national press and gave his own physical description of him. 'He was in his early thirties, about 5'10" tall, medium in build, with dark brown wavy hair; speaking with a London accent which was not cockney. He was wearing a single-breasted charcoal suit with a white shirt and tie. He was smart in appearance and not the sort of person I would expect to go hiking.' Boulton described the woman who was with Roberts as '. . . aged about 35-38, fairly well built with dark hair, wearing a one-piece belted dress with short sleeves.' He concluded by offering further help with hard evidence: 'When required I can produce the copy bill of which the top copy was given to the customer.'

Reported sightings of Roberts continued to flood in to the murder-operations room at Shepherd's Bush and police stations around London and the South-East. At Wisley Common, Surrey, police tracked down a solitary man but he turned out to be a Londoner on a trip to the country to pick mushrooms. In Peacehaven on the Sussex coast every available patrol car converged on the town after another report but again the officers drew a blank. At Brighton and Hastings Regional Crime Squad detectives went to boarding houses and small hotels and showed landladies pictures of Roberts. At Bulow Court in Fulham armed detectives arrived and made a fruitless hour-long search of the block of flats following another tip-off.

On Wednesday, 31 August Jack Witney found himself once again in the company of Detective Constable George and Detective Sergeant Berry while travelling to and from West London Magistrates' Court.

Witney: 'I see you got another photo, then.'

Berry: 'Yes, what do you think of it?'

Witney: 'That's more like him. I have been trying to remember places or people he may have been in touch with. No news yet, is there?'

Berry: 'No, we have not got him yet. Did you ever go to a scrap dealer's place with Duddy and Roberts in the Harlesden area?'

Witney: 'Yes, I went with Duddy and Roberts. Only Roberts went inside. Duddy and I went for a drink in the local – I think it's called the Junction. The place is off the Harrow Road. I think the chap who runs it is called Tony; he's got an Austin 1100 or a red Mini. I have never seen him myself.'

Berry: 'We must have this person seen, then.'

Witney: 'It's very difficult to remember. I was trying to think of some of the fellows who knew Roberts in Maidstone when we were there. Frankie Fraser was there at the time and there was another one called Charlie Wilson – they were always chatting together. Roberts told me he went down to see Charlie when he got nicked for the Train Robbery lot. Roberts told me afterwards that he met Goody's bird there and he strongly fancied her. This amazed me as he hardly spoke about women at all.'

Berry: 'We must trace everyone who knew Roberts.'

Witney: 'I shall never forget that Friday.'

Berry: 'If you are going to say anything about the matters with which you are charged I must caution you. You should talk to your solicitor first.'

Witney: 'Well, I went to call for Duddy at his place at eight o'clock in the morning. Duddy and Roberts were in the Daimler and Roberts said something about the brakes being a bit dodgy so we went off in my van. I drove to Western Avenue first and I went in and saw an uncle of mine and had a cup of tea. I'm not going to tell you his name because I don't want him to get involved; he's getting on a bit. We must have left there about quarter to ten. We floated around Eastcote way. Later we drove around by

East Acton station because, as you know, we had plates made up from the Corsair we had seen around there. We were trying to nick a similar model for something we had in mind. I drove up to the Scrubs and you know what happened afterwards. Roberts must still have two .38s and definitely a Luger because I have seen spare ammunition in the box. Roberts was reloading this when we went across the river after the shooting, he was putting in another magazine.'

Berry: 'Roberts must be getting short of money now.'

Witney: 'I went down to Bristol with him and Lil Perry this year in the Daimler because he wanted me to look over something he planned to do by himself. I thought he was bloody mad but he may have done that job to get some money.'

Berry: 'To avoid anyone else getting killed, if he has this in mind and hasn't done it will you tell me what his plan was?'

Witney: 'Yes, we drove down to Bristol and he told me on the way that a Securicor van pulled up outside a bank in Whiteladies Road and took money in and he wanted to nick the cash. When I saw the set-up I told him he was potty. Afterwards we picked up Lil from her place as we had dropped her there first and then we came back to town.'

Berry: I will inform Bristol police to have that covered in case Roberts should try that, if he hasn't already done so.'

As with previous impromptu conversations that DS Bob Berry had with Witney and Duddy there were useful snippets of information, both about the day of the murders and possible leads to Roberts. Witney's mention of Frankie Fraser and of the Great Train Robbers Charlie Wilson and Gordon Goody was interesting although these men were in a vastly different criminal league from that of Roberts, Duddy and Witney.

In August 1966 Roberts, Witney and Duddy were not gangsters and hard men of this type, although they no doubt aspired to be something more than they were. In the underworld of 'swinging' London there were many minor criminals seeking to make their mark and gain some kind of standing for themselves. Perhaps it was for this reason, to gain respect and some trace of stature, that Witney dropped the names of Frankie Fraser, Gordon Goody and Charlie Wilson into the conversation with DS Berry.

The murder investigation and hunt for Roberts had some competition for public and media attention and even that of Metropolitan Police officers the following day. Crowds gathered along Uxbridge Road, Shepherd's Bush under overcast skies, standing in silence to pay their respects to the funeral cortege of Christopher Head, David Wombwell and Geoffrey Fox.

Chapter 28

On the morning of 1 September 1966, crowds lined the streets of Shepherd's Bush in the wind and the rain, just a mile from where Detective Sergeant Christopher Head, Temporary Detective Constable David Wombwell and Police Constable Geoffrey Fox had been shot down during a routine patrol twenty days earlier.

There were people at every vantage point. They stood six deep in front of shops, most of which had closed for the duration of the funeral service at the Victorian Gothic Church of St Stephen and St Thomas on the corner of Coverdale Road and Uxbridge Road, opposite Shepherd's Bush Police station. On the roof above the CID office on the second floor where the murdered officers had worked, a Union flag hung at half-mast. More than six hundred uniformed police officers stood along the kerbside at close intervals, just as they would for a State occasion, but on that grey Thursday there was little sound or movement amongst the grim-faced onlookers, many of whom were weeping openly.

The hush of the morning was suddenly broken at ten

a.m. by a single bell tolling from the church spire. At the same time in the courtyard of Scotland Yard a lone piper struck up a lament to mark the start of a simple fifteen-minute service conducted by Canon G. R. Dunstan of Westminster Abbey and attended by uniformed and CID personnel and civilian staff who had to remain on duty.

Shortly before 10:15 a.m. a procession of three immaculate hearses, with dark rainclouds reflected in their gleaming black paintwork and a mass of flowers on their rooftops, led fourteen funeral cars at walking pace along Uxbridge Road from the direction of Shepherd's Bush Green. The long convoy drew up with military precision and the relatives of the deceased made their way into church. Commissioner Sir Joseph Simpson greeted and spoke to mourners and then took his place in a pew with Deputy Commander of the CID John Du Rose. The congregation took up every available seat and included the Mayor of Hammersmith, Councillors, local shopkeepers, street traders, publicans and police officers from all over London.

Outside, twelve uniformed policemen wearing white gloves and six plain-clothes detectives in dark suits took the three coffins from the hearses and raised their dead colleagues onto their shoulders, six men to each coffin, hands pressed against wood panelling and steadying the weight. The image captured the comradeship, communal grief and stoic dignity of the occasion and for those who had lost their loved ones perhaps provided some measure of support and comfort too.

The service was led by the Vicar of St Stephen and St Thomas, the Reverend John Ashbridge. The Order of Service simply stated that Christopher Head, David Wombwell and Geoffrey Fox were 'police officers killed whilst on duty'. Three hymns were sung, including 'Abide With Me' and 'On the Resurrection Morning' and PC Bernard Horan, the youngest officer at Shepherd's Bush police station, read the lesson, chapter fifteen of the First Epistle to the Corinthians. The Bishop of Kensington, the Right Reverend Ronald Goodchild, read from the New Testament, the Gospel according to St John, chapter fifteen, verse three: *Greater love hath no man than this that he lay down his life for his friend.*

In his address Goodchild said that everybody, both inside and outside the church, was there, 'to pay homage to three brave men and say thank you.' They had not come to think of all the publicity that had, not unnaturally, been generated by the three men's deaths. 'But to think of one of the fundamental truths of our society which this tragedy has brought home to us. It is a stern reminder of what we really ask of our policemen. We live in a society in which we all belong to one another. The welfare state emphasises this responsibility we have for each other as it seeks to provide for our just needs and our proper security. Let us pause and think that what we ask of our policemen is not only the maintenance of law and order so that our freedoms may be protected. We ask for the protection of our lives, if needs be at the cost of their own. It is a great deal to ask and we are sharply reminded of it with this tragedy.'

Among the hundreds of people who sent flowers was Margaret Roberts, gold and white chrysanthemums, and a card attached on which was written, *With deepest sympathy. Mrs Margaret Roberts, Jnr.*

After the funeral service was over the coffins containing the remains of the three murdered police officers were each taken to their final destinations, Geoff Fox to be buried at Hammersmith, David Wombwell to be cremated at Mortlake and Chris Head to his mother's home town of Torquay where he was later buried. With the crowds still dispersing, police colleagues in the murder-investigation team returned to the operations room at Shepherd's Bush police station to make what they could of the rest of the day.

To ensure the ongoing hunt for Roberts was not fading in the public's mind the police came up with a new idea. The right-hand column of the *Daily Express* front page the following day was headed: *Roberts: Yard Offers £1,000 Reward. A reward of £1,000 was offered by Scotland Yard last night for information leading to the arrest of Harry Roberts.*

This new move in the hunt for Roberts is unprecedented in Yard history. Behind it is the belief that Roberts is being hidden by the underworld and that for £1,000 somebody might give the police a tip-off. Complete anonymity is promised if wanted and the Yard says information can be passed on through a newspaper, lawyer or other channels.

On Friday morning John Duddy was taken back and forth to West London Magistrates' Court where his remand in custody pending further police enquiries was extended. As had now become a familiar routine Duddy was accompanied by Detective Constable George and Detective Sergeant Berry and once again Duddy initiated a conversation.

Duddy: 'You have not had any luck with Roberts, then, sir?'

Berry: 'No, not at present.'

Duddy: 'I suppose you are all a bit worried in case there is going to be another shooting.'

Berry: 'Naturally it would be nice to know if Roberts got rid of the guns or how many he is carrying. He could have buried them after the shooting on the Saturday or Sunday. I believe you were still with him.'

Duddy: 'I can tell you what happened afterwards when I was with him and he definitely did not get rid of the guns then.'

DS Berry then cautioned Duddy and reminded him that he was legally represented.

Duddy: 'After the shooting I went home as I was feeling sick with the whole business and I had to get my kids their tea. I did not see either of them again on that day. On

Saturday morning Roberts came to my place between ten and eleven and we both walked back to Wymering Mansions, by going up Westbourne Park and into Harrow Road. We got to his place at about 11:30. Lil Perry was in the flat and the three kids were there. June Howard came in shortly afterwards. I was still feeling very shaken and about one o'clock Perry and Roberts left the flat with the youngest baby in the pram. That evening about eight o'clock Roberts and Lil went out alone. They did not take the baby this time. I don't know if they went in the car. They both came back about 10:30 p.m. They did not say to me where they had been. I know that evening a lady doctor called at the flat and asked the small boy if mummy was in.

'That night I slept on the settee. On Sunday, Lil came out of the bedroom and asked me if I wanted a cup of tea, this was about nine o'clock. Roberts did ask me if we had better stick together, I said, "No." Roberts told me to go to a holiday place and lose myself.

'To get some fresh air we did go to the park at the back of the flats Sunday morning or it could have been on the Saturday morning. Lil came with us and we took the three children as well. When we went back to the flat, as I only had three quid on me Roberts gave me a fiver so I could go to Glasgow. I was glad to see the back of them and I left the flat and caught a bus to Watford and then caught a late train to Glasgow.'

What was strange about the mostly one-sided conversation

between Duddy and Berry was that Duddy initiated it apparently to offer his help by talking openly about the events after the shootings and his association with Roberts and Lilly Perry. But Duddy first said that he supposed police were worried in case there is going to be another shooting to which Berry replied, 'Naturally it would be nice to know if Roberts got rid of the guns or how many he is carrying.'

Duddy knew the crucial fact that Roberts was no longer armed and so he was in a position to allay fears that if Roberts was cornered he would shoot again. Yet when Berry suggested that Roberts might have buried the guns on the Saturday or Sunday, when Duddy was still with him, Duddy withheld the fact that on Sunday morning he went with Roberts to Hampstead Heath and buried the guns. Instead his reply was deliberately misleading: 'I can tell you what happened afterwards when I was with him and he definitely did not get rid of the guns then.' Unlike Witney, who had helped in the hunt for Roberts, Duddy chose to be selective with the truth and keep some of his inside knowledge to himself.

Meanwhile high-level discussions had been going on between Detective Superintendent Dick Chitty, Sir Joseph Simpson the Commissioner of the Metropolitan Police, and Graham Harrison at the Home Office who in turn consulted Mr D. Taverne, one of the Parliamentary Under-Secretaries of State. Along with an unprecedented £1,000 reward offered by the police for information leading to the arrest of Harry Roberts, it was proposed that a 'wanted' poster should be produced and circulated widely across the country.

There were reservations and Chitty had to argue his case. Having been informed of the conversation between Duddy and Berry, Chitty said, 'I have quite reliable information that Roberts is in possession of three firearms and ammunition for them, and that the other two prisoners who are currently in custody have expressed the opinion that Roberts will not hesitate to shoot again.' Chitty added that he thought it was probable that Roberts 'was being looked after by other criminals of the sort who would do almost anything for money' and publicising the reward could encourage someone to come forward with information. He acknowledged that it was of course a well-established precedent both in the police and at the Home Office that rewards would not be offered for information leading to the discovery of the identity of a person responsible for a serious crime, but this case was different. 'We know who we want and have ample evidence to charge him when he is arrested. There is therefore absolutely no fear that the offer of a reward is likely to induce anyone to fabricate evidence.' After consultation with the Home Office-appointed solicitor Mr E.O. Lane, there were no further concerns or objections raised and the task of producing the wanted poster was given the go-ahead.

A distribution list was drawn up and over 16,000 copies

were sent around the country. The layout was simple, as was the message (see page 6 of plate section for original poster):

£1,000 REWARD
MURDER

A reward or rewards up to a total of £1,000 will be paid for information leading to the arrest of HARRY MAURICE ROBERTS (b. Wanstead, Essex on 21.7.36. 5' 10", photo above) wanted for questioning in connection with the murder of three police officers on 12th August 1966 at Braybrook Street, Shepherd's Bush.

Chapter 29

On Sunday, 4 September Detective Superintendent Dick Chitty made a dramatic and unprecedented appeal to the British nation on television. Viewers noticed that he looked tired, which wasn't surprising considering that he had only slept no more than four hours at a stretch since the day of the murders.

Chitty asked for help in his search for Harry Roberts. He showed photos and pointed out Roberts's distinguishing features – the thick arched eyebrows, the nose, the hair, the scars and the eyelids. He said the reward on offer was made 'to ensure, as far as possible, that if Roberts is discovered it will be handled quietly, without bloodshed, or any kind of battle and without any harm coming to members of the public, policemen and Roberts himself.' Chitty ended his television appearance by repeating the now-familiar warning: 'We are appealing to you for any help you can give us, but I would emphasise that no member of the public who thinks he sees Roberts should take any risk whatsoever. Please contact Scotland Yard or any police station immediately.' Predictably

Chitty's plea sparked a new wave of reported sightings: each one was followed up but none of them led searchers even close to where Roberts was hiding.

In Harry Roberts's account of his time holed up in Thorley Woods, which he insisted on dictating word for word to author Kate Kray during a prison visit a quarter of a century later, he said that after three weeks he was finally forced to break cover. 'My rations had all but run out two days before, I had scraped the green mould off my last slice of bread and, since then, had only eaten ears of corn from a nearby field. I was now very hungry and weak and I knew I had to go out and get some food and supplies. The thought terrified me but I knew I had to go.'

By now Roberts had lost weight and had grown a stubbly beard that he hoped would help disguise his appearance. He made his way across the fields to a main road, found a bus stop and decided to head for Harlow to purchase provisions.

The first shop he went into was apparently a tobacconist's where he said that a picture of him was on the front page of every national newspaper. Unrecognised, he bought tobacco, then found a supermarket and retreated back to the woods as quickly as he could. 'I built a fire, made a big pot of tea and toasted the bread. It was good to eat again and I ate the whole loaf.'

Roberts recalled that his trip to Harlow 'was [on] the very day the three coppers were buried'. He also said the next day was a Tuesday, the day he had arranged to call Lilly Perry each week while she waited at a telephone box in Maida Vale. He gave a detailed account of how he went in person to intercept her and narrowly avoided being spotted by DCI Ginger Hensley. However, although this may have some foundation in fact, his chronology presents an obvious error. The funeral of David Wombwell, Chris Head and Geoff Fox took place on Thursday, 1 September.

Nevertheless, the part of Roberts's version of events that is broadly true is that it was around this time that he decided to go to Hampstead Heath to retrieve his buried guns. 'I didn't like the vulnerable feeling I had had in the town. I had to get my guns because I felt naked without them so the next day I got a Greenline bus to Camden then a bus to Hampstead Heath and walked across to Kenwood.' After unearthing the guns with his bare hands he tucked the malfunctioning Luger into his belt, put the now-tarnished nickel-plated Colt .38 Special in a carrier bag and reburied the .38 Enfield ex-British Army Service revolver.

As it turned out, Duddy's deliberate omission in not telling DS Berry that the guns were buried on Hampstead Heath had two aspects to it that he was unaware of at the time and can only be appreciated in retrospect. First, if the police had known about the buried guns and had recovered them with Duddy's help the weapons would not have been there when Roberts went to retrieve them. Second, and more importantly, Roberts was indeed now armed. Unintentionally, by leading the police to believe that Roberts had firearms and ammunition in his possession Duddy had actually given them good reason to continue their hunt for him with extreme caution.

Twenty-five days after the Braybrook Street murders and less than a week after the funeral of Chris Head, David Wombwell and Geoff Fox at Shepherd's Bush, a memorial service was held in their honour at Westminster Abbey on Tuesday, 6 September. The service was relayed to nearby St Margaret's, packed with police and members of the public, and to other cathedrals and churches throughout the country.

The morning was warm and sunny and long before the service began the streets around Westminster were jammed with traffic and people. Ordinary folk who had no seat in the Abbey simply came to be there and were content to stand or to sit on camping stools and newspapers and watch from any place they could find outside.

It began with marching ranks of policemen and policewomen from all the forces in Britain. There were two thousand of them, from senior officers to new recruits. Sharp-pressed blue serge uniforms, sunlight glinting on silver buttons and buckles, gleaming shoes in step with one another, a show of solidarity and solemn faces.

Acclaimed *Daily Mirror* reporter of forty years, Donald Zec, wrote that day: *'The setting is as familiar as it is famous for the celebrated, the exalted, the royal, the warriors of note and doers of great deeds. But these magnificent and immensely moving proceedings had no touch of ermine, no jingle of spurs. Just police helmets and heavy boots, and ceremonial armaments were no more lethal than the truncheon and the whistle. This was the unique significance of it all. One day just three names on a roster at Shepherd's Bush, a random trio from London's police force, suddenly and tragically projected into history and the national Roll of Honour. Two wives and a mother in the Abbey made suddenly and painfully conspicuous.'*

Harold Wilson, the Prime Minister, Home Secretary Roy Jenkins and Edward Heath, leader of the Opposition, were there. Such an occasion of national moment and recognition demanded the attendance of dignitaries with their gold chains of office, noble lords in top hats and frock coats, members of the senior judiciary and high-ranking civil servants. Her Majesty the Queen was represented by Lord Hilton of Upton, who was stopped and asked for his ticket as he walked up to the main entrance and waited patiently outside while enquiries were made. For on that day the police and organisers were checking everything that could be checked, even though Lord Hilton didn't look like a gatecrasher.

At noon a procession of clergy, police and prison chaplains entered the Abbey and took their allotted positions. Finally from among the silent sea of blue uniforms the opportunity came to let out some pent-up feelings in a thunderous rendition of 'Guide Me, O Thou Great Redeemer' with a crashing crescendo at *'Death of death and hell's destruction . . .'*

Sir Joseph Simpson, the tall, slim Commissioner of the Metropolitan Police with a mane of leonine white hair, read the first lesson from the Book of Revelation, Chapter twenty-one, verses one to seven. Another hymn was sung, 'The Lord's My Shepherd', and then the Dean stood and spoke to the congregation.

'I ask you, whether here or at home, to search your own heart. May not these killings, which have so shocked us, along with the hard realities by which our nation is faced at the present time, mark a turning point in our society in a general revulsion against brutality and a determination that our society shall not slide into violence.'

It didn't seem to matter that the Dean's words sounded like something from a previous century: everyone wholeheartedly agreed with the sense and sentiment of what he said. The Dean then commended Christopher Tippet Head, Geoffrey Roger Fox and David Stanley Bertram Wombwell, 'whose death came suddenly to them in the course of their duty as servants of the law and order of our land.'

The mighty Harrison and Harrison organ of Westminster Abbey, installed for the Coronation of King George VI in 1937, thundered once again and 'Abide With Me' was sung with vigour and volume, with heart and soul. The hymn was followed by prayers for the mourners, especially for the wife and three children of Geoffrey Fox, the wife and two children of David Wombwell and for the widowed mother of Christopher

Head. The memorial service concluded with the police choir singing unaccompanied 'God Be In My Head' and it was so moving that even some hardened policemen cried without embarrassment.

As the congregation filed out slowly, the half-muffled bells of the Abbey were rung by police bell-ringers. A dense crowd was gathered outside the great West Door, among them several people carrying banners calling for the restoration of capital punishment for the murder of police and prison officers.

The following day, on Wednesday, 7 September, while being escorted to and from court Jack Witney again engaged DS Berry in conversation on the pressing subject of Roberts's whereabouts.

Witney: 'I have thought of somewhere else where Roberts may have gone.'

Berry: 'Where is that?'

Witney: 'It was my missis who told me this. When she was chatting to Lil Perry one day and Roberts and I had gone for a drink, Lil Perry told my missis that she had a sister in Devon and Cornwall and Roberts had visited her with Perry. I cannot help you with the address. There was another fellow in Maidstone [prison] at the same time as Roberts and he was doing a three- or four-stretch. I think he came out in the latter part of '62. I think his name is Roy Smith.'

Berry: 'I will have that checked out.'

Witney: 'Does Duddy know where Roberts has gone? He must have seen him after me.'

Berry: 'He does not appear to have any ideas, so he tells me.'

Witney: 'When Roberts and I saw Duddy in his place on Friday evening, there was no talk about guns.'

Berry: 'I have told you before that if you say anything connected with the shootings I must caution you and must remind you that you have a solicitor.'

Witney: 'Yes, all right. Well, after Duddy walked off outside the fire station after I had parked the car, Roberts and me walked to Westminster Bridge and we got a bus. Roberts was carrying a blue raincoat. I know Roberts asked for two tickets to Kentish Town but the bus was not going there so we got off at a stop before Euston Road and we walked down by Euston Station. We went into a café and we had two teas. After about ten minutes we came out and caught a cab and went to Duddy's flat. Jock was there. Roberts had the Luger in his trouser belt. He took it out. We had a cup of tea there until about a quarter to seven and then Roberts drove me in his Daimler to Westbourne Park. I bought a paper and walked home.

'There was another fellow I have just remembered who was in Maidstone called Billy Rocket. I think he married when he came out and lived with his wife who had a café or restaurant.

'How are the wives of the policemen who got killed? I cannot bear to think about the kids they had. Roberts and

Duddy must have been mad. I cannot understand how the Detective Sergeant got run over after being shot. It was not me, you know. When Dave came up to me followed by the sergeant, the sergeant walked around the back and came up by the side where Roberts was sitting. It was then that Roberts fired across my face at Dave. The sergeant ran up the road and stumbled and fell to the ground and Roberts shot him. Duddy followed Roberts and he went across to the police car which was still moving and fired into the car. Roberts and Duddy ran back to my motor and I backed away.'

Berry drew a plan of how Witney explained the scene at Braybrook Street. The events were much as described previously by Witney, Duddy and various eyewitnesses. However, the differing details of every account given – even sometimes by the same person on different occasions – were important to record as it was only by comparison that detectives could work out, second by second, exactly what had taken place.

Nevertheless, it remained hard to envisage how and why the situation had escalated so rapidly from a routine stop of a suspect vehicle to triple murder. But it was only by going over it all again and again that both Witney and the police investigators could begin to process matters into some kind of understandable sequence, even if the actual killings still didn't make sense. It was clear that Roberts had been suddenly panicked by the fear that his unlicensed guns were about to be discovered. But, even so, his reaction was out of all proportion to the situation, especially considering the likely penalty. Still nagging away in the minds of the Operation Shepherd detectives was the question of whether there was some additional critical factor that they had yet to discover.

Chapter 30

On the front page of the *Police Gazette* for 7 September 1966 was:

> Special Notice
> MURDER
> CRO – Re Special Notices, 30-8-66 etc (murder of three police officers).
> Notices offering a reward for information leading to the arrest of HARRY MAURICE ROBERTS CRO No 33943-54 are being distributed to all Forces through Regional Criminal Record Offices for display on police noticeboards and at other suitable places.
> Additional supplies of the notice may be obtained on application to C-5 Branch, New Scotland Yard telephone WHItehall 1212, Extn 32.

Over the next few days the approved wanted poster was pinned on every police station public noticeboard across the UK. It was another way of keeping the face of Harry Roberts firmly in the minds of the public and reminding them of the financial incentive that the police were offering in return for help.

Scotland Yard had by now released several photographs of Roberts. The Thursday, 8 September edition of the *Daily Express* had them all in an article headed *The Sixth Face – A new picture lines up in Roberts gallery*. Number one was the first photograph released by the Yard and is still the best-known image. Number two was of Roberts wearing a hat and had been taken in the Malayan jungle ten years earlier. Number three was another old photo of Roberts as a soldier. Numbers four and five were more recent, taken in a Soho club and also used for the wanted poster. The latest picture to be released was from when Roberts had lived in Bristol. In all six photos he was clean-shaven and looked younger, a good deal less underfed, dishevelled and careworn than he did now.

All the while police switchboard operators were being kept busy with reported sightings from the public. Twelve white Jaguar police cars raced through Leicester with horns blaring and roof lamps flashing after Roberts was supposedly spotted on the Nottingham-to-London express train. Fifty police officers boarded the train at Loughborough and worked their way through the crowded carriages. Signalmen along the track ahead were alerted in case anyone tried to jump off. By the time the train pulled into St Pancras every passenger in every carriage had been checked but despite the quick response it turned out to be yet another false alarm. But undaunted and ever resolute, Dick Chitty told *Daily Express* reporter John Ball: 'It is a hunt that will go on until he is found.'

No task was too great, no detail too small in the dogged, determined effort to gather evidence and build the triple murder case. An example: DCI Hensley arrived at Wymering Mansions with two shopping bags in his hand, one grey-and-black plastic, the other brown canvas. Both had been found in Witney's car.

June Howard identified the plastic shopping bag with a zip as hers and said that Roberts had sometimes used it. The canvas bag, she said, was identical to one that Roberts had carried at times and she'd seen it around the flat. She added, 'I did not know what he actually used the bags for.' The remark was more revealing than she intended: clearly, bags have various different uses so why *would* she know? But Roberts had used the canvas bag in which to carry his three guns and it was that particular use Howard did not want to admit to knowing about.

Later that day Duddy was again in the company of DS Berry on his journey to court. However, this time it was Berry who had something he wanted to discuss with Duddy.

Berry: 'I'm going to show you some bags to see if you can identify them.' He cautioned Duddy and first presented the plastic zip-bag.

Duddy: 'I have seen that before – that was in the back of the van behind Witney. I thought there was a map in that bag, an atlas of London or something like that.'

Berry then showed Duddy the canvas bag.

Duddy: 'I have seen that one before, carried by Roberts with guns in it; it may have been in the Daimler. I thought Roberts pulled out a gun from that bag. I cannot remember this bag being in the van on the day of the shootings although it could have been under the seat.'

Berry drew a diagram of the interior of Witney's car. Duddy pointed out where each of the men had been sitting and Berry indicated where the canvas bag had been found.

Duddy: 'When Roberts and I left the Daimler on Friday morning to get into the van I have a feeling that Roberts was carrying something – it could have been this bag. It could have had the guns in it. I don't know where I got the gun from when I followed Roberts out of the van.'

All the preoccupation with bags may seem incidental or perhaps pointless. However, the bags were physical evidence that would help tie key elements together. The two bags found in Witney's car could now be linked to Roberts. June Howard had identified both bags and had said Roberts had used them. Duddy had clinched it by saying that Roberts used the canvas bag in which to carry his guns which were to become the murder weapons.

The other conclusion that could be drawn was that, as there were no guns in the canvas bag when it was found in Witney's car, Roberts, Witney or Duddy had removed them when the car was left in the railway arches in Vauxhall after the shootings. Neither Witney nor Duddy had guns in their possession or at their homes when they were arrested and that made it all the more likely that Roberts still had the guns with him.

On Monday, 12 September Dorothy Roberts was interviewed again by Detective Inspector Slipper in the presence of Detective Chief Inspector Hensley. Much of what she told them had already been established but, as with other witnesses, there were fresh personal insights and new details.

Reading Dorothy Roberts's dictated statement fifty years later is an opportunity to travel back in time to that day in September 1966, to the interview room with Slipper and Hensley, and get some sense of her as a person.

Shepherd's Bush Police Station
'F' Division
12th September 1966
STATEMENT OF: Dorothy Blanche ROBERTS nee HARRIES
Born: 19.3.1907
21 Kendal House
Augustus Street, NW1
Waitress

I live at the above address with a friend named Jeanette Whitehead. I was married in 1935 at Lambeth Registry Office, Brixton Road, SW2, to Harry Maurice Roberts who was born in Birmingham in 1906. We had one child, a boy, who we named Harry Maurice, the same as his father. He was born on 21st July, 1936.

At that time my husband and I were managing the George Hotel, Wanstead, E11. My husband joined the R.A.F. early in the war and served in Britain throughout the war. I purchased a restaurant in Cardington Street, NW1. My son Harry went to Wales to stay with some friends, Mr and Mrs Hopkins, who are now deceased, at Llanbradach near Cardiff. Mrs Hopkins's daughter, Alice McQuade, resides nearby at 13 Langdale House, Stanhope Street, NW1.

Harry went to school in Wales, but after returning to London in 1945, he has not been back to Wales. I gave the restaurant up soon after the war ended. I then had a house in Varndale Street, NW1, and used to let rooms for a living. I have been in Kendal House for about nine years now. I parted from my husband soon after the war and have since been divorced. It was some years ago when I last heard of my husband, he was in Birmingham at the time.

I kept my son Harry. I even paid for him to attend boarding school where he was a boarder until he was 15 years of age. He then went to work for an engineering company in Camden Town. He stopped there for about 18 months, then left and after that he would not work and the trouble started.

I myself was born in Liverpool. There were three girls in the family, myself, Laurise and May, both my sisters are dead. Laurise died about thirty years ago. I know it was before the war. My parents are also dead. My father's name was John Harries.

And with this Dorothy Roberts ended her short verbal account. It was taken down and read over to her by Jack Slipper. She then refused to sign it.

One of the most revealing things about Dorothy Roberts's recollections is their sketchiness and brevity but it's perhaps not surprising that she left out, or glossed over, certain details and just wanted to get the interview over with. It must have been hard for her to make sense of the fate that had befallen her and her son, let alone talk about it with any clarity or objectivity.

Dorothy Roberts's summary of her life and her son's omitted that he was expelled from boarding school before he was fifteen years old. She was no doubt still trying to work out why, how, and when, 'the trouble started' and she might have forgotten that the first signs of trouble were after her son left boarding school when he was restless, unsettled and sometimes violent towards her. She neglected to say that the army had brought about a change in him and he had been a successful soldier and later married. Her son and daughter-in-law had lived with her for a time and conceived a child. Things then escalated when her son was arrested and convicted for the vicious assault on William Gaylard and it was his pregnant new wife Margaret who had informed the police. And after Roberts's seven-year prison conviction Margaret lost their baby. For this was the more painful, complex and interwoven narrative that had ultimately led Dorothy Roberts and her only son to the disastrous situation in which they now found themselves.

However, three months later Mrs Roberts did speak about her life and her son again, in more depth and with greater insight. But it wasn't to a police officer, it was to crime reporter Tom Tullett from the *Daily Mirror*. She told him: 'I've had a lot of time to think it over . . . I think of nothing else day and night, my son's always with me in my thoughts. I know now where the turning point was.' Later, in the unfolding sequence of events of the Shepherd's Bush Murders, Dorothy Roberts would give a more revealing and insightful version of her side of the story.

There was no let-up in Slipper and Hensley's determination or work schedule. They had also been investigating the source and background of the three guns acquired by Roberts. Lilian Perry was very helpful again and on Tuesday 13 September she agreed to look at a selection of guns with Slipper and Hensley that had been brought to Shepherd's Bush police station from the Metropolitan Police Forensic Laboratory.

After examining the weapons Perry said: 'Amongst the guns laid out on the table was one which was identical to one of the guns which Harry Roberts possessed. I recognise it by its shape and butt and also by the metal container which holds the bullets which slips into the butt of the gun. Harry called this the magazine and I have seen him pulling back a spring button on the side of the magazine and filling it with bullets.

'I also pointed out two other guns which are very similar to the guns I have seen in his possession. I particularly remember [that] the round magazine on these guns flicked out sideways from the gun.'

Four hours later Slipper then got Perry to make a longer statement that elaborated on where Roberts had purchased the guns but, more crucially, on what he'd done with them after the shootings.

'I think I told you last time that Robbie went out on Saturday morning to get rid of the guns – this was not true. It was on Sunday when he and Duddy took them out to dispose of them. They told me they had buried them. Robbie wanted Duddy to go over to Lambeth and burn the car they had used in the shooting, but Duddy would not go so on Saturday night, 13 August 1966, I drove over with Robbie to burn it. He showed me the garage but he couldn't find anything to burn it with. He said he wanted to destroy the fingerprints.

'We had a drink in the pub on the corner. I did discuss with Robbie the method of dying hair. He suggested dying his blond but I told him it was ridiculous as there were not many men about with blond hair.

'I realise how much help I gave him to escape and

wish I had never met him in the first place. Robbie told me on many occasions that no one would ever put him inside prison again and he would shoot them first. He often said when he was carrying his guns that they could not hang him if he shot anyone dead. If I had known that he meant to carry out what he said he would do I would have left him.'

Lilly Perry's statement, combined with other enquiries that Slipper and Hensley had been making amongst contacts in the Greek Cypriot community in Camden Town, gave them a pretty clear idea of who to speak to next.

Early on Sunday morning, at 6:30 a.m., Slipper, Hensley and Detective Sergeant Sutcliffe arrived at 14 Pratt Street, NW1, the home of Christos Costas.

Hensley said to him, 'I have reason to believe that you are one of three men who sold a Luger and two other guns to a man known as Harry Roberts who is wanted for the murder of three police officers.'

Hensley cautioned Costas who replied, unconcerned: 'No, not me. I not know what you talk about – get out of my shop. What you want with me?'

Slipper said, 'You fit the description of a man who got into a large black car with Roberts and you showed Roberts how the guns worked. A woman was in the car at the time.'

Costas, clearly realising there was no getting out of it,

replied: 'Yes, that was me. I sold him the guns. What happens now?'

Hensley said, 'We are taking you to Shepherd's Bush Police Station for further enquiries.'

At Shepherd's Bush, Costas agreed to make a written statement that included a key exchange with Hensley.

Hensley: 'Where did you get the guns from?'

Costas: 'I used to run a gambling place at 33 Pratt Street, NW1, and when some of the boys lost they used to ask £5 or something for the guns and I used to do that. At eight o'clock one night, with two other Cypriots I went to Denmark Street off Shaftesbury Avenue. I don't want to name them because they did not know what I was doing. I went in my friend's car and there met a man on the corner. He walked towards me and asked me if my name was Chris. I said, "Yes." He asked me if I'd got them, meaning the guns, I said, "Yes, I can't give them to you here." He said, "Let's go down to my car."

'We both got into my car with my two friends and drove around some one-way streets until we stopped behind a big black car. I got out with this person and got into his car, into the back seat. There was a woman sitting in the front. I showed him the three guns telling him I had no bullets for two of them. The three guns I had were one revolver, I think it was a .45, another revolver, I think it was a .22 and a Luger 9mm. I told him there were no bullets for the Luger or the .45 but I had a box of bullets for the .22. I asked him £35 each for the guns but he gave

303

me £90 and said he would give me the rest later. I gave him the guns and he gave me the £90. I left his car and got into my friend's car and we drove away. I never thought any more about it until this morning when you came to my shop and questioned me about a woman and the selling of guns in that car.

'If the man I had sold the guns to is Roberts the photograph of him is a bad one. I have been shown another photograph which is better. I only saw him for about half an hour. He is good-looking and his hair is Tony Curtis style. The only reason I know it must be Roberts is because of the questions you put to me about a woman and the sale of the guns in the car.'

Chitty then came into the interview room and Hensley said, 'This is Christos Costas who sold the guns to Roberts. He has made a statement.'

Chitty read the statement, then cautioned Costas and said, 'You realise that three police officers were killed with these guns.'

Costas replied, 'I know now.'

Chitty said, 'You also must have known that these weapons were to be used for committing crime.'

'I don't ask questions,' Costas replied.

'Where did you get these guns?'

'Nearly all Greeks in clubs carry guns.'

Chitty said, 'The courts of this country take a very serious view of persons unlawfully carrying firearms and for selling them the way you have.'

'Your courts. You charge me now, I plead guilty,' Costas said. 'For this, three months at most, I'm not worried.'

Chitty said, 'It is most important that we find Roberts and recover the guns. You will now be taken to the Police Laboratory where you will be given the opportunity to pick out the type of guns which you sold to this man.'

Costas said, 'Yes, all right, I will show you.'

Chapter 31

On the following Friday morning Duddy and Witney were taken independently to court, locked in separate vans, consumed by their own thoughts, each with different involvements in the brutal murders of David Wombwell, Chris Head and Geoff Fox. Handcuffed to police officers, they were brought up from the holding cells at West London Magistrates' Court and placed in the dock together. It was the first time they had seen each other since the day of the shootings exactly six weeks earlier. And it was the first time that Witney and Duddy would hear the accounts of witnesses and face the evidence, diligently assembled by colleagues of the dead policemen, who had been working around the clock on Operation Shepherd to build the case against them.

23 September 1966 was the first of two days of committal proceedings held on consecutive Fridays at West London Magistrates' Court to consider the murder charges against Jack Witney and John Duddy. The hearing was opened by counsel for the prosecution Oliver Nugent with magistrate Seymour Collins presiding. Nugent began

with a summary of the known facts and said he would be calling a number of witnesses to give their accounts.

First to stand in the witness box and tell their stories to the court were a succession of four children. Seymour Collins directed the press that their names should not be published.

Nugent began with a dark-haired girl of fourteen in a blue coat. She said that at about 3:15 p.m. that Friday she saw a car pull up in the middle of Braybrook Street, followed by a blue van. A man got out of the car and went over to the van. There were three men in the van. One of them looked like the footballer Bobby Charlton.

All eyes in the courtroom turned to the dock, to dark-haired Scotsman John Duddy and the other man, Jack Witney, slender, with receding fair hair. At first glance he did have a resemblance to the famous Manchester United midfielder who had played an essential part in England's recent World Cup victory.

'That man was sitting in the driver's seat,' the girl continued and she was the only person in court not looking at Witney. She continued her account and the sequence of events she described did not follow what had actually taken place. She confused the two men who had guns and who had fired shots at whom. But the precise choreography of her story was not of paramount importance. When she reached the point where the blue van reversed away at speed and disappeared from view, Oliver Nugent asked her to look around the courtroom and said, 'Can you identify any of the men you saw in the van?'

The girl pointed to Witney. 'That's the driver.'

A ten-year-old boy was next to give his evidence. He said he was only eight yards away when the three policemen were shot in Braybrook Street on 12 August. 'I thought it was acting,' he said, 'even when the shots were fired.' He ran to get his two sisters aged three and four, in case they should get in the way of the camera and spoil the film. He said, 'A man in a blue suit got out of the van, holding a gun. He started firing at the policeman. The policeman ran back shouting, "No, no, no." The man in the blue suit shouted, "Come on!" and a man in a white jacket got out and they both ran and shot the driver of the police car.'

The two other children followed, recalling what they had witnessed, each able to provide clear recollections and descriptions despite the horror of what they had seen.

Throughout the day there was a procession of adults who followed them including Mrs Renee Pickering of Braybrook Street. She had heard two shots, then her nine-year-old son, who was playing in the street outside, screamed.

Detective Chief Inspector Robert Brown who arrested Duddy recalled, 'On the way to the police office Duddy said, "I was in that car but I did not do the shooting." '

June Howard later told the court what she knew, or was prepared to say. Lilly Perry was the last witness of the day. She was dressed in a smart white coat and spoke so quietly at times that it was hard to hear her. She said she had come to London from Bristol earlier in the year with Harry Roberts, who she referred to as Robby, and they'd been staying with his friend, Mrs Howard. 'I met Jack Witney and John Duddy,' she told the court and then identified them both in the dock.

Perry spoke of conversations she'd overheard between Duddy and Roberts on the day after the shooting. 'Oh God, what a hell of a mess we made of things,' Roberts had said and Duddy had replied, 'Yes, I wish it had never happened.' Perry recalled, 'Robby then said, "We should burn the car because of fingerprints." But Duddy did not want to go. They talked about getting rid of the guns. Duddy brought the guns that morning back to Mrs Howard's flat. He said he had slept with them – two at his feet and one under his pillow.'

After Perry finished giving her evidence, Witney and Duddy were remanded for another week and Seymour Collins adjourned the court until the following Friday, 30 September.

For the journey back from his day in court John Duddy was accompanied by DS Berry and TDC Nadin. Duddy was quiet and preoccupied but finally he spoke to the person he had confided in most over the past six weeks.

Duddy: 'One thing has been worrying me. I have told you a lie about the Friday night.'

DS Berry: 'If you haven't told your solicitor, you had

better do so, but if you are going to say anything to me I must caution you.'

Duddy: 'Roberts and Witney did come back to my place after the shooting. And another thing, I caught a bus to Edgware on the Sunday and then caught the train to Watford. These things are coming back to me but I thought you were going to call my kids to give evidence. That's why I did not tell you Roberts and Witney came back to my place, as they were there.'

Berry: 'It makes little difference, really.'

Duddy: 'You've got the impression that Witney was forced to drive back after the shooting. You can take it from me Witney was the brains of this outfit and on the way back to the garage after the shooting Roberts suggested leaving the car in a mews around Notting Hill. But Witney said we must go back to the garage and clean the van down and then think about cutting it up. June Howard in her evidence talked about Saturday and said something about her being at the flat between four and six o'clock. What did she say that for? She definitely went out as I have told you between two and four in the afternoon and that was the last time I saw her. Another thing, I did go back to my place after leaving Roberts about lunchtime and I saw my nipper.'

The committal hearing on 23 September was the first time that Duddy got a sense of the wider evidence that would be presented against him and was able to consider if what he had told the police fitted with the accounts of others. It was clearly preying on his mind that there were discrepancies. But oddly, despite his deliberations and misgivings about the smaller details, he still chose to withhold the vital information that he and Roberts had buried the guns on Hampstead Heath on the morning of Sunday, 14 August.

In the week before the second part of the committal proceedings to hear the evidence against Witney and Duddy, the search for Harry Roberts continued. Reported sightings from the public were less frequent and the recent arrest of Buster Edwards in connection with the 1963 Great Train Robbery was a reminder to everyone that Roberts might possibly sooner or later run out of options and give himself up. It seemed unlikely, given his limited resources, that Roberts had left the UK and that meant he could be being harboured by someone he knew or was in hiding, probably somewhere he was familiar with and that was not too far away.

In Bristol, on Thursday, 29 September, Lilly Perry was in court again but this time she had instigated the proceedings. The *Daily Mirror* had the story on page twenty-two the following morning.

Two lawyers clashed over Harry Roberts in a courtroom yesterday during a husband and wife maintenance case. The wife, 41-year-old auburn-haired Mrs Lilian Perry, was said to have once lived with Roberts. Her solicitor, Mr F. O. Counsell said, 'Mrs Perry emphatically denies adultery but admits Roberts had been lodging with her.

The husband, former policeman Anthony Perry of Stoke Lane, Westbury-on-Trym, Bristol, was said to have stopped maintenance payments to Mrs Perry after reading about her association with Roberts who is wanted for questioning about the shooting of the London policemen. His solicitor, Mr Anthony Gouldsmith said, 'When he learned certain facts he discontinued the payments. But Mrs Perry has the effrontery to issue a summons herself.

Mrs Perry's solicitor asked for an adjournment so that witnesses could be brought from London. The case was adjourned indefinitely.

Lilly Perry's close association with Harry Roberts had been widely reported after her appearance in the witness box at West London Magistrates' Court the previous Friday. Even though in reality sex between them had been infrequent it was both untrue and naive to assert that her relationship with Roberts was purely platonic. It was perhaps a measure of her desperation to return to some sort of normality and reconstruct her life. But now, without support from either her former husband or Harry Roberts, she had been left without any form of income.

The morning of 30 September was cloudy, there was drizzle in the air and the ambient temperature outside was hovering around 17°C as the committal proceedings reconvened at West London Magistrates' Court with

Seymour Collins again presiding. Evidence came from Detective Inspector Steventon who had arrested Witney.

Counsel for the prosecution, Oliver Nugent, read out Witney's statement, explaining first that it was made after the police had disproved his story about selling his car and had found the vehicle parked in railway arches at Vauxhall shortly after midnight on Sunday, 14 August. At 11:30 that night Witney had finally admitted to his ownership of the Standard Vanguard but had denied involvement in the shootings. 'As God is my judge I had absolutely nothing to do with the shooting of any one of the three policemen . . .'

In the face of the many incriminating statements made by witnesses, and the physical evidence gathered by the police investigation team, Witney and Duddy pleaded Not Guilty to the triple murder charge. Their counsels stated that both men wished to reserve their defence. Without further ado Seymour Collins committed them for trial at the Central Criminal Court, at a future date to be set, charged that with others they murdered Detective Sergeant Head, Detective Constable Wombwell and Police Constable Geoffrey Fox at Braybrook Street, Shepherd's Bush on 12 August.

While Duddy was travelling back from court he was at least in familiar company.

Duddy: 'A thing that has been worrying me is since I told you that my wife was living at Norbury, someone has told her employer that she is my wife and she got the sack and she's got to leave the flat now.'

Berry: 'I can assure you that the police had nothing to do with that.'

Duddy: 'No, don't get me wrong, I know it has nothing to do with you. It's my mad brother. He has been trying to cause trouble between us for some time. I'll get a mate of mine to attend to him.'

After a lull in the conversation Duddy said, 'One thing I have appreciated is the way you have treated me. I expected rough treatment especially after what I have done to one of your mates.'

Berry immediately cautioned Duddy and told him in his own interests to say nothing further about it.

Harry Roberts had by now slipped into habits and routines at his hideaway at Thorley Woods in the Hertfordshire countryside. His fear of being spotted, or stumbled upon, was ever present and he organised his daily life to minimise the danger. By day Roberts remained in the woods and only ventured out at night. His isolated routine became almost an exercise in self-hypnosis. At times he forgot why he was there. It was tempting to think that perhaps the world had forgotten about him. He discovered a nearby poultry farm and local allotments which supplied him with plenty of food and he would sit quite content by his fire, talking to himself and daydreaming in a secret world all of his own making.

The daylight hours shortened and the weather grew colder. There came a particularly wet day in October when Harry Roberts finally decided to turn himself in. For hours he had been lying under a plastic sheet, cold and soaked to the skin. Then he reached breaking point. After packing a few things in a bag he made his way to the woodland edge and stood for a moment looking up at the dark rain clouds drifting ominously overhead. All of a sudden the sun broke through and the fields and woods took on a different aspect. It was just enough to remind him that perhaps the life he had was preferable to what awaited him in the world beyond. He turned around and went back to his camp.

Meanwhile Witney and Duddy were locked away on remand, waiting for a date to be set for their trial at the Central Criminal Court. As Duddy had said in his final conversation with DS Bob Berry, it was a remarkable tribute to the police officers who dealt with them that they had not suffered any mistreatment. Their overriding preoccupation as they sat alone in their respective cells was the defence they could offer to mitigate their involvement in the murders when they came to trial at the Old Bailey.

Those others caught up on the fringes of the Braybrook Street shootings were struggling to get back to some kind of normality. But for the widows, children and other members of the families of David Wombwell, Chis Head and Geoff Fox their worlds had been shattered and the pieces of their lives could never be put back together.

Chapter 32

With the date – Monday, 14 November – set for the trial at the Central Criminal Court of Jack Witney and John Duddy, nearly three hundred witness statements that had been taken during the three months of Operation Shepherd had to be numbered, organised and assembled. DCI Ginger Hensley, DI Jack Slipper and their fellow detectives wrote and prepared their own statements and accounts. Scenes-of-crime officer Detective Sergeant Ronald Lawrence compiled all the physical evidence that would need to be presented in court. Forensics officers at the Metropolitan Police Laboratory in Theobald's Road had written reports on the evidence found at the Braybrook Street murder scene, the finger marks and items found in Witney's Standard Vanguard and Roberts's Daimler, the clothing and other possessions taken from Witney and Duddy when they were arrested. And head of the investigation Detective Superintendent Dick Chitty, provided a twenty-page overview of it all from the police investigation perspective.

*

At 3:30 a.m. on Friday, 11 November, boiler-man and nightwatchman thirty-three-year-old Roy Stanley Yates made a routine tour round the offices, joinery works and timber yard at Walter Lawrence & Son Ltd in Sawbridgeworth, Hertfordshire. His usual routine was to patrol the premises every hour and a half or so to check that the office and factory doors and windows were secure and there was no sign of forced entry. At around four a.m. he was in the factory building when he heard a sound. He wasn't sure what it was at the time but when he was doing his next round at 5:15 a.m. he noticed that a casement window in the office block was broken and realised the sound he had heard earlier was breaking glass.

'I entered the office and saw that a drawer in a desk had been opened. I then went into the accountant's office and saw a filing cabinet had been forced open, drawers were pulled out and papers removed. I then saw that the door in the corridor of the office leading to the factory was also open. I walked towards this door and before I reached it I heard someone shuffling their feet and then the person ran. I could hear the sound of footsteps and it sounded as though there was more than one person. I did not go through the door. I immediately went and made a phone call to inform the police.

'I then returned to the factory and made a search of the buildings and saw that three coffee machines had been forced open. An instrument had been used on the front of the machine and broken the lock. The coin containers of these machines had been removed from their normal position and were empty. I also saw that four chocolate machines in the factory had been forced open in a similar manner and the money taken. There would have been about £2.10s.0d in sixpences missing from the chocolate machines. I did not see anyone in the factory but I was of the opinion that there were two or more thieves from the noise of their footsteps when they made their exit.'

While other police officers were talking to Yates and looking at the office and plundered vending machines, PC Alan Loftin, Dog Section, Old Harlow, Essex, arrived with his Alsatian, 'Shan'.

'On my arrival I was informed that the night watchman had disturbed one or more men who had made off in the general direction of Bishop's Stortford. I cast my dog, Shan, close to the River Stort's bank where he was able to locate a track running towards Bishop's Stortford. This track ran across the top of an old rubbish dump following fairly close to the river and then through into the grounds of another mill. The track came out onto the A414 road, turned for a short distance towards the main A11, crossed the A414 and followed the towpath on the river bank.

'Although dawn was approaching, mist from the river impaired vision. However, there was a very heavy frost and I could clearly see footprints in the grass.

'My dog tracked down the towpath which at this point is very muddy, but because the mud was frozen no footmarks were visible. After about a quarter to half a mile the mud gave way to grass where the towpath leads into fields. At this point I was able to see clear footprints again left by two persons who had only recently walked along the riverbank. Shan at this point was tracking very fast and I had to run to keep up with him. I would estimate that the men were no more than twenty-five minutes in front of me.

'In one or two places the track cut across fields and I deduced that the persons I was following obviously knew the route as, at these points, there were large bends in the river that they had cut off.

'At various points there are wooden swing gates along the riverbank separating one field from another and I could see on these gates where a person's hand had rested to open it. As I progressed down the river these marks became fresher. Shan was still tracking very fast. I estimated I was less than ten minutes behind the men.

'The track followed the towpath until I came to the Bishop's Stortford side of Spellbrook, where it crossed over a bridge over the River Stort, then across very marshy ground between the river and the railway lines, towards the A11. At this stage Shan was tracking even faster and I was running as fast as I could to keep up with him.

'When I reached the A11 I found that I had come out next to the sign indicating that I had entered Thorley. I flagged down a motorist and asked him to call Bishop's Stortford police via the 999 system from the nearest telephone box and inform them of my location.

'The track then carried straight over the road and went in the direction of a large wood. By now Shan was tracking so hard that he kept pulling me over.

'Some distance ahead of me I saw a man sky-lighted against the horizon. He was walking on rough ploughed ground about six feet out from a hedgerow and I thought I saw another man between him and the hedgerow. Suddenly the man looked round and started to run up the field towards the wood.

'With Shan bounding forward as I entered the wood I fell into a deep ditch and the dog ran off after the man without me.

'I was trying to climb out of the ditch when a figure came out of the undergrowth and either purposely jumped on me or fell over me. I tried to take hold of the man but as I was on the ground, and by this time very tired, I was unable to apprehend him.

'I called Shan back but his tracking line became entangled in the bushes and he was unable to pursue the man any further. After freeing the tracking line I called Shan to return to me as I was so tired that had I been attacked by anyone I would not have been able to defend myself and I was in no condition to chase after anyone.

'For about twenty minutes I remained absolutely still in the hope that the men I had been following were still in the wood. After a time it became apparent that these men had left. I again put my dog on the tracking line and he picked up a scent leading out of the wood onto ploughed fields.

'The person I was following obviously had some knowledge of police dogs as he appeared to be attempting to put my dog off the track by zigzagging and doubling back on himself but still progressing generally in the same direction. With considerable difficulty Shan was able to follow the track, which after it entered a stubble field became straightforward.

'About three quarters of a mile from the wood I saw a man walking towards Thorley church and the farm next to it. I could see footprints on the ploughed earth running in his direction only a few minutes old and also two sets coming in the opposite direction that were at least three or four hours old. The track ran through the farmyard onto a concrete road that is covered in mud and then cut across a field directly to two caravans.'

Meanwhile, Detective Constable Peter Simpson was on duty at Bishop's Stortford police station at 6:15 a.m. when a telephone message was received from a member of the public. The caller said that a policeman with a dog had stopped him on the A11 road at Thorley and asked him to call Bishop's Stortford police to inform them that he was following a track through the woods at Thorley, towards the Green Man public house on the A119 road. DC

Simpson immediately left the police station with Police Sergeant Trotter and went to the location.

After fifteen minutes fruitlessly searching the area for the dog handler, Simpson and Sergeant Trotter drove to Thorley Church and turned down a private roadway that ran from the back of the church. After a quarter of a mile they saw two caravans and a lorry parked at the side of a field and Trotter stopped the police car. The officers sat observing the encampment for several minutes but after seeing no signs of life they turned around and headed back towards the main road. They were about 300 yards from Thorley Church when Simpson finally spotted Loftin and his dog, sitting by a barn.

'Both the dog and PC Loftin were covered in mud and very tired. Loftin told me that he had tracked two men from the river at Sawbridgeworth as far as this barn. He said he thought he would probably recognise at least one of the men and we straight away went to the two caravans nearby.

'I knocked on the door of one of the caravans and opened it. Standing immediately inside the doorway was a youth I now know to be John Cunningham. Cunningham was fully dressed and the boots he was wearing were muddy. PC Loftin, who was standing beside me, identified Cunningham as one of the men he had seen in the wood earlier that morning. Loftin then arrested Cunningham and I escorted the youth to the police car.

'A few moments later, Sergeant Trotter and Loftin came towards the police car from the second caravan, accompanied by a man I now know to be Tom Cunningham, father of the youth, John. Loftin asked me to convey the two Cunninghams and himself back to Bishop's Stortford police station.

'When Loftin informed John Cunningham that his dog had tracked him from the A11 road through a wood to within 300 yards of the caravans Cunningham said, "I don't know what you're talking about." Cunningham explained that before our arrival he had gone to the farm and back again to collect water.

On the journey to Bishop's Stortford John Cunningham stated emphatically that he was not responsible for the offence for which he had been arrested but that someone was sleeping in a tent in a wood between Thorley church and the A11 road and that he thought this may be the person that we were looking for. Cunningham did not give the exact location.

'On arrival at Bishop's Stortford police station, John Cunningham and his father were handed over to other officers of the Essex Constabulary to be conveyed to Harlow Police station. PC Loftin then informed me that he was going back to the caravans near Thorley Church to make further enquiries regarding the two arrested men and that with the benefit of daylight he would then backtrack through the wood towards the A11 road in an effort to find any evidence which may relate to the burglary offence at Walter Lawrence & Son Ltd for which the Cunninghams have been arrested.'

At 8:30 a.m. Alan Loftin returned to the caravan camp with Police Constable Fardell where they spoke to Mrs Cunningham. They questioned her about her menfolk having been out all that night and searched the caravans for stolen property but found nothing incriminating.

During the course of the conversation Mrs Cunningham said that they had not got the right men as her husband and son had been in all night. She repeated what her son had said earlier and told them that if they wanted to catch the right person there was a man sleeping rough in the area. The officers tried to ascertain from her in more detail who this man was and pinpoint where he was sleeping but Mrs Cunningham only repeated that the man was sleeping at the edge of a nearby wood.

But even after an exhausting night's work Loftin's instincts were still razor sharp. 'We pressed her for the exact location of the wood as there are a number of woods in the area but she was unwilling or unable to tell us. I felt she knew more than she was prepared to say.

'Still in company of PC Fardell I went to a farm close to Thorley church. where we questioned two farm labourers. I asked them if they had seen or knew of a man sleeping rough in local woods. One man said that two local boys on bicycles had seen smoke coming from a corner of Thorley Wood and from his directions we were able to obtain a rough location of where the smoke was seen.

'We searched for a considerable time in the wood and were about to give up when my dog disappeared in some heavy undergrowth and would not return when called. PC Fardell and myself then decided to investigate the dog's actions. As we forced our way through the tangled undergrowth we came across a well-camouflaged tent. We searched the tent and there found a shoulder holster, also a considerable amount of property that indicated that a man or men were living in it. We decided against searching the tent more thoroughly in order to disturb as little as possible so that should the occupant return they would not know the tent had been found.

'Owing to the isolation of the wood the quickest possible means of communicating our discovery to senior officers was to return to my dog van where I passed the information of the tent to Chief Inspector Tame and DS Jones at the Regional Crime Squad. I also informed Bishop's Stortford police station that I would return there at midday and requested the presence of a senior officer so that I could inform him of the tent and its exact location.'

Chapter 33

While PCs Loftin and Fardell were in Thorley Wood, Thomas and John Cunningham were on their way to Harlow police station as that was the district which covered the part of Sawbridgeworth where the burglary at Walter Lawrence & Son Ltd had taken place.

At Bishop's Stortford police station Detective Sergeant Thomas O'Connor of Hertfordshire Constabulary was also considering another burglary early that morning at the United Sack Company in Sawbridgeworth and he decided to go to Harlow to speak to the Cunninghams.

'During the night of Thursday 10/11 November, the two premises were forcibly entered: the offices of the United Sack Company, Sawbridgeworth in the Hertfordshire police district, and the offices of W. Lawrence & Son Ltd, Sawbridgeworth near Sheering in the Essex police district. Although these premises are in different police districts they are within half a mile of each other.

'On the morning of Friday, 11 November I was informed that two men were in custody at Harlow police station having been arrested by Essex police officers for the W. Lawrence & Son Ltd offence. I went to the scene of both burglaries in order to acquaint myself with the methods used by the thief and possibly to obtain evidence to connect them with the men in custody at Harlow. The two offences were of a similar pattern.

'At 12:30 p.m. that same day, I went to Harlow police station where I saw the two prisoners, Thomas and John Cunningham, father and son respectively. I interrogated both of them separately regarding offence number one. Both men strongly denied having been responsible for any offence whatsoever. The interviews terminated shortly before two p.m. I formed the opinion that neither prisoner was connected with the offences.

'Thomas Cunningham was then bailed under Section 38 of the Magistrates Court Act 1952 in respect of offence number two. John Cunningham was later charged with the offence by Harlow police and bailed later that evening.

'During my interview with each prisoner, both stated that they had been wrongly arrested and that the man the police wanted was living in a tent in a wood near to their caravan at Thorley. When the prisoner Thomas Cunningham was bailed by the Harlow police, I conveyed him back to his caravan at Thorley, near Bishop's Stortford. On reaching his caravan, he indicated Thorley Wood to me, which was approximately half a mile away and said that was where the tent he had mentioned was situated. I returned to Bishop's Stortford police station where I was informed that the Essex police-dog handler had already visited Thorley Wood and had located the tent.'

Despite the discovery of the tent following the recent burglaries and the arrests of the Cunninghams, DS O'Connor and his colleagues did not go to Thorley Wood until late that night. Perhaps there were other matters to attend to that day or they decided that under cover of darkness in the early hours of Saturday morning was the best time to approach the encampment and apprehend the occupant.

At around three a.m. on Saturday, 12 November O'Connor went with other officers to the location at Thorley near the church. 'On the outskirts of the wood I found a brown and green tent hidden in the bracken. It was unoccupied. I went into the tent and saw various household articles. I noticed 30 rounds of what appeared to be .38 revolver ammunition and one other round of a similar nature. I also found a home-made holster made of leather for carrying two pistols. I took possession of the bullets which were in a tin.' DS O'Connor also took away a bottle containing methylated spirit, a blue and white cup and a pill bottle for fingerprint examination.

According to Harry Roberts's account, after almost being apprehended by a policeman and his dog in the early hours of Friday morning he slept most of that day in a small disused aircraft hangar that was being used as a Dutch barn to store straw bales. Early on Saturday morning he crept back into the woods. Approaching his hideout he noticed that the flap of his tent was open. As he crouched in the undergrowth a man came out of the tent and from his manner and the way he was dressed it was obvious he was a policeman.

Roberts only mentioned seeing one police officer when in fact O'Connor went to the woods 'with other officers'. Why none of them heard Roberts approach the camp, if indeed he did, was either a testament to Roberts's stealth or to the fact that he was never there. Nevertheless, what *is* a matter of fact is that Roberts was not in his tent at three a.m. when O'Connor and his colleagues arrived there and that Roberts had abandoned his camp from Friday night and had taken refuge in the straw barn about a mile away.

During PC Loftin and his dog Shan's heroic and remarkable tracking, the trail had become confused and although it was Roberts who had carried out the burglary at Walter Lawrence Ltd in Sawbridgeworth somehow the trail had led Loftin and his dog to the Cunninghams' caravans while Roberts evaded capture.

In daylight, the full extent of the extraordinary tent encampment was examined more closely. Detective Sergeant Frederick Halsey of the Photographic Department, Police Headquarters, Hatfield, arrived and photographed the tent inside and out and carried out a preliminary search.

The tented area measured approximately 10ft 6 inches by 13ft. The end facing the edge of the wood was obscured by a stockade of earth and branches. The tent supports had been constructed with considerable skill, made of interwoven cut branches and covered by tarpaulins that were painted green and brown in a camouflage pattern. Sticking up through the roof of the tent was a makeshift metal chimney connected to a round cast-iron stove inside. The interior of the tent was remarkably well organised: cut wood by the stove, two saucepans and cooking utensils, knives, forks and plates. In the opposite corner was an aluminium folding garden chair, a camp bed with a sleeping bag and neatly folded blankets. There were a number of recent national newspapers that covered the latest developments in the police investigation, the forthcoming trial of Witney and Duddy at the Old Bailey and the search for Roberts. An improvised cupboard made from pieces of wood and cardboard contained a well-stocked larder that provided an insight into Roberts's improvised hideout existence. It included tinned peaches, tins of Libby's fruit cocktail, mandarin oranges and apricots, a tin of Irish stew, Heinz curried beans, tomatoes, spaghetti, an egg box containing four eggs, a 2lb packet of Tate and Lyle sugar, Bird's custard powder, a carton of Saxa salt, Marvel dried milk powder, a jar of marmalade, a jar of mint jelly, a jar of Sun Pat peanut butter, a bottle of Bell's scotch whisky, a bottle of Gordon's gin and a bottle of Schweppes tonic water. Sundries included washing-up liquid, Daz washing powder, wire-wool scouring pads, toilet tissue and a tea strainer.

*

On the first day of the trial of John Witney and John Duddy at the Old Bailey on Monday, 14 November, Dick Chitty was listening to Lilly Perry give her evidence when he was handed a message to telephone Bishop's Stortford police station. Minutes later Chitty was heading for Hertfordshire.

When Chitty was shown the tent in Thorley Woods he was certain that it was where Roberts had been hiding for the past three months while the biggest-ever manhunt mounted by British police had been scouring the country. Chitty deduced that as almost everything that Roberts possessed had been found in the tent he could not have gone far. Although, worryingly, there were the home-made holsters and the ammunition, no guns were found in the tent and that meant Roberts was still armed.

It is not clear from police records and other anecdotal evidence exactly who first suspected that the tent in Thorley Woods was connected with Harry Roberts and decided to contact Chitty. Certainly final confirmation was made through fingerprints on objects found in the tent matching those of Harry Maurice Roberts at the Criminal Records Office.

Chitty contacted Scotland Yard, requesting as many detectives as they could muster to meet him at Bishop's Stortford. By Monday night the area around Thorley was ringed with police officers, dog handlers, and detectives armed with guns and tear gas. They were instructed to move in quietly and make their presence as inconspicuous as possible throughout what turned out to be a bleakly cold night.

On Tuesday morning hundreds more policemen assembled and lines of officers a few yards apart, with sticks and guns and dogs, began to sweep methodically across the autumn fields and woods like an army of beaters flushing birds at an enormous game shoot.

After attending the briefing at Bishop's Stortford, thirty-three-year-old father of two Police Sergeant Peter Smith of Stevenage police was assigned to search Nathans Wood, near Sawbridgeworth. 'On 15 November 1966 I was directed to go to Bishop's Stortford police station respecting a large-scale search for Harry M. Roberts. I left Bishop's Stortford police station with other officers at about 9:30 a.m. We drove to Nathans Wood near Sawbridgeworth. The wood is part of a farm known as Blounts Farm.

'With the other officers I encircled Nathans Wood. We were all spaced out about 200 yards apart and about 500 yards from the outside of the wood on the north side. This would be about three-quarters of a mile from Thorley Wood, which is to the east of Nathans Wood.

'As the search progressed I walked slowly with the searchers until I came to a Dutch barn which was full with straw bales. As I searched amongst the straw I noticed a bottle of spirit and pulled a bale away to have a better look. I then noticed a gun which appeared to be a Luger pistol. I also saw a small torch battery and a hand torch. I pulled another bale of straw down which revealed a sleeping bag laying full length between the trusses of straw. It appeared to me that the sleeping bag was empty so I prodded it with my hand. As I did so a man's head appeared from the end of the sleeping bag. Although unshaven and dishevelled I immediately recognised the man as Roberts, wanted at Shepherd's Bush for the murder of three policemen.

'Your name is Harry Roberts,' I said to him.

'Yes, you won't get any trouble from me, I've had enough,' he replied.

'I am arresting you,' I then cautioned him.

He replied, 'I'm glad you've caught me.'

I said to him, 'Get up.'

'Roberts offered no resistance when I searched him and in the right pocket of the jeans he was wearing I found a full magazine of bullets. I took possession of this and escorted him out of the barn. On the way out I took possession of the Luger pistol.

'Once out of the barn I shouted for Sergeant Thorne to assist me. Thorne came across to me and together we took Roberts to the farmer's Land Rover which I commandeered and we took Roberts to Bishop's Stortford police station where I was present when Chief Inspector Briggs searched him. He was then placed in a cell.'

In London at the Old Bailey Detective Superintendent Dick Chitty left the court first, closely followed by Sir

Elwyn Jones, the Attorney General, while the cross-examination of Perry continued. A few minutes later Sir Elwyn returned. Then the judge's clerk appeared, whispered to the judge, Mr Justice Glyn-Jones, and signalled to the Attorney General to leave the court again.

There were whispered exchanges among the press in the public gallery too as reporters tried to work out what was going on. After a few minutes Chitty returned, picked up his briefcase and left again. Frustratingly, no one was any the wiser when Justice Glyn-Jones adjourned the court for lunch.

By the time the court reconvened, rumour and conjecture were finally resolved when the Attorney General, Sir Elwyn Jones QC informed the judge of the arrest of Roberts. In making an application for an adjournment Sir Elwyn said, 'This quite clearly calls for careful consideration in regard to this case and its effects upon this case.'

Mr Justice Glyn-Jones replied, 'I entirely agree. The prosecution and the defence should consider the best course of action to be taken.' He told the jury, 'We may go on with this trial or I may discharge you from giving a verdict and make other arrangements. I will not say any more now. I shall have to hear what counsel has to say tomorrow morning.'

At 2:55 p.m. on Tuesday, 15 November at Bishop's Stortford police station, Chief Superintendent Newman and Chief Superintendent Rowe were with Dick Chitty when he finally faced the man he'd been hunting for ninety-six days.

Chitty said, 'I am Superintendent Chitty. You know why you are here.'

He cautioned Roberts who replied, 'Yes, I've had enough, you know all about it. I don't know why we were there but I shot the two and Jock shot the other. Witney stopped in the car and got us away.'

'Will you put what you say in writing?'

'Yes.'

'Will you write it yourself or do you want me to write it?'

Roberts said, 'You write it, you've got no axe to grind.'

Chitty wrote out the caution on the statement form and read it to Roberts who read it again before signing it.

Shepherd's Bush Police Station

'F' Division

15th November 1966

STATEMENT OF: Harry Maurice ROBERTS

No fixed address

Unemployed

I, Harry Maurice Roberts, wish to make a statement. I want someone to write down what I say. I have been told that I need not say anything unless I wish to do so and that whatever I say may be given in evidence.

(signed) H.M. Roberts

I'll tell you the truth. I shot the two policemen on that Friday and it was Duddy who shot the driver. I don't know what we were doing up there by the Scrubs. We were going to nick a car but not that particular day. We had the plates in Jack's van. We were going to rob the rent collector. When the police car pulled us and the officers came back to us I thought they were going to find the guns in the car and so I shot the officer who was talking to Jack. And then shot at the one who was talking to Jock. I got out of the car and this officer ran towards the police car and I shot him. Jock got out of the car and went to the police car and shot the driver.

We then got back into the van and Jack drove back to the arches at Vauxhall. We first decided to abandon the van but then decided to take it back to the arches and we were going to burn it later.

After Jack had been arrested and the van had been found by you, I went with Lilly Perry and left the clothes I was wearing in a Left Luggage office at Euston. I bought some camping equipment and then went to Epping Forest with Lilly. I left her there and she went back home to June Howard's place. I then walked to Thorley Woods where I have been ever since.

The reason I was not at the tent when you went there was because on Thursday I went screwing and was followed back to the woods by a policeman with a dog so went to the barn where I was caught.

Chitty: 'How many guns were there in the bag in the

car that Friday afternoon when you were stopped in Braybrook Street?'

Roberts: 'Three – an Army .38, a Colt .38 and the Luger.'

Chitty: 'What happened to the guns?'

Roberts: 'Me and Duddy buried them on Hampstead Heath on the Sunday. I dug two of them up three weeks later. The Luger is the one you have which was with me when I was caught and the .38 you will find in the barn.'

Since I have been living rough, I have lived by thieving either food or money to buy food. What you found in the tent I have stolen or bought with stolen money.

I have read the above statement and I have been told that I can correct, alter or add anything I wish. This statement is true and I have made it of my own free will.

(signed) Harry M. Roberts

Statement taken at Bishop's Stortford Police Station, written down by R. Chitty Detective Superintendent in the presence of Detective Chief Superintendent Newman and Detective Chief Superintendent Rowe. Read over to Roberts and his signature was witnessed by all officers.
Commenced 3 p.m.
Terminated 3:35 p.m.

Harry Roberts's statement, which took just thirty-five minutes to dictate, was concise, simple, straightforward and almost entirely truthful apart from stating 'We were going to nick a car but not that particular day.' Why Roberts chose to lie about that minor detail is strange. The most striking thing about his statement is that it is devoid of any self-recrimination, remorse or emotion. Roberts did not resort to the superficially pleasant manners and seeming amiability that he had used to manipulate and deceive others in the past. He knew they were of no use to him now.

In many ways his terse four-hundred-and-fifty-one-word statement, dictated to Chitty in Bishop's Stortford police station on that Tuesday afternoon, made a mockery of the shock and distress caused by the brutal murders he had committed, the numerous other lives shattered, the efforts of the thousands of policemen who had dedicated themselves to hunting him down over the past three months.

Later that day at about four p.m. the man who finally discovered Harry Roberts, Police Sergeant Peter Smith, went back to the Dutch barn with Superintendent Peat, Detective Inspector Hasted, Detective Sergeant Halsey and Detective Sergeant Bob Berry of the Metropolitan Police. At the spot where he had chanced upon Roberts in a sleeping bag, Smith found hidden amongst the straw bales a rucksack and a holdall containing various items including a loaded .38 Colt revolver, a box containing fifteen .38 cartridges and eight 9mm cartridges. DS Halsey took a series of photographs of the barn and also of the property found.

The Shepherd's Bush Murders

Back at Bishop's Stortford police station Harry Roberts's personal possessions – five £5 notes; forty-two £1 notes; 1/6d in silver; 7½d in copper coins; a metal key; a driving licence in the name of John O'Brien; an Inventic wristwatch; a £5 bank-cash bag, a blue Bank of England cloth bag, along with the holdall, rucksack, two guns and ammunition – were handed over to Detective Sergeant Berry to take back to London where they would be used as evidence in the yet to be resolved trial of the three men charged with the Shepherd's Bush Murders.

But that's not all there was to the story of Harry Roberts, Jack Witney and John Duddy, and the murders of David Wombwell, Chris Head and Geoff Fox. It would never be that simple for the victims' families, the investigating police officers, or the British public. Witney, Duddy and Roberts had been captured and were in police custody – but what would happen to them now? What *should* be done with them when they were brought before judge and jury at the Central Criminal Court? With the impact of the Shepherd's Bush murders still reverberating all through the country, was the law capable of delivering a sense of justice and restoring public confidence? Would the pain and outrage amongst the police, and the public outcry for the recently suspended death penalty to be brought back, influence the outcome in order to send a clear message that killing policemen carried the most serious penalty? Would justice be done? *Could* justice be done? Would the punishment fit the crime?

Chapter 34

At five p.m. on Tuesday, 15 November, Harry Roberts was taken in a police van from Bishop's Stortford to Shepherd's Bush, escorted by Detective Sergeant Bob Berry. Mrs Dorothy Roberts was already waiting at the police station when her son arrived and was allowed to see him for ten minutes. Afterwards she said, 'My son told me the police had been the essence of kindness, but he looked thin and tired, like an old man.'

At 8:10 p.m. Chitty spoke to Roberts in the Charge Room. 'As the result of the enquiries I have made and what you have told me this afternoon, you will now be charged with being concerned with others in killing three police officers at Braybrook Street on Friday, the twelfth of August 1966.'

Roberts made no reply and was formally charged with the murders of TDC David Wombwell, DS Christopher Head and PC Geoffrey Fox. When asked if he had anything to say Roberts replied, 'No, sir' and was put in a cell overnight. It can only be wondered how Roberts managed to sleep that night in the building where the men he murdered had worked and from where they had set off on their nine-to-five Q-car shift on the last day of their lives.

Early on Wednesday morning, at 7:15 a.m. Detective Chief Inspector 'Ginger' Hensley, in the company of Detective Sergeant Bob Berry, spoke to Roberts about a conversation he'd had with Chitty the previous afternoon, after Roberts had made his formal statement. Hensley said to him, 'I understand you want to show me where you buried the guns, one of which is still there.'

Roberts answered, 'Yes, sir.'

'In your own interests you'd better say no more but just take me to the spot.'

They left the police station in an unmarked car and Roberts directed the driver to Hampstead Heath. In Spaniards Road they stopped and walked across the Heath to an area near Kenwood. Roberts pointed out a spot among the trees. He kicked the loose earth away with his foot and six inches beneath the surface Hensley uncovered a rusting revolver, the final gun of Roberts's motley arsenal.

Roberts said curtly, 'That's it. That piece of cardboard was the box the ammo was in. There's nothing else there.'

Roberts was led back to the car and was taken to West London Magistrates' Court, where he was put in the cells until his appearance before the court later that morning.

*

The front page of the *Daily Express* that day had the headline: *After a 96-day search . . . ROBERTS MURDER CHARGE*. There was a small photograph of the arresting officer, Sergeant Peter Smith and the other policeman who had assisted him, Sergeant John Thorne, both of them smiling broadly, and below that was a large image taken the previous evening of the rear entrance of Shepherd's Bush police station. There was a black police van drawing into the gateway, followed by a white Ford Zephyr. A large crowd had gathered either side of the entrance, held back by uniformed police officers. Standing on the rear steps of the police station stood a group of plain-clothes detectives and above them people were leaning out of every window.

The front-page story, by *Express* reporters Percy Hoskins, John Ball and Brian Park, had the details and a couple of surprising insights and developments.

> *After 96 days on the run Harry Roberts was charged in London last night with murdering three policemen.*
>
> *A crowd shouted as he arrived at Shepherd's Bush police station from Bishop's Stortford. Roberts was arrested in Hertfordshire on the second day of the trial in which John Duddy and John Edward Witney are accused of murdering the policemen – and, as a result, an unusual legal problem has arisen.*
>
> *Last night it was believed that the Crown's next course may be to apply for what is called a 'Voluntary Bill of Indictment' against Roberts. This in effect means that he could be brought to trial*

without evidence being called at Committal Proceedings in a magistrates' court.

In the current trial at the Old Bailey the jury would be discharged from giving a verdict. A fresh trial would be held in a few weeks' time with Roberts, Duddy and Witney together in the dock.

At the Law Courts last night a conference to decide the issue was held between the Attorney General, Sir Elwyn Jones, the Director of Public Prosecutions, Sir Norman Skelhorn and counsel assisting Sir Elwyn, Mr. Michael Corkery and Mr. John Mathew. They were joined by police chiefs.

A separate column on the front page was headed *REWARD* and reported on an unexpected new slant.

Last night a gypsy named John Cunningham said, 'I am going to claim the £1,000 reward for the capture of Harry Roberts. After all, it was me that put the police on to him.'

It was last Thursday night when Mr Cunningham, a 21-year-old potato picker, stumbled into Roberts's camp in Thorley Wood, near Bishop's Stortford. 'I was walking my dogs when I saw a light,' he said. 'I got to within 10 yards and could see the outline of a tent covered in branches and leaves, with a light burning inside. There was a noise like someone chopping wood. I was a bit frightened. Next morning the police came to see me for some offence and I told them about the camp. I was released on Friday night and they came to have a look on Saturday.'

Embedded in the article was a photo of the dark-eyed,

dark-haired John Cunningham and he did have a point, albeit an ironic one. If PC Loftin hadn't arrested Cunningham on Friday, Cunningham would not have mentioned the man in a tent in a nearby wood, the tent wouldn't have been discovered and Harry Roberts wouldn't have been captured three days later. Another irony, of course, was that Cunningham had been arrested for a crime committed by Roberts. However, whether John Cunningham's reward claim would be successful remained to be seen.

At ten a.m. Roberts was brought up from the cells at West London Magistrates' Court. As he stood in the dock, his hair shaggy, his face gaunt and with a ginger tinge to his beard, he looked nothing like any of the photographs of him issued by the police to the press. Wearing a grey-brown raincoat over an open-necked brown shirt and a light brown pullover with dark blue jeans tucked inside gumboots, Roberts spoke clearly but quietly when answering questions put to him by the clerk of the court.

Mr Oliver Nugent for the Crown requested that Roberts should be held on remand for one week, referring to the two men on trial on the same charges at the Old Bailey. The magistrate, Mr Seymour Collins, was of course already familiar with the facts. Witney and Duddy had both appeared before him previously. He said that it seemed desirable that all three men should be tried together at the same time. 'There is the additional question of whether the whole of the matter has to be reassessed by this court for committal or whether, perhaps, it might proceed straight to trial at the Central Criminal Court by way of application for a Voluntary Bill of Indictment.'

Roberts was asked if he had the means to instruct a solicitor, to which he replied that he did not. He was granted legal aid. Seymour Collins then asked Roberts if he had anything to say and he replied, 'I have nothing to say today.'

For ninety-six gruelling days Harry Roberts had been hunted with his photos on reward posters all over Britain and seldom out of the newspapers. But now that he'd been finally captured his first appearance in court lasted a little over five minutes and somehow it seemed rather an anti-climax. For the investigating officers of Operation Shepherd there was still work to be done but before they got back to it Dick Chitty took his team for a drink. They had all been working twelve- to fourteen-hour days without let-up for three months. There was talk of how Roberts had managed to stay in Thorley Wood undetected for so long but all the officers knew, and had known all along, that the fugitive's greatest ally is fallible human nature. It was illustrated most vivdly by an item in the newspaper only that morning.

Two miles away from Roberts's hideout was The Farm grocery shop, managed by Mrs Joy Lewin. She had served Roberts once a week for six weeks. When he first went in and stood at her counter she recognised him. 'After he had gone out I said to my assistant and a customer, "My gosh, that chap looks like Harry Roberts." But they laughed and I didn't do anything about it. I was afraid of feeling a little foolish. Now I feel an even bigger fool.'

After his appearance at West London Magistrates' Court Roberts was taken to Brixton Prison, escorted by DS Bob Berry, and, like Duddy and Witney, Roberts struck up a conversation. He had been alone on the run but had still been free to think and dream and hope. Now his alienation was complete and perhaps he felt in need of some kind of human interaction.

Roberts: 'Not so cold today.'

Berry: 'No, I suppose it was getting colder in your tent.'

Roberts: 'It had not been too bad.'

Berry: 'However did you find that place?'

Roberts: 'I used to play in the woods when I was a youngster. My mother had a friend in Thorley High Street named Chappel – he was a motor dealer.'

There was a pause in the conversation while Roberts thought for a moment and then he said, 'Do police dogs only chase after someone running?'

Berry: 'Why do you ask that?'

Roberts: 'Last Friday I crossed the A11 to go into the woods and the police dog was walking with me but it went away again.'

Berry: 'You were very fortunate. Did you go back to your tent then?'

Roberts: 'Only for a few minutes, then I went to the barn. I did go back to the tent on Saturday morning but I saw that police were guarding it so I hid in the barn.'

There was another pause and then Roberts said, 'Do I have to have that blanket over my head? I should have thought everyone has seen my photograph by now.'

Berry: 'We cover you for your own interests. We must ensure that no witness sees you in person.'

And with that the short exchange between Berry and Roberts ended. As with Witney and Duddy, DS Berry had learned a little more while travelling with Harry Roberts – why he had hidden in Thorley Wood and how close he had come to being caught early on that Saturday morning when he was being tracked from Sawbridgeworth by PC Loftin and his dog Shan.

While she'd been giving evidence at the trial of Duddy and Witney, Lilly Perry had been staying with June Howard at Wymering Mansions. By this time June's husband Colin had been released from Wormwood Scrubs prison and was back at home. At around 12:45 p.m. the telephone rang and Perry answered it. A woman's voice said hesitantly, 'Is Colin there, please?'

Perry immediately recognised the voice as that of Dorothy Roberts. Perry said, 'No, Colin's not here. He has taken June to the hospital.'

After a long pause Dorothy Roberts said, 'Is that Lilly?'

'Yes.'

'I saw Robbie yesterday. He looks terrible. He's so thin. If you ever saw a skeleton dug up, that's him.'

Dorothy Roberts then repeated how thin and ill her son looked and Perry said how sorry she was for Mrs Roberts, seeing him like that. Perry added, 'I would like to see him later on when the time is right.'

'You?' Mrs Roberts snapped. 'Who are you? What makes you think he'll want to see you? It's me, his mother, he wants to see.' Perry was taken aback by the outburst and couldn't think what to say. But Mrs Roberts hadn't finished, 'I'm going to get a bloody good QC for him and I'll make damn sure that you and June go down for this.'

Perry said, 'Why, what have I done?'

'You've given evidence, haven't you? You had no business to. Robbie's not going to carry the can for you two and I'm telling you now he is my son and I am going to stand by him like I have in the past. Do you hear me? Do you hear what I am saying?'

Perry hung up without replying. After thinking it over, she called Shepherd's Bush police station and later that afternoon related the conversation in a statement taken by Detective Sergeant Sheila Acton.

Now that the police had recovered three guns – two when they arrested Roberts and the third from Hampstead Heath – the next key step in the investigation was to prove that the recovered guns were indeed the murder weapons.

In Braybrook Street the police had found spent 9mm

cartridge cases and two live rounds. They also knew that a .38 calibre gun had been used but they had two .38 revolvers. The question they were therefore hoping that scientific analysis could decide was which gun had been used. That might also confirm the statements by Witney, Duddy and Roberts that only Roberts and Duddy had taken part in the shootings. Some witnesses had said that all three men had fired guns and Duddy had said in one of his statements, 'We all three had guns but I don't know if Witney used his or not. I believe he did.'

Forensics expert John McCafferty first examined the Luger semi-automatic pistol, Enfield revolver and ammunition that Roberts had had with him when he'd been arrested in Hertfordshire, and then the earth-encrusted and rusty .38 Colt Special recovered from Hampstead Heath. He reached several key conclusions.

First, the cartridge cases and the single live bullet found in Witney's car when it was discovered in Vauxhall could now be proved to have come from the guns that McCafferty examined.

Second, the Luger P08 was the murder weapon used in the shooting of David Wombwell and Chris Head.

Third, the malfunctioning magazines for the Luger provided an explanation why the police had found both spent cartridge cases and live 9mm rounds in Braybrook Street. The shooter had manually ejected rounds when trying 'to restore correct function'.

Fourth, the fact that the Luger was prone to jamming

explained why after Chris Head had been shot in the back he'd had time to get up from the ground and take cover in front of the Q-car without being shot again. The Luger malfunction was also the reason why Geoffrey Fox had reversed the Q-car towards the shooter in a defensive action, having deduced that the gun was jammed or out of ammunition. Fatally, what Fox did not and could not have known was that the men they'd stopped had other guns. He only realised this when Duddy got out of the Vanguard and fired at him.

Fifth, the .38 Enfield was the weapon used to shoot Geoffrey Fox.

Sixth, the .38 Colt Special had not been used. This confirmed that only two of the three men had fired guns, which supported Witney's claim that he had taken no part in the shootings.

Although the second-by-second sequence of events in Braybrook Street on the afternoon of 12 August was made clearer by the ballistic tests on the murder weapons, the case against Roberts, Witney and Duddy was yet to be heard and the charges against each of them proved beyond doubt to a jury.

Chapter 35

Meanwhile John Cunningham's claim on the £1,000 reward offered by the Metropolitan Police was gaining momentum. He had sought the advice of solicitors H. Stanley Tee & Co. of Bishop's Stortford and in turn they wrote a letter on his behalf to the Commissioner of Metropolitan Police, Sir Joseph Simpson, at Scotland Yard. He received it that Thursday, 17 November.

Dear Sir,

We have been consulted by Mr Thomas John Cunningham of The Caravan, Thorley Church, near Bishop's Stortford who wished to make a claim for the reward which we understand had been offered for information leading to the whereabouts and arrest of Mr Harry Roberts.

As you may know, Mr Cunningham was the first person to point out to the police that a man was living in a tent in a wood near Thorley. In fact he suggested to the police that they should direct their enquiries to such person regarding another matter.

As is, of course, now well known, this was the tent which in fact had been occupied by Mr Roberts prior to his arrest.

We do not think there is any need for us to say more in this letter because Mr Cunningham has already been interviewed at length by Police Officers about the whole matter. We are merely writing this letter on his behalf because he is, as you may know, a gypsy and finds it difficult to communicate by letter.

We await hearing from you as soon as possible.

Cunningham's reward claim was also the subject of a report written that day by Detective Chief Inspector Tame, Acting Superintendent at Harlow police station where the Cunninghams were taken after their arrest on Friday, 11 November. Tame summarised, point by point, the events surrounding their arrest following the break-in at Walter Lawrence & Son Ltd. When he got to point number 10 he began to describe a sequence of events that had not so far been recorded and it made the whole matter all the more extraordinary and complicated.

The first revelation concerned an interview that had taken place at Harrow police station after the discovery of the tent, between PC Fardell and John Cunningham's father Thomas, about the man his son had mentioned living in a tent in the woods nearby.

10. Later that morning, Thomas Cunningham, when questioned about the unknown man by PC Fardell, said, 'My boy (John Cunningham) has been messing about with him. He's been down there for some time in that tent. I told my boy to keep away.'

PC Fardell said to him, 'Surely you must have some knowledge as to who this man is?'

Cunningham replied, 'I don't know but I suppose it might be Jetty (meaning William Porter aka Loveridge, a prison escapee). My son hasn't said anything about him.'

Point twelve of Tame's report turns to the arrest of Harry Roberts:

12. When Harry Maurice Roberts was questioned at Bishop's Stortford police station by Detective Superintendent Chitty (Metropolitan Police) and Chief Superintendent Rowe (Hertfordshire Constabulary) he admitted being responsible for the offence at Sawbridgeworth for which the Cunninghams had been arrested and claimed he had been alone.

13. As previously reported there is evidence that at least two persons were involved, therefore this verbal statement by Roberts would appear to be an attempt on his part to cover up for his accomplice.

In his statement to the police, nightwatchman Roy Yates at Walter Lawrence & Son said, *'I did not see anyone in the factory but I was of the opinion that there were two or more thieves from the noise of their footsteps when they ran.'* PC Loftin reported tracking two sets of footprints visible in the morning frost. It is possible, therefore, that Roberts was not alone when he robbed the vending machines at the joinery works and that he was in the company of Cunningham. If that is true then it's another strange twist in the character of Harry Roberts that following his capture and when facing a triple murder charge he should bother to exonerate John Cunningham.

As far as the police were concerned, for the time being the matter of whether John Cunningham's claim had any merit or whether he was simply trying it on was left in the balance. As far as Cunningham was concerned his claim on the £1,000 reward was a matter of urgency: with the help of solicitors H. Stanley Tee & Co. the illiterate John Cunningham was determined not to let Sir Joseph Simpson conveniently forget about him.

The following day the press and other news media reported the 5 December date for the trial of all three men arrested for the Shepherd's Bush Murders. The presiding judge, Mr Justice Glyn-Jones had decided that nineteen days, including weekends, was enough time for the police and prosecution counsel to amass the evidence against Roberts and sufficient for Roberts's solicitors and counsel, Mr Kenneth Richardson, to prepare the defence.

The Times also reported that day on another important and pressing decision concerning the murderers of David Wombwell, Chris Head and Geoff Fox.

Scotland Yard yesterday said the fund for dependants of the three officers shot at Shepherd's Bush in August was expected to total £210,000 [about £3m in 2016's money].

Sir Joseph Simpson, Metropolitan Police Commissioner, proposes to divide the money into eight parts, each of £26,250 [£342,000 in 2016's money]. One eighth each will be paid to the widows of Police Constable Geoffrey Fox and Detective Constable David Wombwell, a further eighth to Mrs Head, mother of Detective Sergeant Christopher Head, and the remainder to be distributed by depositing three shares with the Public Trustee to provide a trust fund for Mrs Fox's three children and two shares for a similar fund for the two children of Mrs Wombwell.

The two widows and Mrs Head have agreed and it is hoped that the distribution will take place in the middle of next month.

While the police and legal teams were hurriedly assembling the evidence and paperwork required for the much anticipated triple-murder trial of Harry Roberts, Jack Witney and John Duddy at the Central Criminal Court, the Commissioner of the Metropolitan Police, Sir Joseph Simpson received another letter from John Cunningham's solicitor, H. Stanley Tee & Co.

Dear Sir,

We wrote to you on the 16th November on behalf of Mr John Cunningham who claims the Reward offered for information leading to the whereabouts of Mr Harry Roberts.

We have not had a reply to our letter although we have received a postcard acknowledgement from the Shepherd's Bush police station under the writer's reference but acknowledging a letter we are supposed to have written on the '18th November'.

Will you please let us hear from you in answer to our letter as soon as possible.

By the beginning of December John Cunningham's reward claim had been passed to Detective Superintendent Chitty – as if he didn't have enough to do. On Thursday,

1 December solicitors H. Stanley Tee & Co. telephoned him and followed the conversation with a letter the same day.

> *Dear Sir,*
>
> *Our Client Mr John Cunningham*
>
> *We write to confirm our telephone conversation today when you told us that more than one application has been made for the Roberts Reward and that none of these applications would be considered until after the proceedings against Mr Roberts are concluded.*
>
> *We understood you to say that a senior police officer would then be appointed to consider all the applications in detail.*
>
> *We further understand that at that stage you will be in touch with us again.*
>
> *If in the meantime you will be kind enough to let us know the exact wording of the Reward which was offered we shall be very grateful.*

There is no record of Chitty's reaction to his telephone call from Cunningham's solicitor but the call was certainly ill-timed, coming as it did with just five days to go until the opening of the trial of Witney, Duddy and Roberts for the murders of David Wombwell, Chris Head and Geoff Fox at the Central Criminal Court.

Chapter 36

When Jack Witney, John Duddy and Harry Roberts were brought up from the holding cells at the Old Bailey to the dock of Court No.1 on the opening morning of their trial on Monday, 5 December 1966, it was the first time that all three had been together since the day of the murders.

Their individual crimes in Braybrook Street that afternoon for which they had been arrested were formalised in eleven separate counts. The wording of the indictment is, on the face of it, laborious and repetitive to read. However, on closer examination the offences for which Witney, Roberts and Duddy were charged prompt reflection on their individual actions and respective culpabilities, set against the subsequent legal framework constructed for their trial.

THE QUEEN
against
HARRY MAURICE ROBERTS
JOHN DUDDY
and
JOHN EDWARD WITNEY

357

1. STATEMENT OF OFFENCE:

MURDER.

PARTICULARS OF OFFENCE:

Harry Maurice ROBERTS, John DUDDY and John Edward WITNEY on the 12th day of August 1966 within the jurisdiction of the Central Criminal Court murdered David Stanley Bertram WOMBWELL.

2. STATEMENT OF OFFENCE:

ACCESSORY AFTER THE FACT TO MURDER.

PARTICULARS OF OFFENCE:

John DUDDY, well knowing that Harry Maurice ROBERTS and John Edward WITNEY had murdered David Stanley Bertram WOMBWELL, did on the 12th day of August 1966 and on other days thereafter within the jurisdiction of the Central Criminal Court, comfort, harbour, assist and maintain Harry Maurice ROBERTS and John Edward WITNEY.

3. STATEMENT OF OFFENCE:

ACCESSORY AFTER THE FACT TO MURDER.

PARTICULARS OF OFFENCE:

John Edward WITNEY, well knowing that Harry Maurice ROBERTS and John DUDDY had murdered David Stanley Bertram WOMBWELL, did on the 12th day of August 1966 within the jurisdiction of the Central Criminal Court, comfort, harbour, assist and maintain Harry Maurice ROBERTS and John DUDDY.

4. STATEMENT OF OFFENCE:

MURDER.

PARTICULARS OF OFFENCE:

Harry Maurice ROBERTS, John DUDDY and John Edward WITNEY on the 12ᵗʰ day of August 1966 within the jurisdiction of the Central Criminal Court murdered Christopher Tippet HEAD.

5. STATEMENT OF OFFENCE:

ACCESSORY AFTER THE FACT TO MURDER.

PARTICULARS OF OFFENCE:

John DUDDY, well knowing that Harry Maurice ROBERTS and John Edward WITNEY had murdered Christopher Tippet HEAD, did on the 12ᵗʰ day of August 1966 and on other days thereafter within the jurisdiction of the Central Criminal Court, comfort, harbour, assist and maintain Harry Maurice ROBERTS and John Edward WITNEY.

6. STATEMENT OF OFFENCE:

ACCESSORY AFTER THE FACT TO MURDER.

PARTICULARS OF OFFENCE:

John Edward WITNEY, well knowing that Harry Maurice ROBERTS and John DUDDY had murdered Christopher Tippet HEAD, did on the 12ᵗʰ day of August 1966 within the jurisdiction of the Central Criminal Court, comfort, harbour, assist and maintain Harry Maurice ROBERTS and John DUDDY.

7. STATEMENT OF OFFENCE:

MURDER.

PARTICULARS OF OFFENCE:

Harry Maurice ROBERTS, John DUDDY and John

Edward WITNEY on the 12th day of August 1966 within the jurisdiction of the Central Criminal Court murdered Geoffrey Roger FOX.

8. STATEMENT OF OFFENCE:
ACCESSORY AFTER THE FACT TO MURDER.
PARTICULARS OF OFFENCE:
Harry Maurice ROBERTS, well knowing that John DUDDY and John Edward WITNEY had murdered Geoffrey Roger FOX, did on the 12th day of August 1966 and on other days thereafter within the jurisdiction of the Central Criminal Court, comfort, harbour, assist and maintain John DUDDY and John Edward WITNEY.

9. STATEMENT OF OFFENCE:
ACCESSORY AFTER THE FACT TO MURDER.
PARTICULARS OF OFFENCE:
John Edward WITNEY, well knowing that Harry Maurice ROBERTS and John DUDDY had murdered Christopher Tippet HEAD, did on the 12th day of August 1966 within the jurisdiction of the Central Criminal Court, comfort, harbour, assist and maintain John DUDDY and Harry Maurice ROBERTS.

10. STATEMENT OF OFFENCE:
HAVING A FIREARM WITH INTENT, contrary to Section 1 of the Firearms Act 1965.
PARTICULARS OF OFFENCE:
Harry Maurice ROBERTS, John DUDDY and John Edward WITNEY on the 12th day of August 1966 within the jurisdiction of the Central Criminal Court

had with them firearms with intent to commit an indictable offence, or to resist their arrest, in either case while they had the said firearms with them.

11. STATEMENT OF OFFENCE:

HAVING A FIREARM TOGETHER WITH AMMUNITION SUITABLE FOR USE IN THAT FIREARM IN A PUBLIC PLACE WITHOUT AUTHORITY OR REASONABLE EXCUSE, contrary to Section 2 of the Firearms Act 1965.

PARTICULARS OF OFFENCE:

Harry Maurice ROBERTS, John DUDDY and John Edward WITNEY on the 12th day of August 1966 within the jurisdiction of the Central Criminal Court had with them in a public place firearms together with ammunition suitable for use in the said firearms without lawful authority or reasonable excuse.

These eleven counts were the foundation of the prosecution's case upon which the jury would be asked to consider their verdict.

After the list of offences was read aloud by the clerk to the assembled court, the accused in turn were asked how they pleaded on each of the counts. Duddy and Witney pleaded not guilty to the whole indictment. Roberts pleaded guilty to murdering Detective Constable Wombwell and Detective Sergeant Head. He further pleaded guilty to being an accessory after the fact in the murder of Police Constable Fox and guilty to possessing a firearm and ammunition in a public place (Count 11), the lesser of the two firearms offences detailed in Counts 10 and 11. Roberts pleaded not guilty to Count 7, the murder of PC Fox, and Count 10, possessing firearms with intent to commit an indictable offence or to resist arrest.

As all three men were put on trial together, a stronger starting point for their defence would have been to coordinate their responses to the charges in the indictment and for each of them to have offered a guilty plea for those crimes which they had actually committed and to which they had confessed in their statements to the police.

Roberts for murdering Wombwell and Head; being an accessory after the fact in the murder of Fox; possessing firearms and ammunition in a public place. The three guns belonged to Roberts. He alone had purchased them in March 1966 and had brought them with him in a bag that day, as he was in the habit of doing for no specific purpose.

Duddy for the murder of Geoffrey Fox; being an accessory after the fact to the murders of Wombwell and Head.

Witney for being an accessory after the fact to all three murders.

For this was the truth of the matter. And it would have made each of their actions and respective legal defences clear to the jury at the outset.

*

Looking like a character from a Charles Dickens novel, with a full-length ceremonial judicial wig framing his long, thin, deeply-lined face and round wire-rimmed spectacles, seventy-one-year-old Justice Sir Hildreth Glyn-Jones (born 19 March 1895), had the appearance and manner of a man from a bygone age, an epoch away from the unsettled Britain of the mid-1960s.

The judge asked the leading counsel for the prosecution, the Solicitor-General, Sir Dingle Mackintosh Foot QC: 'Do you accept the pleas of Roberts?'

Sir Dingle replied, 'No, my Lord.'

Glyn-Jones simply said, 'Then I need say no more.'

With this brief exchange between two knights of the realm the trial commenced on the counts in the indictment to which the three accused men had pleaded not guilty. The Voluntary Bill of Indictment against Roberts had dispensed with the evidence against him being heard first in committal proceedings at West London Magistrates' Court. However, that meant witnesses who had given evidence at committal proceedings against Witney and Duddy in September would now have to be called again to give testimony against Roberts.

The prosecution team was led by Foot with Mr John Mathew (counsel for the defence of Great Train Robber Charlie Wilson at his 1964 trial) and Mr Michael Cockrey. The Solicitor-General had stepped in to lead the prosecution instead of the Attorney General, Sir Elwyn Jones, who by that time was involved in the Aberfan disaster inquiry.

Sir Dingle, striking in appearance – statesmanlike, square-jawed, a full head of silver hair swept to the right by a side parting, still good-looking for a man of sixty-one years – began his opening for the prosecution by telling the jury there could be no question of accident, provocation, or self-defence. 'The Crown says this was a case of deliberate, cold-blooded murder.'

He then set out his narrative of events which, although necessary, added little to the story that the jury, everyone else in the courtroom and the rest of the British public had already read in the press.

Sir Dingle made a point of reinforcing that when Head was shot in the back 'he fell dying in the road,' although that was not strictly true, or at least not proven or medically certain. The complications surrounding Head's cause of death muddied the simplicity of a triple murder charge. It is possible this was anticipated at the time of Home Office Pathologist Dr Donald Teare's post-mortem report on the evening of the shootings and was now, therefore, beyond question or debate.

The Solicitor-General explained that the prosecution case was supported by a number of written depositions. He was going to call other witnesses to provide their testimony in court, including four children who would describe what they saw during the 'two or three terrible minutes of the shootings.' He foreshadowed decisive things that his witnesses would say – Patricia Deacon, for example, and how her taking note of the car number had led to the arrest of Witney. He quoted from Lilly Perry's statements to the police, which gave an account of Roberts's movements and what he said to her when he returned home after the shootings.

The jury were told that after Witney's story about selling his car had been disproved he said in a statement to the police, ' "Honestly, I didn't shoot the coppers. As God is my judge I had absolutely nothing to do with the shooting of any of the three." As Roberts raced back to the Vanguard after the shooting I said, "You must be [profanity omitted] potty," and Roberts replied, "Drive [profanity omitted] unless you want some of the same." I was petrified with fear and shock. I reversed back round the corner and put the car in the garage where you found it.'

A notable omission in Sir Dingle's summary of Witney's role was that Jack Witney had greatly assisted the police by not only naming the men who were with him in his car that Friday afternoon but had also shown detectives where each of them lived. Without Witney's help the police investigation team would not have so quickly learned how the three officers were murdered, or by whom, nor traced John Duddy, nor immediately known that Harry Maurice Roberts was the third man. Strangely, no acknowledgment or direct reference to Witney's considerable assistance and cooperation was given throughout the trial, even by his own defence lawyers. No doubt because Witney wished to avoid any suspicion by the men who were with him in the dock that he had grassed them up. The consequences that might follow could have been serious.

In the grand sweep of the prosecution's summary there were many thumbnail sketches of people and events, quotes of things allegedly said by the accused men, statements of what numerous policemen had said, done and seen and accounts of what had been found in forensic and physical evidence. Sir Dingle's oratory was all delivered with such confidence and eloquence that it was hard for anyone listening to consider that the prosecution's version of events was not necessarily the only – or, indeed, definitive – one.

Sir Dingle then came to the crux of the matter. The prosecution's case was that Roberts had shot two of the officers and Duddy had shot the third. Witney had been the driver of the Vanguard, '. . . although he was probably armed he did not press any trigger. But in the submission of the Crown, he is just as guilty in law of these murders as the other two.'

In terms of criminal charges, as opposed to any moral perspective, equal guilt arose from the legal definition of 'common purpose' or 'joint enterprise'. This was the basis in law upon which it had been decided by the Crown that Witney, Duddy and Roberts should all be charged with all three murders.

Under the Accessories and Abettors Act 1861, secondary liability can be applied to most offences. The principles are commonly used in crimes of violence, theft, fraud and public order. A joint enterprise may or may not be pre-planned. Sometimes a jointly committed crime occurs spontaneously. The applicable law is the same in either case. However, secondary liability should only be applied if it can be proven that a person has assisted or encouraged the offence, intended to assist or encourage the offence, or must have foreseen the offence that the other party or parties would or might carry out. Yet none of these conditions applied to Jack Witney's unwitting involvement.

The Solicitor-General was still opening the case for the Crown when the trial was adjourned until the following day.

On Tuesday morning, the second day of the trial of Witney, Duddy and Roberts at the Central Criminal Court, Sir Dingle Foot concluded his opening remarks with quotes from written statements of the accused. For some reason he also mentioned a remark that Witney had made on 7 September while in transit with Detective Sergeant Robert Berry. 'How are the wives of the policemen who got killed? I cannot bear to think about the kids they had. Roberts and Duddy must have been mad.'

It was a strange quote for the prosecution to seize upon, for rather than corroborate or help prove any of the eleven charges against Witney and the other two men it gave the jury a glimpse of Witney's character. He had shown remorse and concern for the families of the victims. Something never expressed by the other two.

After concluding his long opening address Sir Dingle called a number of eyewitnesses who were in Braybrook Street on the afternoon of 12 August, including the four children he had mentioned in his introduction the previous day. It was an emotional start to the first-hand accounts of those who had been caught up in the horror of the shootings.

Later Lilian Perry came to the witness box. Dressed in an apple-green coat and white high-button jumper, she spoke quietly of her involvement. That was by now common knowledge, but there was one response she gave that was new and had a bearing on the charge that Witney, Duddy and Roberts '. . . *had with them firearms with intent to commit an indictable offence*'. In answer to an interjection from Justice Glyn-Jones, 'Did he [Roberts] say what would have happened if they [the police officers] had searched the car?' Perry replied: 'He said if the police had found the guns they would have done time for nothing because they were not out to do anything.'

What Roberts meant by 'done time for nothing' and 'not out to do anything' was that they were not out to commit a crime for which they needed or had planned to use his guns. And that was central to the 'common purpose' of the three men that the prosecution asserted linked them all to the three murders and made them equally culpable.

The rest of Perry's evidence covered events until she and

Roberts had parted in Epping Forest and he had said, 'This is as far as we go together. I am on my own now.' All the while as Perry was giving her evidence from the witness box Harry Roberts was just a few yards away. It was the first time she had seen him since that Monday afternoon at the bus stop on the edge of Epping Forest. She occasionally glanced over at him sitting in the dock and it was clearly hard for her to reconcile the contradictory feelings for the man she had taken into her home and life, had cared for, loyally supported and loved. Now she was left with no alternative but to assist in his prosecution for murder.

On page ten of *The Times* on Wednesday, 7 December under the report of the murder trial at the Old Bailey was a short column headed: *NO CASE AGAINST REWARD MAN. John Cunningham, aged 21, a farm worker who is claiming the £1,000 reward for leading police to the hideout of Harry Roberts, made a three-minute appearance at Harlow Magistrates' Court yesterday.*

Cunningham's solicitor had said that while the case had been pending another man had admitted responsibility for the offence. After consideration the Director of Public Prosecutions had no objection to the proceedings against Cunningham and his father being withdrawn.

On the third day of the murder trial at the Old Bailey Mrs June Howard was called to the witness box. Dressed in a check yellow coat, patterned white stockings and with a jewellery clip in her dark hair, she said she'd known Roberts for ten years. On one of his visits to London from Bristol he'd asked her if she was in a position to get him guns. 'He mentioned the subject several times,' Howard said. He sent her £65 or £70 to buy him a gun but she never did so.

She recalled that in her flat, towards the end of last year, Roberts had thrown a canvas bag towards her and told her to catch it. She'd asked him what it contained and he'd said, 'A gun.' She said that she told him to take it out of her flat. Roberts replied the gun was only for frightening people.

Mrs Howard also remembered Witney and Duddy coming to her flat at Wymering Mansions, 'in June and July this year.' She claimed to have once heard Witney say to Roberts in her kitchen, 'If we have them we must be prepared to use them.' Howard was asked what she thought Roberts and Witney were talking about and she suggested they were talking about guns.

On another occasion in Roberts's Daimler Witney said to her, 'Would you pass me my right hand [meaning the gun] – it's in the glove compartment.' She opened it and saw two guns and told Witney she did not want to handle them. Howard said that Witney replied, 'Don't be silly, it is only a small one.'

Howard recalled finding the ammunition in her flat in June, in a tin and in the pocket of a jacket belonging to Roberts. 'I told Roberts that I didn't like having them in my place.'

Under cross-examination, counsel for the defence of Duddy, James Comyn QC, asked June Howard, 'When Roberts asked if you could get him guns, didn't you ask him why he wanted them?'

'No, I shouldn't imagine he would have told me if I had asked,' Howard replied.

It was a fair point but Comyn was not to be put off. 'Did you suspect it was for criminal purposes?'

Howard twisted her hands on the edge of the witness box and paused, sensing where Comyn's questions were leading. 'I suppose so,' she said almost inaudibly.

Comyn: 'As Roberts was not working when he and Mrs Perry were staying with you, did you suspect he was living on crime?'

'There was no reason to suspect. He never seemed to have any money,' Howard replied pithily.

'Did you know he was keeping guns at your flat?'

'No,' Howard said emphatically, although by her own admission she had discovered ammunition in Roberts's jacket.

It was then counsel for Witney, Mr Barry Hudson's turn to cross-examine June Howard. He asked her about Post Office Savings Bank forgeries and drugs. 'The day on which you were to give evidence three weeks ago, you were taken to hospital with an overdose of drugs,' he stated. It was hard for the jury to see what counsel for the defence was driving at, or what relevance it had, but the judge did not intervene.

'Not an overdose,' Howard retorted. 'I was taking pethidine for rheumatic pains.'

'You were taking a good many at the time?' Hudson asked hectoringly and still no one objected on June Howard's behalf.

'I was taking a tablet every four hours.'

'Is it right that you have been questioned by the police about forging documents and getting money from the Post Office on them?'

'Yes.'

'In fact, you have admitted to the police that you forged a signature. You did that in the presence of all three defendants?'

Howard nodded. 'Yes, knowing that two of them were carrying guns, I didn't quite know what might happen to me if I didn't agree to.'

Mr Comyn and Mr Hudson's questioning of June Howard didn't appear to accomplish anything in defence of their clients. In fact, it seemed that in their efforts to discredit June Howard's good character all they had achieved was an own goal.

Chief Inspector Hensley followed later and gave his account of the arrest of Duddy in Glasgow when Hensley had been accompanied by Detective Inspector Slipper.

When it was Slipper's turn he recalled that under caution Duddy had said during the flight back to London, 'It was Roberts who started the shooting. He shot the two who got out of the car and shouted at me to shoot. I just grabbed a gun, ran to the police car and shot the driver through the window.' Slipper said he wrote down Duddy's remark in his notebook and immediately showed it to Hensley.

Comyn informed Slipper, 'Duddy's instructions to me are that no statement was made on the aircraft, do you understand?'

'I understand.' Slipper said firmly. He understood that Comyn was referring to 'verballing' – incriminating remarks or confessions alleged to have been made at a place outside a formal interview under caution.

Mr John O'Brien was called by the prosecution. Thirty-eight-year-old O'Brien said that a year ago he and Witney had been working at the same firm in Acton. They often used to go to Tom's Bar café in Horn Lane nearby. 'We were talking once about being in trouble with the police and how far you would go to keep out of trouble,' O'Brien recalled. 'Witney said life was his freedom and if necessary he would kill to keep that freedom. I told him I would not kill to keep my freedom, I would not kill to get away.'

Mr O'Brien said that on the Tuesday before the shootings he sold his driving licence to Witney for £6. After learning of Witney's arrest in the newspaper, on 15 August he went to the police station and told them about the transaction. At the time O'Brien made a five-page statement in which he said that he had been with Witney when he once went to Tinworth Street to collect money from the governor [William Keeley, although he wasn't named in court] of Crown Engineering who took 'bent gear'. O'Brien admitted that he had also stolen metal from his employers and sold it to the same man.

It was not revealed to the jury that between the time of John O'Brien telling the police about selling his driving licence and attending court that day, he had been serving a custodial sentence in Brixton prison for an unrelated matter. Not that it would have invalidated his evidence but the jury would have had a clearer understanding of the character and context of the prosecution's witness.

Nevertheless, the purpose of the evidence elicited in court from June Howard and John O'Brien on days two and three of the triple murder trial at the Old Bailey was clear. There were unsubstantiated recollections that Witney knew about Roberts's guns. Combined with Howard stating that Witney had asked her to pass him a gun in Roberts's car, her claim to have overheard Witney say, 'If we have them we must be prepared to use them,' and O'Brien's conversation with Witney in Tom's Café – 'he had said that he would kill to protect his freedom' – the prosecution was hoping this would be enough to convince the jury of Witney's intent and complicity.

But even if these accounts were true and accurate, Witney's childish showing-off to June Howard with the gun in Roberts's Daimler, his overheard bravado about being prepared to use guns and his bragging to O'Brien over a cup of tea about what he would theoretically do to protect his freedom, all sounded more naive than truly menacing or indeed conclusive. And it was a long way from providing compelling evidence that habitual petty thief Jack Witney had uncharacteristically recently acquired more sinister criminal characteristics and was a willing participant in the murder of David Wombwell, Christopher Head and Geoffrey Fox.

Chapter 37

On Thursday, 8 December at the Old Bailey, counsel for the defence of Roberts, Duddy and Witney offered the jury an alternative view of the Shepherd's Bush Murders. Roberts was represented by Mr James Burge QC and solicitor Mr John Richardson; Duddy by Mr John Comyns QC and solicitor Mr Batt; Witney by Mr Barry Hudson, instructed by solicitor Mr Michael Wrightson.

The perspective was limited in that only Jack Witney elected to give evidence in his defence. In the witness box Witney appeared intelligent, in command of himself and clear in what he had to say. In response to the first question put to him he confirmed that around the end of June or beginning of July he bought a Standard Vanguard, registration number PGT 726, in poor condition, for £20. He insured the car but had not registered the change of ownership and because it needed work to pass an MOT test he could not obtain a road fund licence.

The subject then moved to the car number plates, registration JJJ 285D, that were found in Witney's car. Witney said that a few days before the shooting he had ordered the set of number plates. It was his intention that they should be fitted to a stolen vehicle.

His counsel, Barry Hudson, asked, 'What did you intend to do with the stolen car?'

Witney: 'Nothing particularly. Probably it would have been sold.'

'Was anyone going to help you?'

'I would have stolen the car myself. The two gentlemen in the dock might have helped me to change the plates and perhaps dispose of the car.' Witney said he rented the garage at Vauxhall to house the car after it was stolen.

He was asked to explain his whereabouts and the sequence of events on Friday, 12 August. He began by saying he left home just before eight a.m. and drove to Duddy's flat. He had arranged to meet Duddy and Roberts there. 'We were going to look out for a car to steal. Roberts was carrying a shopping bag in which was a pair of dungarees.'

Hudson: 'Had you the slightest idea that underneath those overalls were firearms?'

Witney: 'I had not the slightest idea.'

'Did the use of firearms come within your contemplation?'

'No. It would be utterly ridiculous. If you are caught the maximum penalty you are likely to get for taking and driving away is six months.'

Witney explained how he, Duddy and Roberts had looked at a number of railway-station car parks while searching for a suitable car to steal, but they had not found what they'd had in mind.

'We arrived at East Acton station at about three o'clock. There we decided to give up the venture for the day but I could not go home because my wife thought I was at work.'

Hudson: 'I want you to tell us, slowly and clearly, what happened after you got into Braybrook Street.'

Witney did as he was asked and it was detailed and accurate. He explained why he had backed his car away from the scene at speed up Econwald Street, which had up to then been a mystery.

'I reversed up because I could not stomach driving past the policemen. My mind was in such a state I did not realise where I was driving.' With Roberts beside him holding a gun in his hand, Witney said he drove to the railway arches in Tinworth Street.

After parking his Vanguard in the garage Witney and Roberts went to a café at Euston. 'Roberts said to me, "You look as though you are going to keel over." I was shaking like a leaf, sweating buckets. I could only drink half my cup of tea. Then we got a cab to Duddy's place.'

Hudson: 'Have you ever carried a firearm?'

Witney: 'Never in any circumstances, except during my army training.'

'What picture did you have of Roberts after this terrible thing?'

'He was a different person to the one I had known.'

'Had you ever seen him like that before?'

'No, never.'

'What was your attitude to him after this happened?'

'I was petrified. Later Roberts asked, "You wouldn't grass us, would you?" I said, "No" and he said, "Don't make that mistake. You know what happened to Jack Spot and his wife and that was minor in comparison."' *[In 1956, on Billy Hill's instructions, Jack Comer aka Jack Spot and his wife Rita were attacked outside their Paddington home by 'Mad' Frankie Fraser, Bobby Warren and others. Both Fraser and Warren were later given seven years in prison.]*

Justice Glyn-Jones, who had remained silent throughout Witney's testimony interjected, 'You mean in comparison with what was going to happen to you?'

Witney turned to the judge and replied, 'That's what I took it to mean, sir.'

Under cross-examination Witney maintained he was 'terrorised' by Roberts and when it was put to him that in his statement Duddy had said, 'Witney was the brains of the outfit', Witney replied that was 'nonsense'.

By the time Jack Witney stepped down from the witness box and returned to the dock, he had created a reasonable impression: a small-time thief who had found himself caught up in something that he'd neither foreseen nor could have done anything to change the outcome of in the heat of the moment. And later he'd panicked and then tried to cover things up and had constructed a rather feeble alibi when questioned by the police that night.

There were a few inconsistencies in his account of the shootings when compared with what other witnesses had said. But it was clear that the turning point had been when Detective Sergeant Head had asked Duddy to show him what was in the canvas bag on the floor between the front seats and it had become clear that the guns were going to be discovered. There was nothing in what Witney said to invite suspicion that he was lying about his involvement and any discrepancy seemed due to nothing more than the fallibility of human memory, which was understandable in the circumstances.

The weakest part of Witney's testimony was his feigned ignorance of Roberts having the guns in the 'shopping bag' that he was carrying when Witney had met him that morning. Being led by his counsel to say he had 'not the *slightest* idea' that underneath the overalls in the bag were Roberts's three guns overstepped the mark. The statement seemed unlikely and inevitably undermined Witney's plausibility and his claim of complete innocence. And that was the problem faced by Witney's defence counsel. If Witney knew that Roberts had brought guns with him that day, wasn't Witney complicit in the intention to use them and complicit in the actual use of them to murder Wombwell, Head and Fox?

Yet when Witney, Duddy and Roberts had set off that morning in Witney's car their only 'common purpose' was to steal a car. When they were stopped later by the Q-car crew, it was Roberts who unilaterally decided to shoot

Wombwell and Head and then, after his Luger jammed, incited Duddy to shoot Fox by shouting 'Come on!' and 'Get the driver!'

In his final speech Duddy's counsel, Mr James Comyns QC, said the accused men presented 'a dirty picture', not of gangsters, but of small-time 'almost pathetic criminals'. 'Is it not the real truth,' he suggested to the jury, 'that Harry Roberts carried guns because it made him feel bigger than the petty criminal he and the others were?' Describing Roberts as 'trigger-happy' Comyns said, 'It was he who initiated the quite pointless massacre at Braybrook Street. Neither in conscience nor in fairness can you find Mr Duddy guilty of murdering Sergeant Head and Detective Wombwell. Roberts shot the officer standing at the car window as he was taking Witney's particulars. He went on in the most callous cold blood to shoot the second officer in the back as he was running to safety. Roberts is the man who started it all.'

Mr James Burge QC, who had taken over the defence of Roberts, had little to offer in defence of his client. There was, however, the way the charges in the indictment had been constructed and Burge said that it was clear from the accounts of all the witnesses, and the statements made to the police by all three of the defendants, that Roberts had not shot Police Constable Geoffrey Fox. Roberts had admitted he was the 'prime mover' of what happened and that he fired the first and second shots, but before the jury could find him guilty of the third murder they must be satisfied that there was a common purpose between the defendants to use guns.

The distinction Burge made was both true and, of course, also had some bearing on the actions and culpability of all three men. If Roberts had been charged with two murders and had pleaded guilty their would have been no need for the Crown to present a prosecution case against him, thereby saving time and public money. If Duddy had been charged with the murder of Fox the same would have applied to his plea and to the case against him. And guilty pleas would have been taken into consideration by the judge when sentencing. Nevertheless, the Crown had opted for 'common purpose' as this allowed for all three men to be linked together on a triple murder charge. As far as Duddy and Roberts were concerned the distinction was less significant but it was a very different matter as far as the case against Witney was concerned.

Burge's closing remarks offered Mr W.M. F. Hudson a neat starting point for his objections to the charges against his client, Jack Witney. He said the condition of Witney's car, without a road-fund licence and with a defective exhaust tied on with wire, made it an open invitation for the police to stop him. 'In view of the car's condition do you really believe Witney was party to an enterprise involving the carrying of loaded firearms? He was only out to steal a car, an easy offence to commit these days.'

In response Sir Dingle Foot QC said no one had suggested that the shooting of the police officers was anything but murder. That being so, there were only three questions for the jury to consider: Who did the shooting? Did the accused have the common purpose of using guns in order to avoid or resist arrest? And if Witney was not a party to a common design was he an accessory after the fact because he helped the others to escape? And so it was that on Friday, 9 December 1966 the trial was adjourned for the weekend.

On the morning of Monday, 12 December at the Old Bailey Justice Hildreth Glyn-Jones summed up the case against Roberts, Witney and Duddy for the jury, giving guidance on what had been presented by counsel for the prosecution and defence and framing how the charges against the accused worked in law.

The jury then retired to the jury room to consider the overwhelming abundance of personal testimony given in court and also in numerous written depositions. In total, 401 witnesses had contributed their observations and opinions and then there was the wealth of physical and forensic evidence to weigh up before each jury member voted on their conclusions.

Just forty minutes later the jury filed back into Court No. 1 and the foreman of the jury was asked if they had reached a verdict upon which they were all agreed. He declared that the jury was unanimous. The main counts in the indictment were read out and the foreman's reply to each one was a single decisive word: 'Guilty'. All three men were guilty of all three murders. All that remained was for Justice Glyn-Jones to pass sentence.

Witney, Duddy and Roberts stood in the dock, showing no visible reaction or emotion as the sentences were handed down on each of them. 'Life' was the statutory tariff for murder, thirty years apiece was what they each got for that crime and ten years to run concurrently for possessing 'firearms with intent to commit an indictable offence or to resist their arrest'.

Glyn-Jones concluded his duties by saying, 'You have been justly convicted of what is perhaps the most heinous crime to have been committed in the country for a generation or more.

'I think it unlikely that any Home Secretary in the future, regarding the enormity of the crime, will ever think fit to show mercy by releasing you on licence. It is one of the cases in which a sentence of imprisonment for life may well be treated as meaning exactly what it says. But, lest any Home Secretary in the future shall be minded to consider your release on licence, I propose to make a recommendation.

'I recommend that you should not be released on licence – any of you – until a period of thirty years has gone by from today's date.'

As the prisoners were led away down to the cells, lawyers' clerks packed away thick bundles of papers into bags and detectives began collecting the exhibits, including items of clothing and the three guns.

The Shepherd's Bush Murders

For the Crown prosecution team it was an unqualified victory. For the victims and the families of the murdered policemen and the countless police officers who had worked without rest during four months of dedicated and determined investigation, there was some sense of retribution and closure in that the three men responsible for the shootings in Braybrook Street on the afternoon of 12 August had been caught and tried before judge and jury, found guilty and sentenced to life imprisonment.

But for others not emotionally connected with the events and looking back at the case of the Shepherd's Bush murders fifty years later, there remains a nagging concern that still divides opinion: Was this fair? Was this right? Had the law served its purpose? Had justice been done? Did the man who instigated the shootings and killed two of the officers deserve the same punishment as the two other men he was with? Did the second man who killed one officer after being incited to do so deserve that same punishment? Did the third man who killed no one, and later helped the police, deserve to be sent to prison for the same length of time as the other two men?

When the legal principle of 'joint enterprise' or 'common purpose' was applied to the charges against Roberts, Duddy and Witney, the individual actions of each man were never in much dispute. However, their 'common purpose', in legal terms, which the prosecution asserted tied all three men together and made them equally culpable, was never proven conclusively and was open to considerable doubt. But – because three policemen had been murdered, because of the callous cold-bloodedness of the killings and the pointlessness of them, because of the national publicity, the impact and shock and outrage, the reaction of the police and the Establishment, the strength of public feeling – the Shepherd's Bush Murders trial at the Central Criminal Court in December 1966 was always going to be a law unto itself.

Chapter 38

When Witney, Duddy and Roberts were taken down to the holding cells at the Old Bailey to await transportation to prison, they were each allowed a short visit from a spouse or a close family member. Afterwards reporters intercepted and interviewed Lillian Witney, Teresa Duddy and Dorothy Roberts as they left the Central Criminal Court building.

The following morning, Tuesday, 13 December, under the front page headline *NOT LESS THAN 30 YEARS FOR ROBERTS DUDDY AND WITNEY* the *Daily Express* reported:

> 'Mrs Duddy said, "After you've known a man for 15 years you can hardly desert him at such a time. When I saw him in the cells a few moments ago he offered me a divorce but I refused."
>
> 'Mrs Witney said, "I don't think my husband should have received such a long sentence as he didn't fire any of the shots. I shall go on loving him."'

Dorothy Roberts, like all human beings, didn't always

387

say in public – particularly to newspaper reporters – what she thought and felt privately. On this occasion her remarks were an attempt to temper public feeling rather than a true expression of what she must have felt. *'It's a mystery to me why he didn't turn the gun on himself. I imagine he was a coward. But I suppose I will still visit him in jail. After all, I am his mother.'*

With her four-month ordeal finally over, Dorothy Roberts later agreed to be interviewed by author Tom Tullet for his 1967 book, *No Answer From Foxtrot Eleven*. Perhaps she imagined that by doing so she could distance herself from the crimes of her son, cushion herself against the inevitable assumptions that, as mother of the vilified Harry Roberts, she must in some way have been partly responsible for his actions. Indelibly tainted by the sins of her son it would appear that self-preservation was her understandable motive, an attempt to defuse any public hostility, directed against anyone connected with her only child and to claw back some kind of workable life, normality and respectability for herself.

Fifty-three-year-old Dorothy Roberts spoke softly, undramatically, in a quite educated English accent. She called her son 'Robin' – a nickname, she said, that he was given by a nanny when he was an infant. In many ways what Dorothy Roberts said, although it was not her intention, provided not only a deeper insight into her son, his background and their relationship, but also a revealing view of what kind of person and what sort of parent she was.

*

'It's easy to be wise after the event, but I've had a lot of time to think since Robin was caught. I think of nothing else day and night, my son's always with me in my thoughts.

'The first I knew he was involved in the murders was when the police came to see me. But they didn't turn me over then. As soon as they had gone I burned everything that might incriminate my son, like addresses and that. I set fire to it all in the sink, then flushed it down the lavatory. I was terrified if they found him they'd kill him, or he would shoot himself.

'The funny thing was that about three-thirty that Friday afternoon, a blackbird flew in my kitchen window. I couldn't get rid of it, and it frightened me. I phoned down for the caretaker to get it out for me. I said to him I was sure the bird had brought me a message, that it was an omen of some kind.

'Once before I had had a strange premonition like that, during the war. I was staying with my Aunt Ada, who kept an apartment house near the Astoria in Brixton. She had a reinforced basement against the bombing, and I had felt quite safe in there. This night the raids started, and I suddenly picked Robin up and said I was going down the Tube with him.

'My aunt thought I was mad, but I just knew I had to. We got into the Underground at Leicester Square, and it was packed out. An old Jew was lying down, and when he saw we had to stand, he gave up his bed to my boy. "He's still got a life ahead of him," he said. I never forgot that. In the morning when we went back to Brixton the street was cordoned off, and swarming with police and ARP. Aunt Ada's house had disappeared, everyone was dead. The police were very good to us then too, they gave us a hot meal and a travel warrant to Devonshire, where I had a relative.

'My husband, Harry, was in the Air Force by then. He wasn't a nice man; he even tried to cheat me out of my Air Force allowance. I'll say this for my husband; he was never a beast to the boy. But when he left me, when Robin was at college, my son didn't care.

'I always paid for his education. Same as I paid for his evacuation to Wales in the bombing. I'm proud and independent, and I never took anything from the State that I could work for myself.

'I was convent-educated in Ireland, and all my life I have tried to be respectable and work hard. My son had a nanny as a baby. It was from her he got nicknamed Robin – and the best education I could afford. He always had good clothes, and plenty of good food. He was a strong, healthy, intelligent boy, and affectionate to me, too. I can only think he inherited his father's nature.

'My husband used to knock me about. I often thought he was mental. His father committed suicide – it was his second attempt. His wife had left him because he was so violent to her, but my husband always blamed his mother for that. His grandfather ruined the family, who were well-to-do in those days, and was found dead in the snow, with his wife. They were selling matches and laces. That's what they had come down to. Mind you, I only know about the Birmingham lot from what my husband told me. I can't vouch for it. He was always taking money off me and putting it on the dogs or drinking it. When my son was born, we were running the George public house in Wanstead then – he did the fortnight's takings. I had to sell my jewellery to pay the staff.

'My baby was overdue, and he weighed 11 lb. 2 oz. It was touch and go whether I would live or die. I had him in the Maycroft Nursing Home, which cost me 14 guineas a week – a lot of money in those days. My son was born at 8 p.m. on Tuesday, 21 July 1936.

'My mistake was taking him away from boarding school. He'd been a boarder there since he was seven or thereabouts, and always well behaved. But when he was about thirteen he kept asking me if he could be a day boy instead. Well, the school was expensive, and he was old enough to look after himself when I was working, so I gave in. He stayed at the same college but as a day boy.

'He started pilfering from my bag then, and playing truant. I didn't know he was playing truant until the headmaster rang me up one day and told me Robin was always absent. I marched him up to the headmaster then, and I told him Robin kept stealing from my handbag. He told me not to leave money around the house to tempt him, and he arranged to ring me any morning Robin didn't turn up to school.

'Stealing from me was nothing new. He had been doing it for years. When I had my restaurant I sacked several staff because I thought they had been dishonest, until one day I caught Robin red-handed. An old member of the staff then confessed she'd known for years Robin had been helping himself to the till, but hadn't liked to tell me, because she didn't think I would have believed her.

'Every time my boy got into trouble and I tried to thrash things out with him, I got nowhere. I just couldn't seem to get through to him somehow. He always knew better than everybody else. He was very clever – too clever for his own good, I used to tell him.

'The funny thing is that when he was at college he used to say he'd be a policeman when he was grown-up. He said he would like to be in the CID. I had hoped he would be a lawyer. That's why I worked hard to give him a good education.

'When he left school I was always fixing jobs up for him, but he wouldn't turn up at the interviews. He had two engineering jobs, but when the second one packed up he wouldn't work, no matter what I said.

'I know now where the turning point was. It was when he was 16 or 17, and I hauled him out of a fellow's flat. He hadn't been working, but he would go out all dressed up, obviously up to something. I got a lady friend of mine to follow him and find out where he went. It was a block of flats not far from here, and the man was a no-good, a criminal type.

'I went up one afternoon and banged on the door till they let me in. In front of my son, and this man's wife, I told him I knew he was no bottle, not fit company for a young lad, and he was never to see my son again. I made Robin come home with me.

'He said nothing until he got into my flat, then he turned on me like a savage and punched me in the face, splitting my lip open. I'd never seen him like that before. I couldn't believe he would do such a thing to his mother. I ran out of the flat, and told him I was going to the police station. Instead I just walked out, then I went into a pub and had a drink to think things over. That's when I made the mistake. I didn't go to the police. I couldn't bring myself to turn my own boy in. If I had, it might have made a difference.

'I cried my eyes out when the police came to me the first time and arrested my son for stealing. I couldn't believe it. After he was sent to Borstal I never missed a visit, and I thought they were putting him right. I thought they would teach him to work there.

'When he went into the Army I thought it would be the making of him. He wrote to me from Malaya once, when he was in the Army, thanking me for the education I had given him. He said when he saw some of the other fellows out there, how little they knew, how they could hardly write their own name, he was glad he had been educated. He never forgot he was a college boy. He spoke beautifully, and had beautiful hand-writing.

'But he came home before his time in the Army was finished. I knew he still had a bit of time to do and I kept telling him to go back but the military police had to fetch him. He was a fool.

'He met a nice girl from Andover then, who came to spend a week-end. I can't remember her name, but she was a nice respectable type and I hoped something would come of it. But no, he met that woman he married.

'When he did his four-and-a-half-year stretch for coshing the old man he swore he was going straight when he came out. The day he was released I cried like a baby. When he asked me why I was crying, I kept telling him it wasn't tears of sorrow, but tears of happiness. I took him to Camden Town, and rigged him out with all new clothes. I spent well over £10 on him so he would feel smart and not have an inferiority complex.

'If I had known then what was going to happen I would have done away with myself. I did try when he was on the run. I took an overdose. Then I was sorry I'd done it and I called the police and they brought a doctor and I swore I hadn't taken anything. It felt like the most terrible hangover. The police were very kind, they said I had had a lot to put up with, and it had been too much for me.

'I will say this for the police. They were good all the time. I had them billeted on me for ages. But they gave no trouble. They used to bring their own tea, milk and sugar, and put shillings in the meter when they boiled a kettle. Sometimes they would even go and do a bit of shopping for me if I wasn't well.

'I think if that Mrs Perry had been a stronger type she might have kept him straight. She seemed a nice respectable type of woman, and as far as I'm concerned, and from what my son told me, she was just his landlady and no funny business. But she might have been stronger with him just the same, because he minded her. That was the thing with my boy; he always did well under discipline. In the Army he did well, at college the same, and when he was in the Scrubs and at Maidstone he was a trusty.

'I can't forgive June Howard and Lilly Perry for not telling me they knew Robin was involved. I started my holiday that Friday [the 12ᵗʰ] and I rang June Howard on Saturday to say I would take one of her children to Margate for a couple of days. She said he might have the measles and made excuses and I could sense an atmosphere. I went up to Camden Town to meet my girlfriend in the Wine Lodge, and we discussed the murders. I said what a shocking thing it was, and what was the world coming to. If anybody had told me my boy was involved I'd have called them a dirty liar. I thought he was safely in Bristol. I must be daft, because even when I knew Witney was involved, and I'd met him with Robin, I still didn't think my son had anything to do with it.

'I always think Robin pulled people down. Witney

and Duddy were only small-time petty criminals. There's no doubt in my mind that my boy was the ringleader. All his life he has liked the company of rotten people. I was always telling him about it, but he wouldn't listen. Yet sometimes he could be good. He was good to Mrs Howard's children, and when he was a lad, when I had pneumonia for six weeks, he cooked all my meals for me, and cleared up for me.

'He was a very tidy boy. Spotlessly clean. That was college and army training. Even when I saw him at Shepherd's Bush when they caught him, and I walked past him at first because of his beard and long hair, he was clean. The police told me everything in his camp was spotless, too.

'I cried when I saw him, and he hugged me. I asked him if the police had touched him, and he said, "No, they have been the essence of kindness." Even now he is in prison, he says the same.

'I asked him if he had seen me on television when I made my appeal, or heard me on the radio. But he hadn't. I told him I had tried to call him in for his own good. Colin Howard, husband of June, who saw me on television, told me he saw other people cry. He said I had gone over so well. I thought it was best to call Robin in for his own good. Do you know, in a way, I am glad he is in prison; at least he can't get into trouble again.

'I had some terrible letters when Robin was on the run, telling me if I paid certain sums they would tell me where my son's dead body was. I also had very kind ones from strangers, enclosing money, which I gave to police funds. I work at a hotel now, which means getting up and out by 6 a.m. I have an old lodger, and do some clerking at home. Going back to work saved my reason. My bosses, who are Irish and very religious, came and fetched me. They said I needed hardness not sympathy, and I was to start work the next day. I did, and I was glad. They never mentioned anything to me, they were very good.

'At my age this shock, and a lifetime's hard work – in the war I often worked 22 hours a day – have taken it out of me. I have lost one and a half stones since the shooting. I am now down to nine stone and still losing. When I come home from work I shut myself away and keep myself to myself. Everybody round here knows who I am. It's not pleasant. There doesn't seem much point in living now and most nights I cry myself to sleep. But I've got to go on living for my son's sake. When everybody else has forgotten him, I will still be visiting him.'

Chapter 39

There were two other women in the life of Harry Roberts who were vitally important to detectives throughout the Shepherd's Bush Murders investigation and later as key witnesses in court. One was Lilly Perry who, in recent years, had known Roberts better than anyone else. The other was his oldest friend and sometime landlady, June Howard.

After the murder trial and convictions at the Old Bailey in December 1966, Perry was still staying with the Howards at Wymering Mansions. Several months after the murders, Perry sat with June Howard on the scarlet leather suite in the sitting room. It was several months, too, after the last time they'd seen Harry Roberts, but there was little they could not recall about him. Lilly Perry called Roberts 'Robbie' and remembered him as the kindest man she ever knew.

'We never had a cross word the whole time we were together. He told me he hated rows, and would walk out of the room to avoid one. He said he had often rowed with his mother and used to walk out.

'He was a very quiet man who kept himself to himself. He hated pubs and clubs and just liked to sit at home and watch television or read. Wrestling was his favourite programme and he read all the James Bond books. He was a deeply lonely man and wanted me to go everywhere with him, even if he just wanted to take his car to the garage to fill it up, I had to go with him. It seemed he couldn't bear to do anything alone. If he was working late on the building site I would take his tea over to him, and then he would insist on me staying there until he finished his work.

'When he bought the big Daimler he would go and fetch his workmen in the morning and drive them over to the site. If they were hard-up he would give them money. He didn't believe in lending. He always seemed to be very popular and he was most generous. I could have anything I wanted. He used to come home from work, throw his pay packet on the table and say, "Have what you want and save the rest." There was often more than £40 in the packet.

'When my daughter married he bought me a whole new outfit, everything from top to toe. I had a three-quarter length off-white swagger coat, a turquoise silk dress and matching lemon shoes, hat, bag and gloves. The gloves were real leather and they cost nearly £3. Altogether he spent more than £30. He paid all the bills and would often give me a tenner to give to June. His only personal extravagance was his car. It was his idol and he would often take me on long drives and stop at the best hotels for food.'

Both Lilly Perry and June Howard were insistent on how much Roberts cared for kids. Mrs Howard spoke from her own knowledge of the way he treated her three children, Paul, aged eight, Barry, aged four and Samantha, aged two. She said Roberts was particularly fond of Barry, the child his mother offered to take on holiday to Margate.

June Howard said, 'He did care for young people. I remember one night he was babysitting for us when one of the boys got cramp in his leg. The next morning he insisted on taking him down to the hospital to see if it was anything serious. Another time it was Parents' Day at Paul's school and I couldn't go and his father was in the country [in prison]. Robbie was very upset about that. He told me I was a rotten mother, and said he would make the effort to go instead because he couldn't bear to see the boy unhappy. When he came back he was quite chuffed because Paul had pretended that he was his father. Another time when our dog took sick one night, Robbie wrapped it in a blanket and took it out in the night to look for a vet.

'He used to worry about us living in such a big, cold and damp flat, which is a constant headache because of the high rent. He was always saying that if he ever made it big he would buy a house for us, so that the children could be secure.'

Both women said that Roberts liked living in comfortable surroundings and was always prepared to do any jobs around the house. He decorated Perry's house in

Bristol and also the Howards' flat. But, said Mrs Howard, 'He had his lazy side, though. He often told me so, and I understood him because I'm the same. If you can get plenty of money the easy way, why work for a little the hard way. That's my philosophy and Robbie was the same.'

Lilly Perry disagreed. She had a different view. She said, 'Robbie explained it to me. He said it was the Labour Government's fault. If they hadn't put the squeeze on and killed the building trade, Robbie wouldn't be inside now. It was only when the building trade flopped that he took to doing jobs. He told me he would have to and I didn't try to stop him because you can't order a man of thirty about. But I hoped he didn't really mean it, and I thought if we never discussed it he would drop it.

'Robbie had to have money. He always had money as a boy. His mother gave him plenty, because she was working and could not spend much time with him. He reckoned it salved her conscience. At least, that's how Robbie sees it. So he could always buy friends with money but he could never rid himself, even as a boy, of his horrible loneliness. That's why he was happy with me, I think. There was no sex between us. I'm sexless, and Robbie didn't like it either.'

June Howard had known Roberts for more than ten years. 'I've only known him with two women, that wife of his and Lilly. He had a funny puritan streak. If my husband went with birds, or told dirty jokes, or I undressed in front of him in the flat, he got really shocked and angry.'

Perry agreed. 'Yes, he was like that,' she said. 'He hated younger girls, especially if they were all made up, or dressed sexy. He was much younger than me, but I never felt that, because he was so quiet and homely. I think he had never had a real home life before. He loved getting home at night, seeing a big fire and finding a steak grilling for him. He used to say that was the life, and we'd sit there so peaceful and happy. I had never had that sort of kindness from my husband. That's why I'll stick to Robbie, and keep visiting him. He'll only be sixty when he comes out, and he's a good prisoner. He told me he's taken an interest in gardening, and he's planting roses. You see, even in prison he has to make a home of it. He's always needed that.'

They both remembered that Roberts had said he would do anything to avoid going inside again. When he'd come out of prison after his last sentence he'd sworn he would never go back.

On the day of the murders, Lilly Perry was expecting Roberts home by half-past five. 'He didn't come in until seven o'clock,' she said. 'I knew at once something was wrong. He looked as if he had been running; he was all breathless and very flushed. I told him I had some nice rock-salmon and chips for his tea. He looked disgusted. "I can't eat anything," he said, "I'm sick up to here," and he put a hand on his throat.

'I couldn't get him to take anything. June went out of the house then and I said: "Did you hear about the three policemen?" And he said: "Shut up – it was us." He said they had been cruising round looking for a car to knock off to do a job. They couldn't find one, and he decided to pack it in and go home when the police stopped them. Over and over again Robbie kept saying: "If only that fool hadn't asked to look inside the car it wouldn't have happened. June has been warning us for over twelve months that if we were caught with guns we'd get fifteen years. I kept thinking about that. I knew if the coppers turned the car over they'd find the guns and put us all away. I thought it was better to shoot it out than go down for fifteen years."

'Robbie couldn't eat anything that night. He couldn't face a cup of tea. He kept staring at TV all the evening but I don't think he saw one programme. His eyes looked far away and when he turned to me if I spoke to him, they were all misted over. I didn't know what to say to him. I knew he wanted to keep quiet and think. But he stayed very flushed all evening, as if he had a fever.

'I went to bed when TV closed down. I slept with June's little girl. Robbie said he would make himself up a bed on the put-you-up in the lounge. He kept on saying he wanted to burn the van. June came home around three in the morning with some friends, and they were discussing the murders. Robbie jumped out of bed and told them to shut up with their theories because he couldn't sleep.

'In the morning we went shopping for the groceries and when we came back Duddy arrived. He said he had slept with the guns under his bed. Robbie said he wished he had kept one. He said he would feel safer with one in his hand, although he never wanted to use one again. Robbie took the guns from Duddy and hid them under a bed. In the afternoon we took Barry and Samantha for a walk in Paddington recreation grounds. Duddy walked in front with us and Barry. I pushed the pram and Robbie carried Samantha in his arms, to hide his face. We didn't talk among ourselves, only to the children.

'Robbie insisted, as usual, on getting back to the flat in time to watch the wrestling on TV. We all went back and he kept on asking Duddy to go with him and get rid of the Vanguard. He said he was worried about the fingerprints all over it. But Duddy was too scared. He said he didn't want to go anywhere near the car.

'About eight o'clock in the evening he asked me to go with him. I said I didn't want to, but he begged, me to go. We left Duddy behind, babysitting for the Howards and we went to Lambeth together and looked at the car in the garage. We didn't go in, but looked through the wooden slats. The car was still there. He kept on saying he wished Duddy would help him get rid of it.

'When we got home he went on at Duddy again, but he refused to have anything to do with the idea.

'I had hardly slept a wink the night before for worry and I was covered in bumps on the skin which irritated like mad. Robbie said it was nerves. On Sunday morning he said he was going with Duddy to bury the guns. I can't remember if they took bags – I seem to remember they tucked them in their trousers. There were three guns. They were gone about two hours. When they came back I asked if they had thrown them into the river. Robbie said no, they had buried them, but for my own good he wouldn't tell me where. But he said they had walked for miles.

'Robbie couldn't eat any dinner. In the afternoon, when we were looking after the children, he rang Mrs Howard and said she had to come back to take care of the children as he had to go somewhere on urgent business. He told me he had to get out of London and hide away.

'We went to a café and, although I wasn't hungry, I ordered a salad. I told Robbie to eat a solid meal. He ordered his favourite, steak and chips but, after a couple of mouthfuls, he pushed it away and said he felt too sick to eat. We went to the hotel but Robbie talked very little. He was thinking and thinking all the time. After he had booked in we went straight to our room. There were twin beds. Neither of us undressed. People who think we were lovers because we spent the night together must be crazy. No man with the worry Rob had on his mind could have wanted sex. Robbie just lay on top of his bed staring at the ceiling and smoking. I knew he was thinking and I didn't like to speak to him. We didn't sleep at all that night.

'Every now and again Robbie would say: "What a mess I've made of things. What a bloody mess. If only that fool hadn't wanted to inspect the car." In the early hours of the morning he said: "I've got to get away, pet. If I can keep hidden, lie low for a while, the whole thing may blow over. Perhaps we'll be together again in a few months."

'We left the hotel about nine o'clock. Neither of us could eat any breakfast. We left his case in the left luggage place at Euston and we went and brought his camping equipment. Then we got a bus to Epping and he hardly spoke a word on the journey. When he got out he said: "This is as far as you go, love." He cried like a baby then, and I hugged him and cried too. He took his money from his pocket – he had about six pounds – and he gave me six shillings and sixpence. He showed me which bus to get and said: "That should be enough for your fare into town. Sorry to leave you short, but I reckon I'm going to need it more than you."

'I wanted to stay with him but he wouldn't let me. He doesn't hold it against me that I turned evidence. He said: "There was nothing else you could do, pet, you had to do it."'

Mrs Howard was less certain on this sensitive point. 'I think he felt I had said a lot more than I should,' she said. 'We've been friends for eleven years. But what else could I do? The police would have found out anyhow. I am still disgusted and amazed at what happened. I wouldn't have said any of those three were capable of it. Duddy was always a bag of nerves, chewing his fingernails and getting worked up before a job. He was definitely the bottom man of the three. But which of the other two was the Guv'nor is hard to say.'

'Before the weekend was over Roberts read in the newspapers that one man had been detained and that a car had been found. He said: "Christ! That's it. They've got poor Jack. If only Duddy had helped me get rid of the car we'd all be in the clear."'

Perry said Roberts was very fond of Jack. 'He was in a terrible state. He was frightened for himself then, but he was upset on Jack's account as well. If only they hadn't had the guns. Robbie always swore they were only for frighteners. He kept on saying that it would never have happened if only the sergeant hadn't decided to search the van.'

June Howard had a different view about the guns. 'If they were only for frighteners they wouldn't have been loaded, would they? I feel, in a way, it was my fault the whole thing happened. Over and over again I told the boys they would get fifteen years if they were caught with guns. That must have been on their minds when the coppers stopped them. It was panic, sheer bloody stupid panic.'

Chapter 40

At 10:45 a.m. on Thursday, 15 December Detective Superintendent Dick Chitty and Detective Sergeant Berry went to visit Roberts in Wandsworth Prison. Chitty told Roberts that the meeting concerned the disposal of his property but Chitty had another, more pressing motive that he planned to come to later and slip it into the conversation.

'I said to Roberts, "I have come to see you mainly about your personal property and the disposal of it. I want you to check these property sheets and if they are correct I want you to sign them. The property you do not require I want an authorisation from you, which we call a disclaimer. This authorises us to dispose of it."

'Roberts said, "Well, the Daimler is on hire purchase, so I will not be keeping up the repayments on that. Goulston Finance Company must have it back. Lil Perry can have my wristwatch and my small red wireless set and the property which I left in the luggage office at Euston Station, that's the suitcase and whatever was in it. She may not want it. If she doesn't, then get rid of it."

'Roberts then went through the property sheets which he signed as being correct and wrote his directions as to the disposal of the stuff on a disclaimer which he also signed.

'Roberts said, "On the papers you have shown me I can tell you roughly where I nicked some of it and possibly you could get it back to the people. The Tilley lamp I got from a Boys' Club near Bishop's Stortford. The cash you found on me and what you found in the rucksack all came from Lawrences at Sheering. I did that place twice, the last time on that Friday before I was caught. The fire buckets I got from the railways near Stortford. The cheque books and papers I got hold of when I broke into a metalising firm just before you get into Stortford. I really cannot remember where half this stuff came from but if you find out, try and get it back or get rid of it."

'I said, "That has cleared the property as far as we are concerned. We will do as you have requested. There is something else now I want to discuss with you. Mrs Perry has made a statement in which she says she was with you when you bought the guns. The man who sold them to you was a Greek – Christos Costas – at the Moulin Rouge. This man has made a written statement admitting it."

'At this stage Roberts appeared to break down and tears came to his eyes for some reason. I then handed to him the statement made by Costas which he read. He was then handed the statement made by Mrs Perry which he read thoroughly and said, "She is right about what she has said – what do you expect me to do now?"

'I said, "The only thing I want to impress upon you is that there has been enough killing with guns and a stop must be made to this illegal transaction in firearms by certain people. Are you prepared to cooperate in this matter by making a written statement concerning your purchase of the guns?"

'Roberts said, "You said this Greek's name is Christos Costas. I never knew his name as far as I can remember."

'I said, "Did you know him as Alexis?"'

'Roberts said, "What's the difference? You have got what you want and he can take his bloody chances on this lot. I would like to help you because I like you. You have been very fair with me but you will get him down without me. I am not going to make a statement. He did me a favour and I just can't grass on him."

'I said, "So you will not help at all, then."

'Roberts said, "No, I will not. I have no axe to grind with you as I have said before, but I am not grassing on anyone even if they are Greek. What Lil has told you is right; you have got it in writing from her. I am not having anything more to do with that. I'm sorry but that is final."

'I said, "Very good, Roberts, we will leave it at that."'

Detective Sergeant Berry said, 'To clear up a point, and you need not answer this question, when Witney referred to a notebook whilst he was giving evidence, this was in connection with Detective Wombwell. Was there ever such a book in existence?'

Roberts said, 'If you mean when Wombwell was taking down the name and address of Witney by the van, that was right, he had my bloody name and address as well in that book. That is why Wombwell had to go.'

Detective Sergeant Berry said, 'What happened to the book then?'

Roberts said, 'Witney took that from Wombwell after he was shot and I put it down the toilet at Duddy's place.'

Detective Sergeant Berry said, 'I suppose you wore gloves when you did the break-ins around Bishop's Stortford.'

Roberts said, 'Yes, all the time and I carried a gun. Anyway, can I have my guns back? I promise you this, that I will not be kept inside and when I get out and anyone tries to nick me, I would do the same again.'

I said, 'No doubt the prison authorities will look after you well.'

Roberts said, 'They will have to. That wedding photograph you got of me. I know where that came from and I shall do something about that when I get out. It is the only one I ever had taken.'

Detective Sergeant Berry said, 'Have you heard from your wife at all?'

Roberts said, 'No, I will shoot her if I get the chance. I never got to know where she was living up North, otherwise you might have had another one to sort out at the time.'

Berry said, 'Anyway, it is all over now and it has not done anyone any good.'

Roberts said, 'I suppose Witney is still whining. He certainly opened his mouth at the trial to put everything on to us. You know we each had a gun when we left the van, so I don't know what he was frightened about.'

During his interview at HMP Wandsworth with Chitty and Berry, Roberts began by sounding rational, reasonable and cooperative. He was helpful and surprisingly thoughtful, suggesting that the property he stole should be returned to the rightful owners. He then became tearful at one point, perhaps because of the reminder of Lilly Perry and the life with her he had lost. He expressed his appreciation and gratitude for the way Chitty had been 'very fair' with him. But then when Berry began asking questions Roberts changed. He became menacing and the other side of his character was suddenly revealed. He showed no remorse for the killings. He said he would 'not be kept inside' and he'd kill again if anyone tried to 'nick him.' He said he'd shoot his wife Margaret and would have done it when he'd been on the run if he had known where she was.

His final remark about Witney revealed his bitterness towards his old friend. Roberts said that he didn't know why, when Witney was in the witness box, he'd said he was frightened of him, because 'we each had a gun when we left the van' – he meant when they'd left Witney's Vanguard at Vauxhall. That may or may not have been true but what was known for certain by that stage was that when Witney was arrested at his home on Friday night he was not in possession of a firearm. Lilly Perry, Duddy and Roberts himself said in their statements to the police that Duddy looked after the three guns that Friday night. And on Sunday morning all three guns were buried on Hampstead Heath by Duddy and Roberts.

On the following day, Friday, 16 December, Roberts, Duddy and Witney were suddenly moved to top-security prisons – Duddy to the secure wing at Leicester gaol, Witney to Wakefield and Roberts to Parkhurst on the Isle of Wight. During his interview with Chitty, Roberts had made it clear: 'I will not be kept inside'. Following the escapes of two of the 1963 train robbers Charlie Wilson (12 August 1964) and Ronald Biggs (8 July 1965) and the recent embarrassment over the escape of the spy George Blake, the prison authorities were taking no chances. Roberts was driven to Portsmouth in a police van escorted by police cars. After a ninety-minute wait the van was driven aboard the ferry *Camber Queen*. During the crossing to the island the decks were patrolled by a tracker dog and its handler.

Duddy was handcuffed during the two-hour high-speed drive from Pentonville to Leicester. Witney's destination, Wakefield prison, held about 100 murderers serving life sentences. The walls were floodlit at night and scanned by closed-circuit television twenty-four hours a day.

*

Christmas came and went and the unsettling year of 1966 came to an end. On the second day of the New Year the man who had sold the guns to Harry Roberts, thirty-year-old Greek Cypriot Christos Costas was arrested. The following morning Costas appeared at Bow Street Magistrates' Court and was remanded on bail until 7 February in his own recognisance (a security entered into before a court with a condition to perform some act required by law) of £500 and a further surety of £500.

On Wednesday, 18 January, applications were lodged at the Court of Appeal by the legal representatives of Harry Maurice Roberts and John Edward Witney. In trying to build his appeal Witney, who had by now been moved to Durham Prison, wrote to Roberts at Parkhurst asking for his help. This was Roberts's reply:

To: 8797 Jack 'The Grass' Witney,
Durham Prison,
Durham,
England.
From: 2372 H. M. Roberts, Parkhurst Prison.
24-1-1967

To, Jack, the grass, Witney,
    You were right when you thought that your letter would come as a surprise to me. As I have been grassed before, but have never known a man to have the front to

write to me and rub it in, then ask me to help him. You must be out of your tiny mind, in my book you are nothing more than an 18ct slag.

In answer to your question, as to what you should do with the three murder charges on your plate, it is to keep your great big trap shut. Because it did not do you any good to put three murder charges on me, did it?

As for that bit about the guns being in your motor and me being the only one who could explain why they were there, I believe that was the question you put in the sick thing you called a letter. Well, if I may jog your memory for you, it was you who carried the guns from my car to your car on 'that Friday' as you put it so you can stop racking your brains over and over (if you've got any).

As for your appeal I hope it goes down as I know mine will, thanks to your big mouth. As for clearing your name I would not spit on you if you were on fire. You try to remind me that before this 'horrible business' as you put it, we were good friends. I have doubts if I could have been a friend of yours after the way you put me in it.

Well let me remind you that before every job we went on you were the first to tell us, that if the police got in the way we were to shoot to kill so as to help us get away and this was brought up and agreed upon on the Friday morning in question before we went out to get the motors, so why bother with all this 'don't know' screams?

The bit in your letter about not to leave you to rot in prison for something [of] which you are innocent, really killed us here, me and the chaps did not stop laughing for two days, you should be on stage, you toe rag.

That load of 'old codswallop' about your counsel not being able to question me at the trial because I would not go into the witness box, is because you asked me not to go into the box at the Old Bailey and I agreed. I also said that although I would not help you, I would not hinder you and I kept my counsel from questioning you, or is it not convenient for you to remember this now?

As for it being no good you appealing to Duddy to help you, I can promise you it is no good you appealing to me either. And now I think about it I'm double glad that Duddy rowed you well in at the trial, because you are nothing more than an 18ct Grass and don't deserve any better, in fact the two of you were a right 'win double'.

In answer to your question, it's lovely down here on the Island, it's a prison just like any other and if I behave myself I might get out by the year 2000. But one consolation that I've got is that I'm the youngest of us and I will live to be released, that's something you and the other fellow won't be able to do, I hope.

I'm glad it's cold up there where you are. Maybe your tongue will drop off with the cold before you can grass anyone else.

If you write and bother me any more, I shall open my mouth as to where you buried a few bodies.

I'm writing this letter in green ink as it suits you better.

Your 'old friend' that you grassed,

Harry M. Roberts.

On 7 February at Bow Street Magistrates' Court committal proceedings evidence was heard in respect of the charges against Christos Costas, and after time to consider his prospects more carefully he took a surprising turn. In his statement to Chitty on 15 September Costas had said, 'I plead guilty. This means three months at the most. I am not worried.' But after taking legal advice during the intervening four months Costas had come to the conclusion that he really did have something to worry about.

Chapter 41

On Saturday, 11 February a short column on the front page of *The Times* had the headline *GYPSY'S SHARE IN ROBERTS CASE REWARD*. *Mr John Cunningham, the gypsy who was living in a field near the tent hideout of Harry Roberts, was one of three men handed rewards by Detective Superintendent Richard Chitty at Bishop's Stortford police station, Hertfordshire yesterday. Roberts was sentenced to life imprisonment for the murder of three London policemen last year.*

Mr Cunningham received the largest part of the reward. Superintendent Chitty handed over the money on behalf of Sir Joseph Simpson, the Metropolitan Police Commissioner, who during the hunt for Roberts offered a reward of up to £1,000.

Frustratingly for them, readers of *The Times* were not told the amount that Cunningham had received – which was £300. It was not the £1,000 that John Cunningham was hoping for but, given the circumstances, he no doubt counted himself very fortunate.

On Monday, 3 April, the *Daily Mirror* reported: *ROBERTS IN JAIL SWITCH. A prisoner believed to be Harry Roberts, who was jailed for life for the murder of three policemen, was moved secretly to a London prison yesterday. A heavy police escort took the prisoner from Parkhurst Prison on the Isle of Wight, across to the mainland by ferry. The London jail is believed to be Wandsworth. Roberts is due to give evidence at Inner London Sessions this week in connection with charges against a man who is alleged to have sold him three guns last year.*

On Tuesday, 4 April at the trial of Christos Costas before Inner London Sessions Roberts duly appeared in the witness box. In the weeks leading up to the trial there had been concerns that in monitored correspondence between Roberts and Lilly Perry, Roberts had been trying to dissuade her from giving evidence for the prosecution. But despite the pressure Perry stood her ground and stuck to her account of the evening when Roberts had bought the guns from a man in the West End of London. Mr John Mathew for the Crown took Perry through her story of that evening. They'd parked near the Moulin Rouge restaurant. She'd looked after £90 in cash while Roberts went off. Later he'd returned with a man and they'd sat in the back of the car. The man had showed Roberts how the guns worked. She hadn't seen his face because the man had been sitting behind her and it was dark. After the transaction she and Roberts had left and later he had showed her the three guns which she had recently identified to the police.

Perhaps to show who was boss Roberts had agreed to give evidence for the defence. In any case it was at least an opportunity for him to escape briefly from the daily routine of the high-security wing at HMP Parkhurst.

Costas's defence counsel, Mr Joseph Yahuda, came under fire at one point for referring to Harry Roberts as 'Mr' Roberts. The court chairman, Mr Reginald Seaton, said, 'This man is a murderer. Call him Roberts.'

Yahuda suggested, 'We should have respect for witnesses.'

But Seaton was having none of it. 'I told you to call him Roberts. Please don't argue.'

In the witness box Roberts stood in a charcoal-grey suit and appeared to be enjoying the situation, knowing that all eyes were on him. He denied the conversation he'd had with Chitty when he was visited at Wandsworth Prison on the morning of 15 December. Roberts added, '. . . the interview was obtained under false pretences.' He said that it was the first time he had seen the accused, Mr Costas. He had bought the guns from another man in South London, '. . . somewhere near the Old Kent Road.' Roberts's position on the matter was perhaps why Mr Yahuda felt he should be treated with respect. Under cross-examination from prosecution counsel Mr John Mathew, Roberts added, 'I have said that Costas didn't sell me the guns and I will not grass on the man who did.'

Harry Roberts was clearly enjoying being in the witness box. He smiled frequently, and looked relaxed and composed. There was little doubt, however, that the jury believed the evidence of Perry and the police detectives rather than that of Roberts and it took the jury only an hour to decide their verdict. They found Christos Costas guilty on all three counts.

Before sentence was passed, Mr Achilles Antoniades made a plea on behalf of his client. 'It is impossible for anyone in this court to erase from his, or her, mind what happened on that tragic day in August last year. But I would like the court to accept that this simple, uneducated, friendly and fundamentally good-hearted man would never have allowed himself, if he had known, to get involved in a case like this for all the gold in the world.'

It was clearly true that Costas did not, and could not, have foreseen exactly to what use the guns would be put. But whether Costas was 'good-hearted' or not it was self-evident that guns sold illegally and indiscriminately are likely to be used for crime.

The chairman Mr Reginald Seaton had the final word. 'This is a classic example of the dangers of people who transact matters concerning firearms in the criminal world. It is quite apparent that when you went into this you knew quite clearly what was likely to happen. At your door, indirectly, lie the deaths of three courageous policemen. I cannot help but take a serious view of these offences.'

Seaton gave Costas three years for possessing firearms without certificate, contrary to Section 1 of the Firearms Act of 1937 and three years for selling firearms contrary to Section 11 of the same Act, the sentences to run consecutively. He was sentenced to a further three years to run concurrently for having a firearm and ammunition in a public place, contrary to Section 2 of the Firearms Act of 1965.

And so it was that on Thursday, 6 April 1967 the case and files of the Shepherd's Bush Murders were closed. The view of London policing throughout the 1960s is often tarnished by notorious cases of corruption, of questionable methods by which evidence was obtained and criminals caught, of money changing hands and of favours done in shady deals between police officers and members of the underworld. But Operation Shepherd remains a shining example of the diligence, determination and discipline that was more often applied to fighting London's burgeoning – at times bordering on epidemic – levels of crime.

On Tuesday, 30 May 1967 at the Court of Appeal, *Regina v. Roberts and Witney* was considered by the Lord Chief Justice, Lord Justice Sachs and Mr Justice Walker. Roberts was represented by Mr James Burge QC and Mr Kenneth Richardson; Witney by Mr W.M.F. Hudson.

For the legal representatives of Roberts and Witney there had been a good deal of discussion, between themselves as well as with their clients, on whether applying for leave to appeal had sufficient grounds. But there was a chance that five months after the intense pressure and publicity surrounding the Shepherd's Bush Murders trial at the Old Bailey, the Court of Appeal might view things differently in hindsight and see more objectively where there were anomalies.

Summarising the background and facts of the case the Lord Chief Justice said that Roberts had pleaded guilty to the murders of Constable Wombwell and Sergeant Head and had been found guilty of the murder of Constable Fox. He had applied for leave to appeal against the conviction in the case of Fox and his sentence on the firearms charge (with intent to commit an indictable offence or to resist their arrest). Witney had pleaded not guilty to all three murders and sought leave to appeal against his convictions and sentence.

It was reasonably clear, his Lordship said, that as Roberts had admitted he shot Constable Wombwell and Sergeant Head and that Duddy shot Constable Fox, the real question regarding Roberts's conviction was whether the three men had gone out on a common enterprise and that each knew that guns would be used if necessary. He said there was plenty of evidence for that.

But what was the evidence that all three men, knowing that Roberts owned guns and was in the habit of taking them around with him, had agreed to use the guns for anything more than frightening people?

The supporting evidence was slim at best the testimony of June Howard allegedly overhearing Witney say 'If we have them we must be prepared to use them' and John

O'Brien alleging that Witney had said that 'life was his freedom and if necessary he would kill to keep that freedom.' Even if these testimonies could be relied upon and could stand alone, there was never any evidence presented by the prosecution – let alone 'plenty of evidence' – that Roberts and/or Duddy had been parties to the common purpose of *possessing firearms with intent to commit an indictable offence or to resist their arrest.*' And that created the paradox that the man who had shot no one had allegedly said he would shoot to avoid arrest whereas the two men who had shot the police officers had never said this was their preconceived intention.

At the Old Bailey trial in December this was a matter that had been left to the jury to decide. If they were left in no reasonable doubt that there was a common purpose, a conviction on Counts 1, 4 and 7 – the murder charges – and Count 10 – possessing firearms with intent to commit an indictable offence or to resist their arrest – followed inevitably.

What is notable in the original indictment is that Counts 5, 6, 8 and 9 – *Accessory after the fact to murder* – were included to allow for the jury not finding that common purpose was proven and instead finding Roberts and Duddy guilty of the murders they did commit. Being accessories after the fact could then be applied to those murders they did not commit. In the case against Roberts and Duddy they would have still received life sentences for murder. It would only have been Witney who received a lesser sentence for being an accessory after the fact.

Witney's main grounds for appeal was that the trial judge had been wrong in admitting the evidence of O'Brien about an uncorroborated conversation between them in a café in July 1965, a year before the shootings in Braybrook Street, when Witney was alleged to have said that 'he could get a gun at any time, that his freedom was his life and that he would kill for it if necessary.'

The objection to this evidence was, first, that it had no relation in point of time to any matter in this case and, secondly, that it was highly prejudicial to the point that it exceeded its probative value and should have been excluded in the exercise of the judge's discretion. However, the Appeal Court would not say that the judge was wrong in admitting it.

The Lord Chief Justice said that counsel for Roberts had raised another point. The judge had failed to direct the jury that they should not rely on Witney's evidence against Roberts, an accomplice, unless it was corroborated. The Appeal Court's view was that there was ample evidence to the contrary and that it was not a case where the judge should have made such a direction.

The Court of Appeal dismissed Harry Roberts and Jack Witney's applications for leave to appeal against their convictions and sentences and in doing so the jail door was finally shut firmly on Roberts, Witney and Duddy who now had to serve out their life sentences with the recommendation of a minimum of thirty years in prison for each of them.

Four months later on Wednesday, 27 September it was the turn of Christos Costas to be heard by the Court of Appeal before the Master of the Rolls, Mr Justice Widgery and Mr Justice MacKenna. Mr Victor Durand QC and Mr Achilles Antoniades represented the appellant.

Durand said that the chairman at the Inner London Sessions had sentenced his client to the maximum of three years on each count to run consecutively – three years for selling firearms and three years for possessing the same three weapons. The sting of the matter was that the sale of the three guns had been to Harry Roberts, who was later convicted with two other men of murdering three policemen. Durand pointed out that the date of his client's offences were put at March 1966. On 15 November when Roberts was arrested two of the weapons were found among his camp equipment. These dates were important for if Costas's offences had taken place in March, more than six months had passed and he had therefore to be tried on indictment. If he had been tried summarily (without delay) the maximum penalty could have been a year plus a fine of £600. Mr Victor Durand QC's estimation of the likely penalty Costas could have received was another clear reminder of the modest penalties in those days for possessing and carrying unlicensed firearms – nothing like the fifteen years in prison that Roberts said he feared when he murdered Wombwell and then Head.

The Master of the Rolls, giving the judgement of the Court of Appeal, said it was plain that Costas, when he sold the guns, must have known that they were likely to be used in a criminal enterprise and the case had to be regarded broadly. The court dismissed the appeal against the six-year sentence given by the chairman, Mr. R.E. Seaton, of Inner London Quarter Sessions on 5 April. But the fact remained that, while Christos Costas must have known that the guns were likely to be used in some kind of 'criminal enterprise', the offences for which he'd been found guilty were possession of unlicensed firearms and selling them, not the purpose to which they were later put. And if the guns he sold had not been used several months later to murder three police officers, Costas would have received a considerably lighter sentence in the first place.

Chapter 42

The lives and day-to-day existences of Harry Maurice Roberts, John Edward Witney and John Duddy, after they were found guilty of the murders of David Wombwell, Chris Head and Geoff Fox and sent to prison for thirty years, are stories all of their own. They warrant inclusion in the fifty-year-long epilogue. Some are significant, others are bizarre and amusing, one is shocking and arguably tragic. Without them the arc of the story is not complete.

By the autumn of 1972 Harry Roberts was still being held in the high-security wing, known as The Cage, at Parkhurst Prison. His mother had been true to her word. After Roberts's trial at the Old Bailey six years earlier she had told newspaper reporters, 'I suppose I will still visit him in jail. After all, I am his mother.'

On Thursday, 30 November 1972 seventy-three-year-old Dorothy Roberts travelled from her flat in Augustus Street, NW1, taking the train from Waterloo station to Portsmouth and a ferry to the Isle of Wight. Prison staff later recalled that she was wearing a fur coat and trousers that day and they had not seen her wearing trousers before.

The following morning a routine fortnightly search was made of Harry Roberts's cell, No. 218, which he had occupied since 1970. The prison officer noticed a square of board fixed to the wall behind Roberts's bed. The thin plywood was barely noticeable because it was painted the same colour as the cell walls. The bed was pulled out and when the board was removed the officer discovered a sizeable hole in the wall. The cell was then searched meticulously and various prohibited items were discovered skilfully concealed: a pair of wire cutters, a short-bladed dinner knife with a sharpened end, a pair of sunglasses, a home-made wood brace and some drill bits, a gas lighter, newspaper cuttings containing maps of the Isle of Wight, a list of addresses, screwdrivers, a business reply card containing details of replica guns and four £5 notes.

When a pair of bolt cutters was discovered in a washroom adjoining the prison visiting area at Parkhurst, the prison authorities concluded that there was a connection between Harry Roberts's plan to escape through the wall of his cell and the recent visit from his mother.

Dorothy Roberts was arrested and charged with attempting to aid her son's escape and in February the following year she appeared at Newport Magistrates' Court on the Isle of Wight. After hearing the evidence the magistrate referred the matter to Winchester Crown Court.

On Wednesday, 21 March 1973, Mrs Dorothy Roberts, represented by John Mortimer QC (also a dramatist, screenwriter and author), pleaded not guilty to intent to facilitate the escape of her son, Harry Maurice Roberts, on 30 November 1972.

Opening the case for the prosecution, Mr Victor Watts said, 'The Crown say that while on a visit to her son at Parkhurst, Mrs Roberts took with her a pair of bolt cutters and left them for him concealed in a washroom.' Watts mentioned that Mrs Roberts was wearing trousers that day and that had surprised prison officers as they had never seen her wearing trousers on previous visits. He explained to the jury that during a routine search of Roberts's cell the day after his mother's visit a large hole in the wall was found covered by a piece of board to disguise it.

In the witness box at Winchester Crown Court the following day, Mr Victor Easen, principal security officer for the maximum-security block at Parkhurst, told the court that Roberts had been constructing a two-and-a-half-foot model power boat over the last twenty months and had a full set of carpentry tools at his disposal. He added that it was unlikely that there would be a pair of bolt cutters in the tool chest. But such a tool would be vital in an attempt to escape and indeed if Roberts had dug his tunnel another two inches his next obstacle would have been the wire security fencing.

When asked by Mortimer about access to the washroom Easen replied that about twenty people might have been in a position to have access to the washroom door key. To cement the point Mortimer suggested that the bolt cutters could, therefore, have been left by any one of those key holders or other prison visitors on that day and there was no evidence to connect them to his client, Mrs Roberts.

Mr Bernard Wilson, another security officer for the maximum-security block, made the startling revelation that this was not the first time Roberts had attempted to escape in this way. Prior to being moved to cell No. 218 an identical hole in the wall, disguised in an identical way, had been discovered in Roberts's previous cell. Wilson said that in his opinion the tunnel in cell 218 would have taken three or four months to construct.

Mortimer suggested that cooperation by a member of staff could not be ruled out and Wilson conceded. Mortimer asked, 'There was an absolute breakdown in security?' Again, Wilson had to agree.

The prosecution case became ever more fragile as other prison officers were questioned by the astute and articulate John Mortimer QC over the course of the trial. Mr Gordon Duffield said that Mrs Roberts had not been searched properly on 20 November. They were very short of staff. Duffield said, 'We try to be humane over visitors and give people as long together as possible.' He added that as far as he knew no one had looked in the bags of visitors, including that of Mrs Roberts.

On Monday, 26 March, the fourth day of her trial, it was Dorothy Roberts's turn to stand in the witness box at Winchester Crown Court. In response to a question from the prosecution counsel she denied talking to Harry Roberts during the six years since he had been convicted for murder about any plans for escape. She wept openly as she told of her fortnightly visits to the Isle of Wight to take her son 'a little food and cigarettes'. She said. 'I visit him because he is my son. But he did not confide in me. He used to say I am too old.'

The following day, in closing the case for the defence, Mortimer said, 'Roberts had collected a veritable armoury of escape equipment without her help. Are we to believe he needed the help of a septuagenarian arthritic cook to come hobbling in with one of the implements?'

The jury were in retirement for five and a half hours debating what seemed to be a straightforward enough case. It was possible that Dorothy Roberts had smuggled a pair of bolt cutters into Parkhurst prison for the purpose of helping her son to escape. Given the lax security there was certainly the opportunity to do so. It was even conceivable that Mrs Roberts would have liked nothing better than to see her son escape and might have discussed it with him. But where was the proof beyond circumstance and conjecture that she had actually attempted to aid him? Finally the jury returned, the foreman announced their verdict and after a week and a half of legal ping-pong at considerable public expense Dorothy Roberts was finally free to escape the torment of Winchester Crown Court and take the train back home to London.

With time on his hands Harry Roberts built models and whiled away the hours painting, an activity at which he was quite accomplished. On page three of the *Daily Express* on Monday, 4 October 1976 the infamous photograph of Harry Roberts appeared next to the headline: *How Anne and Anoushka were both captured on canvas in HM Prison.* The article below reported that portraits of Princess Anne by Colin Wood and a portrait of German-born model and actress Anoushka Hempel by 'police killer Harry Roberts' had been offered for sale at an auction of ninety-five lots held in the Thomas à Becket public house in South London the previous day. The Princess Anne painting was sold for the princely sum of £6 but there was no mention of how much Roberts's artwork fetched.

Five years later John Duddy was at Parkhurst prison when he was taken ill in his cell. The following morning, Monday, 9 February 1981, under HOME NEWS on page 5 of *The Times* was a perfunctory six-line report: '*John Duddy, aged 52, serving life imprisonment for his part in the murder of three policemen in London in 1966, died last night after falling ill in his cell at Parkhurst prison, Isle of Wight.*'

Having served nineteen years of his 30-year sentence the entreaties of Jack Witney finally bore fruit in 1985. After consultation with the Lord Chief Justice, the Conservative Home Secretary Leon Brittan decided that a distinction could be drawn between Witney, who had not fired any shots, and the other two co-defendants who had. Witney was transferred to Leyhill open prison in South Gloucestershire. In November 1988 the Parole Board advised that Witney no longer presented a risk to the public. In February 1989 Brittan's successor Douglas Hurd decided that Witney could be released after a further two years.

In 1991, despite strong objections raised in both houses of Parliament and by the Police Federation that Witney had not served the full thirty years recommended by the trial judge, Mr Justice Glyn-Jones, Home Secretary Kenneth Baker approved the Parole Board's recommendation that sixty-one-year-old John Edward Witney should be released on licence.

Witney was first placed in a hostel in Douglas Road, Horfield, Bristol and later moved to an alms house in Hotwells. Across the road Witney drank in the Rose of Denmark pub. Simon, one of many friends he made there, still remembers him clearly.

'Jack Witney may have been involved with the killing of three policemen but I knew him well for the whole eight years that he lived in Bristol. He was a very kind and generous person who deserved to live out his days among the many friends he had made here since being released.

'The first time I met him in the Rose of Denmark pub

in Hotwells he was very quiet but after a few days he said that he had just moved into the alms house opposite after a long prison sentence. He told us the complete story, expecting to be shunned by everyone and he was obviously ashamed of his past and humbled by the last twenty-five years in jail.

'I think everyone just saw what a nice chap he was and decided that he had paid his dues and deserved a chance for a life. Jack often came to the pub after that and to others in the area too where he also made many good friends.

'He was doing really well and after about two years he managed to get himself a job with a haulage firm driving a van. He worked hard for about three years but was then involved in an accident with an out-of-control HGV. He was badly injured and after a few weeks he realised he was having trouble with the stairs at the alms house and moved into the ex-prisoner accommodation in Horfield.

'About eight months after the move he said that he hated living there and tried to move back to the alms house but it was full. He started looking for a flat in Hotwells and after a little while he found one but the probation service said he could not move and had to stay put.

'After that he caught the bus from Horfield to Hotwells most days and visited his friends. After the accident Jack applied for compensation and a year or so later it arrived. Jack discussed what he should do with the money with several of us in the pub. He came to the conclusion that

Premium Bonds were a safe bet and he could always cash them in if he needed the money. A few weeks later he came in with two £10,000 bonds; almost every penny from the compensation was in his bonds and he was very happy.'

On Sunday, 15 August 1999 Witney had a row with fellow resident Nigel Evans at the hostel in Horfield where they both lived. Evans, who had a history of minor crime, was living at the hostel after his release from prison. Thirty-eight-year-old Evans had a heroin habit which led to him running up £750 of rent arrears.

On Monday morning, Jack Witney was found dead in a pool of blood at his home. A post-mortem revealed that he had suffered horrific head injuries.

Evans appeared before Bristol Magistrates' Court on Wednesday, 18 August 1999, charged with the murder of John Edward Witney. Detective Chief Inspector Mike Hems told the court, 'We are investigating the murder here as opposed to the events in 1966. There is no connection with his convictions in 1966.'

At Bristol Crown Court on Thursday, 25 May 2000 Nigel Evans stood trial for murder. It was said that Evans and Witney had rowed over money and daily household chores like washing-up. Evans attacked Witney, beating him around the head with a hammer. He grabbed him by the throat and Witney, who by then was quite frail, was throttled to death. Evans then stole a chequebook and credit card.

The Shepherd's Bush Murders

Nigel Peter Evans was found guilty by unanimous verdict and when sentencing him to life imprisonment, Mrs Justice Janet Smith told him: 'It is my view that there was much more behind the way in which this dispute arose than you have told us.'

Witney's drinking pal Simon at the Rose of Denmark has a theory about that. 'Within the year Jack was murdered at the hands of Nigel Peter Evans, a petty thief and heroin addict who was sharing the hostel with Jack. We heard at the time that Evans was under the impression that he could just cash in the bonds at a post office – I guess the heroin had fried his brain. Jack will always be missed by those of us lucky enough to know him in the eight years he lived among us.'

Some may take the view that the murder of Witney was poetic justice or just deserts. But it was a cruel twist of fate that Jack Witney – convicted of murder despite having killed no one and after serving nearly twenty-five years in prison – at the age of sixty-nine, when there was a chance for him to enjoy the remaining years of his life, should end up becoming the victim of a brutal murder.

Chapter 43

On Saturday, 25 November 1995, the *Week-ending* magazine of the *Daily Express* ran a feature article entitled: *Why brutal killer Harry Roberts should not be freed after 30 years in jail. When Life really has to be life.* The report recapped the story of the 1966 Shepherd's Bush Murders but the point of it all was to remind readers that in a little over a year *'Britain's most hunted and hated man'* would have served the minimum time in prison recommended by the trial judge, '. . . *although the sentence is up for review next year a final decision can only come from the Home Secretary . . . Even 30 years on, the callous killing of three policemen sears into the mind. It will be long before the Massacre of Braybrook Street can be forgotten.'*

Despite the hyperbole and the political stance of the newspaper, the wider view in 1995 was that the words of the trial judge, Mr Justice Glyn-Jones, when sentencing Roberts still held true: 'I think it unlikely that any Home Secretary in the future, regarding the enormity of the crime, will ever think fit to show mercy by releasing you on licence. It is one of the cases in which a sentence of imprisonment for life may well be treated as meaning exactly what it says.'

However, on Wednesday, 29 May 2002 the *Daily Express* had a new twist in the story of Harry Roberts and the Shepherd's Bush Murders, by which time Roberts had been in prison for thirty-six years. On page ten was the familiar black and white image of Harry Roberts in his late twenties. The headline was: *The mad ruling gives freedom to 1,300 killers.* And the double-page article had the details. *More than 1,300 convicted murderers will have their sentences reviewed after a European court yesterday stripped David Blunkett of the power to decide their fate. The Court of Human Rights removed the right of British Home Secretaries to decide when murderers should be released, once they have served minimum jail terms.*

The repercussions of the Strasbourg Court ruling sparked another article three days later on 1 June 2002 in the *Daily Express*, whose editors now had the Harry Roberts release story firmly fixed in their sights. A double-page feature on pages six and seven was entitled: *Cop killer's fun – EXCLUSIVE. Another monster to be freed by Euro court slips away to party with Kray widow. As relatives of the murdered officers still struggle to come to terms with their grief, Roberts has been living it up on the outside as the day for his release draws nearer.*

In one sickening display, the silver-haired triple killer is seen smirking, surrounded by red balloons and blowing out candles on a cake as he celebrates his 65th birthday.

There were two large colour photographs of Roberts

on the opposite page, one smiling inanely amongst the red balloons and the second in an amusement arcade, playing a slot machine with Kate Kray chatting at his side.

The report recapped the European Court of Human Rights ruling and highlighted a perverse paradox that in focusing on the rights of convicted murderers sentenced to life imprisonment it appeared to take less account of the lifelong anguish suffered by their victims' families. '. . . *It must be pure hell to see this man living it up like this. Geoffrey Fox's son Paul, 52, said, "He looks as if he's had a whale of a time allegedly serving a life sentence. What a joke the criminal justice system is. While I've had to suffer the pain and torture of growing up without a father since the age of 15 this man is having a ball.*

"I'm disgusted and outraged. He ruined my life and I will never forget what happened. But he seems to have forgotten easily enough. My dad was protecting his country and what has happened here is a total lack of respect." '

Of course, the prison authorities had not approved Roberts's impromptu birthday party ten months earlier but the criminal justice system had provided the opportunity. At the time Roberts was living in the relative comfort of a category 'C' prison at Sudbury Park, Derbyshire. As part of his rehabilitation programme he was working on day release in an animal sanctuary at Alfreton several miles away. But that trust and freedom had allowed Roberts to bunk off work to enjoy the party held in his honour at the Hollywood Bowl leisure centre in Sheffield the previous summer.

*

A former employee at the sanctuary told how he worked alongside one of Britain's most notorious killers. 'Harry Roberts had been coming here for two days a week and would do odd jobs around the place as well as walking the dogs. But more recently he had been coming here five days a week. No one knew who Harry was when he started coming here. We knew he was a prisoner but we had no idea what he was inside for. He never spoke about the prison to any of us. He seemed to have lots of money, I don't know where he could have got it from, but he was always buying the dogs little presents – toys and treats. He would even buy them new beds out of his own pocket if any of them were in need of a better place to sleep. He had a real thing for the dogs here.

'I was watching TV one night and it featured what Harry Roberts had done. I suddenly realised that the man on the television was the man I had been working with. I couldn't believe that this old man was capable of what he had done in his past. It was a real shock.'

Just when things were looking promising for Harry Roberts and he was working unsupervised at the animal sanctuary he had proved incapable of living up to the trust that had been placed in him. There was the press report of his sixty-fifth birthday celebrations. Some reports claimed he was supposed to be working; others said that it had happened while he was on five days' 'home leave'. The association with Kate Kray, widow of notorious East End gangster Ronnie Kray, breached the conditions of his release that he should not associate with known criminals or their fraternity. Later in October 2001 it was alleged that Roberts was involved in drug dealing and bringing contraband into the prison. He admitted to having bank accounts containing £10,000 but denied that the money had come from criminal activities. However, with no means of earning money legitimately and with no family, if the funds were not income generated from crime his bank balance could only have been made up from accumulated handouts from admiring fellow criminals.

Three weeks before the 1 June 2002 *Daily Express* article Roberts's work placement at the animal sanctuary was suddenly terminated. He was transferred first to Lincoln prison and then to Channings Wood, Devon. A prison service spokesman said, 'He has been transferred for taking unauthorised trips when he should have been reporting to the dogs' home for community resettlement.' There was no explanation why Roberts's daily excursions from prison had not been subject to any kind of monitoring or supervision.

On the subject of Harry Roberts's parole David Wombwell's widow, Gillian, added her voice to the chorus of protests in a personal letter to the Prime Minister, Tony Blair, asking for 'victims' rights to be heard.' Gillian Wombwell, who had been left to bring up two young children, was understandably horrified by the prospect of Roberts's release but she also raised the important point that he had never voiced any remorse. 'How can this man hope to be rehabilitated into life outside prison? What if he murders again? Yet more families will have to endure what I have had to suffer for years. By committing cold-blooded murder, he has forgone the right to freedom – for ever.'

However, with no other purpose or direction to his life in prison Harry Roberts remained resolute and undeterred. Solicitor Simon Creighton of Bhatt Murphy, representing Roberts, made a challenge on behalf of his client that his continued detention breached Roberts's rights under Article Six of the Human Rights Act 1998. On 20 April 2005 an appeal was made to the House of Lords in which Roberts, now aged sixty-eight and having served thirty-eight years in prison, claimed he was being denied parole because of 'secret evidence' and accused former Home Secretary David Blunkett of trampling on his human rights by using 'secret allegations, secret evidence and a secret trial.'

Roberts was told that following further investigations he would be given the opportunity to respond when his case came before the Parole Board. However, behind the scenes the question of Harry Roberts' release on licence had become ever more complex. Step by step the Parole Board had unwittingly constructed an untenable situation of their own making. There was another factor in assessing Roberts's suitability for parole that pushed the Board into 'breaking new ground.' Although a prisoner would normally have a chance to challenge allegations made against them the Board announced that the information it had received was 'too sensitive' for disclosure, even to his solicitor. After Roberts's April 2005 appeal to the House of Lords, and several lengthy hearings the following autumn, the Parole Board finally wrote to Roberts on 12 December 2006, saying that it would not be recommending his release from jail. It stated: 'While in open conditions, you demonstrated that you are untrustworthy, utterly egocentric and highly manipulative.'

Roberts's solicitor, Simon Creighton, made a comment to the press: 'I have never believed in conspiracy theories until this case. I feel there is a concerted effort to prevent Roberts from ever leaving prison.'

On the face of it the whole thing did sound rather bizarre and arguably unfair from a legal standpoint. But the problem the Parole Board faced was that if Roberts was allowed to see the evidence against him it would be immediately obvious who had provided it. And the Board had guaranteed anonymity to the source of the information because of the source's fear of retaliation. And reprisals were one of the most worrying aspects of the confidential evidence.

The Parole Board was forced to come up with an unprecedented solution and eventually agreed to disclose the 'secret evidence' to an independent lawyer who would then represent Roberts at a future hearing. But Roberts would still not be allowed to hear the evidence against him.

On Saturday, 28 February 2009 Harry Roberts was back in the news. The *Daily Telegraph* headline was: *The notorious killer Harry Roberts could be freed from prison within months after serving 42 years in jail.*

> *Roberts, who was jailed for life for the murder of three unarmed policemen in a west London street, has already completed the first stage of a Parole Board hearing, which he believes will pave the way for his release, it has been reported. The killer hopes a final hearing will find that he is no longer a risk to the public and will order his immediate release. He has already served 12 years more than the minimum sentence recommended by his trial judge. A detailed plan to resettle Roberts in the community will have to be drawn up by the prison and Probation Service, including the provision of housing and benefits. He would have to report at least once a week to a probation officer. Ministers will be powerless to halt his release, even though they remain concerned that any such decision will provoke public fury and that his personal safety could be at risk.*

The report included comments from chairman of the Metropolitan Police Federation, Peter Smyth: 'There are some evil acts for which there is no forgiveness. Every police officer still considers these murders to be one of the most awful events in our history.'

Chris Head's eldest sister, eighty-five-year-old Edna Palmer from Gillingham, Kent, told *The Times*: 'Harry Roberts should never be released. There will never be enough time to make up for the terrible thing that he did. He is a dangerous man and, despite the time, he should remain in jail.'

The *Daily Telegraph* article reviewed Roberts's previous Parole Board hearings, so far as they were known, and the unusual circumstances that had surrounded them.

Last year it was revealed that bugging devices planted in a prison telephone were used illegally to record privileged conversations between Roberts and his solicitor. Roberts had first been transferred to an open prison in 2001 in what was thought to be a prelude to his release. He was returned to closed conditions after allegations that he was involved in drug dealing and bringing contraband into prison. The Home Office used anti-terrorist legislation to prevent Roberts or his lawyers from seeing the evidence presented to the Parole Board to keep him in a secure jail, on the grounds that the sources of the information would be placed at risk.

Roberts lost an appeal to the House of Lords seeking disclosure of the evidence in 2005 and the next year he was turned down for parole. However, the confidential letters and statements containing the allegations were leaked and sent to Roberts at his cell in 2007. The case was referred back to the Parole Board.

It was not until later in 2009 that the mysterious and disturbing story behind Harry Roberts's past parole applications finally became public knowledge after an injunction was lifted on Friday, 17 April in the High Court, enabling Joan Cartwright to tell about her ordeal for the first time.

On 19 April Chief Reporter for the *Mail on Sunday*, Ian Gallagher, broke the story in an article headlined: *Police killer Harry Roberts's five-year terror campaign to silence woman who kept him behind bars.*

Until today, her identity shielded by a court order, she has never spoken about the time Roberts spent at her sanctuary, or what happened after he left. Justice Secretary Jack Straw was last night facing urgent questions about how Britain's most notorious police killer was able to terrorise a woman whose evidence blocked his release from jail. From his cell, Harry Roberts orchestrated a horrifying five-year campaign of intimidation designed to silence 65-year-old Joan Cartwright and her son James.

It began at the end of 2000 when Roberts wrote to Joan Cartwright's animal sanctuary explaining that he had spent 35 years in jail. Now aged 64, he wanted to make the best of what remained of his life and needed to get a job before he could be released. He was a trained bricklayer. Could they help? There was no mention that his crime was murder. Joan Cartwright assumed that Roberts had heard through the probation service of how she had taken in community-service offenders. Her family had been taking on young offenders doing community service for some years. The scheme worked well. The sanctuary got jobs done for nothing and the workers were always supervised by probation officers, who liaised closely with Joan.

In an exclusive interview Cartwright told the *Mail on Sunday*: 'If any problems arose, the Probation Service would simply tell the offender they were needed elsewhere and move them. There was no mention of a complaint, so there was no risk of a grudge.'

Before starting work, Roberts and a prison officer met Joan's son James, 44, who runs a farm near his mother's sanctuary. It struck him as odd that the officer appeared to defer to his prisoner. 'Harry seemed to be the dominant one of the two. He was very forthright and was asking all the questions,' he told the *Mail* reporter. 'The prison officer didn't tell us what Harry had done and, because Harry was standing next to him, we didn't have the opportunity to ask. The officer stayed about ten minutes and after that we had no contact with anyone from the prison for ten months. No letters, no phone calls, much less a visit.'

Weeks later, Roberts started working at the farm, first for three days a week, which was later extended to five. At first, Joan and her family were too busy to be unduly worried by Roberts. Besides, they had decided not to prejudge him.

'We are liberal, community-minded people and we thought it a wonderful opportunity to help someone,' said Joan. 'We didn't ask about his past. He was very good at making us feel sorry for him and stressed it was of the utmost importance that the prison must never receive an adverse report about him. He told us he'd never get out if that happened. And his freedom meant everything to him.'

On his first day as a 'prison outworker' at the East Midlands animal sanctuary and farm run by Joan's family, Roberts betrayed no hint of the terrors that lay in store for his hosts. He was charming and polite. And if Joan found his request for tea a little impertinent, it was quickly forgotten as he recounted a story about his mother and his difficult childhood.

'Looking back, it was a technique to arouse my sympathy, and it worked,' she said. 'He was appreciative of the simplest things. He praised everything; he was sympathetic, easy to talk to and well versed in current affairs. Like me, he was keenly interested in books – although he preferred thrillers and horror stories – and he always knew what was on the paperback bestseller list. He is a clever and eloquent man.'

However, something about the name Harry Roberts troubled Joan's accountant husband, Peter, and while in the library one day he decided to do some digging. Within minutes he found the face of his bricklayer staring at him from the front cover of a book about infamous criminals. 'When he came home and told me I was horrified,' said Joan.

Their perception of Harry instantly altered. 'He was no longer a cheerful old man. We saw him from then on as a dark and dangerous criminal,' Joan explained. 'A very fit, tough guy, whose cold eyes looked at you in a different way. From that point on, nothing was ever the same again. We were trapped.

'Harry is intuitive and although I maintained the veneer of normality and friendship, he very quickly picked up on the fact that we knew. We were out in the car one day and he started telling me that he was famous, that people sang songs about him. He said someone had recognised him at the railway station and given him £10.

'From then on, Roberts began to open up about his past, and talk expansively about his "lifestyle philosophy". He told me one day, "*You can never trust honest people because they always let you down*". Everything bad was good to him. People who committed heinous crimes were his heroes.'

'He particularly revered Kenneth Noye, the Brinks Mat gold bullion robber, who had also killed a police officer. He thought he was brilliant because he was successful and spoke about how, even though he was in prison, he had done so well for himself with all his money and mansion,' said Joan.

'Harry was always saying kidnapping was underrated. He thought there should be more kidnapping as it was an easy way to make money. He would talk more and more about horrible crimes. He didn't understand that people are revolted by things that are normal and everyday to him. It was horrible to hear him talk like this. He suddenly became the boss; he effectively took control.'

With the truth about him in the open, Roberts allowed his temper, which he'd hitherto kept in check, to manifest itself. 'He got me to cook him breakfast most mornings and everything had to be just so,' said Joan. 'Once he held his knife and fork so they were pointing towards the ceiling, banged them on the table and said, "I'm not eating that."

'Then he flung his fried egg on the floor. The yolk was too hard. He said the white had to be firm and the yolk "soft but not too soft". He was really angry and stomped off outside. After that I never got them wrong.'

Afraid of Roberts's temper and suspecting that either he had prison officers under his control or that police had him under surveillance, Joan did not go to the authorities, despite his increasingly demanding behaviour. By spring 2001, Roberts was ordering either Joan or her husband to pick him up from the railway station in the morning, even though he was supposed to make his own way to the sanctuary. 'We'd be in bed and the phone would ring. He'd say, "Good morning, Harry here." He was very specific and would say he'd be at the station in, say, 17 minutes. One of us would scramble out of bed and drive there. We were thinking he'd kill us if we didn't. Once, when I was three minutes late, he stood there fuming. His piercing blue eyes flashed and his cheeks turned red. It was like a headmaster ticking off a child. He said, "I'm cold and I've been waiting. What happened this time?" '

Within weeks, members of what Roberts called 'the serious crime fraternity' began turning up at the sanctuary to take him out to lunch and pay their respects.

'They were people he'd been in prison with, cellmates, and some of them, the police told us later when we identified them from mugshots, were among the most serious criminals in the country,' recalled Joan. 'They had smart suits and drove big, expensive cars and looked as if they'd come straight out of *The Sopranos*.'

She witnessed them handing him wads of cash – thousands of pounds on one occasion. 'They worshipped him and Harry loved it. They turned up at the house and he behaved as though the farm belonged to him, as if he was delighting in how well he'd done. They'd come into the kitchen and I would make them tea. They were dreadful people and talked about people they knew, people they'd been in prison with, and they talked about crime. One of them referred to Harry as "The Butcher". I'm sure it was a joke but it freaked me out; it really scared me.

'In July that year, a few of his friends, along with Kate Kray, the widow of East End gangster Ronnie Kray, took him out to a TGI Friday restaurant to celebrate his birthday. He was in a bad mood because he didn't get to sit next to Kate, whom he adored,' said Joan, who was also at the party. 'He kicked up a fuss about his steak, which wasn't cooked to his liking. He summoned the waitress over and had it sent back.'

With no one monitoring his progress, Roberts found he had time on his hands and decided to buy a car – a flagrant breach of rules for prisoners like him.

'He said he was going to apply for a driving licence and said he would use our address on the application because he obviously couldn't use the prison,' said Joan. 'Our eyes rolled.'

A few weeks later he bought a Volvo for £1,800 in cash from a nearby garage. The money, the Parole Board later said, came from the ex-convicts whom he met while on day release.

'I had to go with him and he told the man there that it would be in my name. He then made me ring up my insurers to get him added to my policy. This filled me with absolute dread. From this point on, every time I went somewhere – to the shops or a friend's house, he'd say, "I'll drive you." That set a dreadful precedent.'

Chapter 44

Joan Cartwright's account continued:

'Everywhere I went, I had this horrible man with me. All my driving had to be done with Harry Roberts. It was getting more and more desperate every day. He would even drive the car, illegally, without me. I remember him picking up one of his prison visitors and bringing him to the house on his birthday.

'He drove back to the prison one day because he'd missed his train. I assumed he would park nearby and walk the rest of the way so no one would see him but he drove straight up to the gate and pulled up outside the prison officer's little hut.

'I thought the officer would see the pleading in my face, but he said something like, "Hi, Harry, how are you?" He was not in the least alarmed and that moment crystalised things for me: I knew we could never go to the prison for help.'

To increase his hold over the family, explained Joan, Roberts talked of how he had 'prison officers in his pocket' and said if anyone rang the prison he would get to hear about it. 'We didn't know whether that was true or not but it terrified us. The more time passed without any contact from the prison, the more we feared what he said was true.

'And while he was with us he sent a package to the prison officer who brought him to us that first day. There was what looked like a private address on it, rather than the prison. After Harry eventually left, the police found the recorded-delivery receipt in the glove compartment of his car. We asked them over a period of time whether they had investigated, but they kept fudging the issue.

'We agonised over whether to go to the police, but didn't do so for the same reason. We did think, as well, that perhaps the police were secretly monitoring Roberts and that they would see what he was up to and pull him out. What fools we were. He was doing more entertaining than working and there was nothing we could do.'

After six months, Roberts's placement at the sanctuary should theoretically have come to an end. Only by proving he was being paid could he extend it. 'He forced my husband to falsify the accounts to make it seem as though he was getting paid,' Joan said. 'My husband hated doing this. He is as straight as a die, a religious, decent man. He is the treasurer of a lot of voluntary organisations and doing this made him ill.'

At this point, Joan and her family could see no end in sight. For his eventual release, Roberts had already been allocated a flat near the sanctuary and he spoke of 'walking across the fields to see us every day,' Joan said. 'I envisaged cooking him these perfect fried eggs for the rest of my life.'

Sometimes, as Roberts sat at the kitchen table, shocking her with gory stories of his criminal past, Joan would strike back, admonishing him for the path he'd chosen in life. 'I would be bold and say how wrong it all was. And sometimes I would tell him that I was off to Mass to say a prayer for him and light a candle for him. He hated that, and told me not to do it.'

Little by little, Roberts was trapping Joan and her family further. James Cartwright recalled: 'I mentioned one day that I was going to the bank. He said he'd come with me. You can't say no to him. While there, he surprised me and said, "I have got to open an account."'

Roberts had a driver's licence, which was all he needed to open a savings account at that time – even though this was another serious breach of prison rules. 'I had been banking there for years,' James said. 'So when the question of his address came up, Harry said he'd been overseas and was now staying with me. Because the guy at the bank knew me he said that was fine.

'I remember that as the man went away to get the forms, Harry said the last time he was in a bank he was robbing it. He explained that it was his job to jump over the counter with a bat in his hand to frighten the tellers. He said that was the part he really enjoyed.'

By autumn 2001, he became more threatening towards Joan, and James devised a plan to extricate themselves from their terrifying predicament using an intermediary with political contacts who would 'go straight to the top'.

'We were just so frightened. Our every waking hour was spent wondering how we could get out of this without being kidnapped or killed. But at this stage, no matter how frightened we were, something had to happen. He had made some terrible remarks and something had to break.

'All we wanted was for Harry to be transferred somewhere else without implicating us so we could get back to our nice, ordinary lives and forget all about this awful time. But in spite of our friend stressing that this was a matter requiring the utmost diplomacy, the Prison Service reacted in an incomprehensible way that immediately put us in danger.

'Instead of coming up with an excuse for moving him on, they told Roberts that serious allegations had been made against him, which sent him into a fury. He wanted to know who had done this.

'Then they tried to keep us out of it and told him that the allegations concerned contraband and visits to London. The next day, the police came round to see us and said Harry was in closed conditions and that we'd never see him again.'

However, Roberts was still allowed to proceed with his parole case, although he was told that it would be opposed by evidence supplied by witnesses whose identity would not be revealed to him.

'Our sense of relief was short-lived, though,' recalled Joan. 'By the time the police had got to the end of the drive, Harry was on the phone spitting blood and spelling out what was going to happen to whoever was responsible. He was going to have them torn limb from limb.'

Joan and her family were catapulted into a nightmarish world of panic alarms and witness-protection plans and the very real fear that 'any one of us might be killed'. But despite assurances from the police and Prison Service that he would never bother Joan and her family again, Roberts's return to a closed jail was simply the beginning of what she describes as 'a spiral of fear even worse than before.'

Roberts rang her five nights a week, always around seven p.m. Sometimes he would be angry, threatening to tear to shreds the 'secret witnesses' denying him his chance of freedom after nearly four decades in jail.

More terrifying still was the sinister way in which he continually asked about her welfare and pretended they were friends, ringing off with the words, 'Love you lots'. Joan had to maintain her part in the phoney friendship so Roberts would not suspect that she was the one who had lodged the complaint. Coached about what to say by Prison Service officials, she expressed mock dismay at the way Roberts had been treated. 'It was horrendous, so stressful and every fibre of my being hated it,' she said. 'Sometimes he'd say he was sending one of his friends round to take me out for a "nice drive", which was truly terrifying. I had to think of excuses fast.'

Joan knew all about his friends because he had brought them to the sanctuary and, later, delighted in shocking her with tales of their exploits. 'There was one, a man from the North-East, who Harry said was a specialist with chainsaws,' she said. 'Harry described very graphically how he cut people up with them. And he later sent me a newspaper article about him. This man had been in my house and I'd made him a cup of tea.'

It was impossible to avoid Roberts. 'It got so our whole lives were geared around not missing his seven p.m. call,' Joan said.

After several months of constant phone calls and demands that she write to him on an almost daily basis, Joan, sick with stress, went on holiday to Lanzarote with her daughter-in-law. 'I knew I couldn't say I was simply going on holiday. We came up with the excuse that I was going into hospital, but he still said – threateningly – that he'd get me back home in days. How right he was.'

On 1 May, 2002, Joan was enjoying the last of the day's sunshine when her mobile phone rang. 'It was the vet to say that he was going to have to shoot Bella, one of my horses. He explained that Bella had been struck with tremendous force on the back of the leg. Likening it to the injuries inflicted on charging cavalry horses by soldiers with clubs during the Crimean War, he said he had never seen a horse in so much pain.'

The attack happened a few days after her husband refused to sign a false witness statement, a glowing character reference that Roberts needed for his parole hearing. He had not wanted to pretend Roberts was a good worker – 'one of the family,' as the killer put it – when the truth was that Roberts had broken the rules and subjected the Cartwright family to months of misery and intimidation.

'But when we heard about Bella,' said Joan, 'we returned home the next day and my husband signed his statement straight away.'

Worse than the calls were the times when Roberts demanded Joan visit him in prison. There, they'd be free from listening devices. He was aware that all his calls to Joan were bugged. The threats would be more direct and his tone more accusative.

She recalls a trip she made with her husband to Channings Wood prison near Newton Abbot in Devon three months after Bella was killed. Initially she had resisted, blaming a troublesome knee, but changed her mind when Roberts told her 'he was going to send the chainsaw man round to see me.' She added, 'We were like puppets on a string. I felt I had to go along with everything because I was fighting for my family's survival.'

Roberts took a disturbingly close interest in their journey to the prison, asking which train they intended coming on and suggesting a hotel to stay in. 'We found this frightening and decided to do something completely different. We went down a few days early and rented a cottage, hired a car and drove to the prison,' said Joan. 'Harry was particularly angry that day and at one point asked, "You are the secret witnesses, aren't you?" We denied it, of course, and I repeated that it might possibly be one of his friends.

'I believe he knew then it was us but said he was going to have this other man kidnapped and tortured and said he'd organised the men to do it. I felt sick, dizzy, and thought I was going to black out.

'Shortly afterwards, my husband's cat Inky was very poorly that morning and he rushed him to the vet who said he'd been electrocuted. She had to put him to sleep and he died in my husband's arms. He came back and sobbed and sobbed.

'In his phone call later that day, Harry asked me if we still had the old black cat. I said that it was very strange that he asked that and said what had happened. He said it was very easy to electrocute a cat, all you had to do was tie it to a battery.'

Over the next five years, there would be many more attacks, some even more horrifying, on the animals nurtured on the East Midlands farm and for which a secret Parole Board hearing later concluded Roberts was responsible 'through the agency of others.'

However, it is understood that during a subsequent hearing – at which Roberts's legal team was present – a new panel could reach no decision as to whether Roberts was responsible for the attacks. He denies all the allegations the Cartwrights have made against him.

The most brutal happened the day before Joan and her son James were due give evidence against him at the most critical of a series of parole hearings, which on this occasion would be closed to Roberts, on 8 November, 2005.

Several intruders had got on to their land and attacked another of the horses, Digby, hacking off part of her head after trying to hang her from a tree. 'My other son and daughter-in-law came across her body while walking with the dogs. There was a rope tied around her back legs and for 50 yards the grass was scored where she fought. It was a total bloodbath. Her rear end had been mutilated and part of her head was missing. My daughter-in-law was so traumatised that her hair fell out. It was just so awful. The horse was such a lovely, gentle, beautiful animal and had particularly taken to my husband.'

By now, police had installed panic alarms at the homes of Joan and her family and there were numerous other sinister events to which police were called, including reports of prowlers and one incident in which the brake pipes were cut on James's wife's car.

'On another occasion, James spotted one of Harry's associates (whom he recognised as he once visited the sanctuary) lurking outside his 13-year-old daughter's school. 'I told the police, but they said there was nothing they could do,' he said.

This was not the first time the family had been threatened. A few months earlier, Joan had felt that her own life was in danger. 'Most Saturday mornings I would visit an auction house in Nottingham, something Harry was aware of. I was there in late August when I saw one of Harry's ex-convict friends who had been to the house standing on the steps. He was shaven-headed, wearing a leather jacket. There was a group of men standing with him.

'I thought they were going to grab me and bundle me away somewhere. I had to think quickly. I was going to make a run for it back to the car park but then worried that it was too isolated. I thought it best to keep walking. I put my head down and bolted past them. I was frightened he would grab me as I went past. Instead of going into the auction, I went into the office and hid behind the door. I was terrified and asked the women inside if I could use the phone as there were some people after me. We could see on the CCTV screen these men fanning out through the auction rooms, looking for me. But by the time the police turned up, they had shot off in a Transit van.

'The police took me out through a back entrance and gave me an escort home, with a car in front of and behind me. Later, I viewed the CCTV with the police who said they recognised some of the men as local criminals.'

After several hearings, the Parole Board wrote to Roberts on 12 December 2006, saying that it would not be recommending his release from jail.

While in open conditions, you demonstrated that you are untrustworthy, utterly egocentric and highly manipulative.

In your evidence at the hearing, it was plain that you had no appreciation of why your dishonest and devious conduct might be regarded by others as giving rise to serious concerns about the risks that you pose.

Controversially, Roberts now has another chance of parole, with a final hearing this summer [2009] ruling on his future risk to the public.

But whatever the outcome, the Cartwrights' nightmare will not be over. 'If he stays in prison, we are worried we might be in danger from his associates on the outside,' Joan says. 'If he comes out, he may come looking for us.'

The following week in the *Mail on Sunday*'s exclusive interview Joan Cartwright spoke of the 'unforgivable failure' of the authorities to protect her family both during and after the ten months Roberts spent at the sanctuary. 'We were told by the Prison Service that if we didn't give evidence he would come out and be released back to our area. They said there would be nothing they could do to stop him walking back up our drive. It was a terrifying situation.'

The first hearing, in early 2005, was adjourned when Roberts discovered the date and location. The second, in November that year, was also adjourned because one of the Cartwrights' horses was hacked to death the day before it was due to start.

*

'It was a tense, frightening time,' said James Cartwright. 'We viewed the third occasion, fixed for the following February, with growing dread.'

Around this time Joan received two letters from Roberts which the Parole Board would later conclude had been intended to intimidate her. In one he addresses the question of whether he would be able to sue the 'secret witnesses' for libel. '*If I win I can sue the witnesses for libel because their statements have caused this case to be brought. The authorities will step aside and leave the witnesses holding the can. It could take away every penny they have got . . . The only thing for the witnesses to do is not give their evidence at a hearing. No one can be forced to give evidence, and I would tell them that if I knew who they were, but the secrecy stops me from doing that.*'

A week before the third hearing was due to start, another horse, Crystal, was attacked with an iron bar. James Cartwright recalled, 'The bone above the eye had been hit and pushed into her skull. The vet said she had to lose the eye. We took it as another warning but we were told that if we didn't give evidence this time, he would walk free.'

They did give evidence, reassured by an undertaking they had received in 2003 from the then Home Secretary, David Blunkett, that Roberts would never see their evidence or learn who had supplied it.

He gave an added assurance that should the Parole Board direct that the material should be disclosed, '*the Secretary of State will withdraw that material.*' In the event, the

Parole Board decided that the 'gist' of the material should be disclosed to Roberts but only after a 'robust' plan to protect the witnesses was put in place.

'Despite talks about relocating the family and possible round-the-clock protection, nothing, was forthcoming,' said James. The Ministry of Justice accused the Cartwrights of being uncooperative, which they vehemently deny, and the result was that the Parole Board decided not to supply Roberts with the secret evidence.

There the matter rested, although not for Roberts, who has denied all the Cartwrights' allegations. He was still engaged in a long-running, highly expensive legal challenge to the decision to protect the identity of the sources.

He took his claim to the High Court and Appeal Court, but was frustrated. When his claim was heading towards Europe a computer disk proving that Joan and James were the secret sources found its way to Roberts's prison cell and his legal team was then able to compel them to repeat their evidence at yet another parole hearing. This time it would not be secret, but in front of their tormentor at Littlehey prison in Cambridgeshire.

'It was terrifying,' James said. 'Roberts sat fifteen feet away silhouetted behind a blue canvas screen. It diminished our evidence. I held back about thirty per cent of it because I felt intimidated.'

Joan said, 'If simple common-sense measures had been carried out we would not have been required to give secret evidence, our animals would still be alive, and the hundreds of thousands of pounds spent on legal fees, security, relocating horses and police protection would not have been spent.'

Derbyshire Police said in a statement: '*In May 2007 Harry Roberts received confidential information relating to a closed parole hearing. Derbyshire Constabulary investigated this leak of documentation, which was in the possession of only a small number of people. Two people were arrested in connection with the inquiry. Following a full investigation, the Crown Prosecution Service decided there was insufficient evidence to prosecute anyone.*'

Assistant Chief Constable Peter Goodman added: '*A team of liaison officers was dedicated to the family and I am satisfied that each allegation made by them has been fully investigated. I believe the Derbyshire Constabulary could not have done more to protect the family and ensure their safety.*'

Chapter 45

The front-page headline of the *Sun* on Thursday, 23 October 2014 was: *COP KILLER FREED AFTER 48 YRS. Police were furious last night over the planned release of Britain's most notorious cop killer. They echoed the 1966 trial judge who said that Harry Roberts should never be freed. Ex-Met Commissioner Baron Stevens – a rookie when Roberts murdered three officers in Shepherd's Bush, West London – said, 'The impact of this terrible crime was horrendous. This is a case where life imprisonment should mean exactly that – life.'*

Police Federation leader Steve White said, 'This decision by the Parole Board is a slap in the face for the families of the three police officers he brutally murdered who, once again, are forced to relive their pain and loss. This is a betrayal of the police officers who died.'

It was not only a controversial but also a contradictory decision by the Parole Board, given the proposal of Home Secretary Theresa May earlier in 2014 for whole-life tariffs for killers of police and prison officers that was going through Parliament at the time. She had recently told the

Police Federation, 'To attack and kill a police officer is to attack the fundamental basis of our society.'

To avoid press attention, late on Thursday, 13 November 2014 Harry Maurice Roberts was released on licence from Littlehey Prison, Cambridgeshire. It was impossible for the families of the murdered police officers to make sense of the Parole Board's decision. In an interview for BBC Television News Gillian Wombwell said, 'I think it's unjust. He has been institutionalised for forty-eight years – what is the point of him coming out now? And it just dredges up old feelings, old sadnesses. The judge at the time said that in this case, life should mean life. I think that the families, the victims, are serving a life sentence. My children had no father. My grandchildren don't have a grandfather. Ours is a life sentence.'

Roberts's release was headline news across Britain's media. There was an echo of the hunt for Roberts in 1966. Some newspapers asked their readers to report sightings of Roberts who was secretly placed at a covert location. Reports in the press ventured into inevitable speculation about Roberts's new life – how much it cost, had he been given a new identity, was the community in which he had been resettled in any danger, not knowing Harry Roberts was living amongst them?

*

By Tuesday, 10 March 2015 the *Sun* had tracked seventy-eight-year-old Roberts down. The headline was: *Cop Killer Roberts's Easy Life*. On pages eight and nine was a double-page feature: *CUSHY LIFER – Triple cop killer at gym, park and shops. 25K lodgings bill is paid by you*. There was the familiar black and white image of Roberts and recent photographs of him sitting on a park bench talking on a mobile phone captioned *FREE TIME*; joking with a supermarket check-out cashier – *TILL JOKER*; waiting at a bus stop – *EASY RIDE*; lifting weights at a gym and emerging from the entrance – *WORKOUTS*.

The dominating photograph was the full height of the page: Roberts with closely cropped white hair, in a grey T-shirt, black tracksuit bottoms, with a bag slung over one shoulder and wearing trendy sunglasses. One unnamed local resident was quoted as saying, 'He's in unbelievable shape for his age. Five decades behind bars hasn't done him any harm at all.'

There were comments from Joan Cartwright, 'Criminal Justice Expert' Harry Fletcher and Metropolitan Police Chief Sir Bernard Hogan-Howe. All of them damning, outraged and dismayed. The *Sun* report conspicuously did not reveal Roberts's secret whereabouts but the sign above the gym entrance – *Fitness Station* – was an easy giveaway. Anyone with Internet access and a few minutes to spare could work out that the gym that Roberts used daily was in Peterborough, Cambridgeshire and he must therefore be living in 'Approved Premises' at the local Probation and Bail Hostel, just twenty-nine miles and thirty-four minutes' drive from HMP Littlehey.

Three months later, on 7 June, the *Daily Star* and *Daily Mail* ran much the same story in much shorter form. What else was there to say, really? There were more photos of Roberts walking around the shops, getting on a bus, talking to a man in the street and jogging in a grey tracksuit. The *Star* report said that Roberts was living at '*a state-funded hostel in the East of England. Forty-eight years behind bars have not tamed Roberts's temper. When our reporter approached him, he clenched his fists and warned: "I'll f**king smash you."*'

It is unlikely, even if he'd been permitted to, that Roberts would have had anything more enlightening to say. Consciously or otherwise human memory constructs unreliable narratives. The recollections of most people, to a greater or lesser extent, are edited, polished and rehearsed to gloss over shortcomings, errors and painful truths. In the case of convicted criminals there's a stronger motive to rewrite their past in order make sense of failures and there's the temptation to brag and glamorise or even reinvent themselves as the kind anti-heroes of criminal fiction. Harry Roberts has been defined and defines himself as a high-ranking British criminal despite having accomplished nothing but the pointless killings of three defenceless police officers. And in that act of mindless fear, rage and stupidity he robbed himself of any meaningful existence.

Harry Maurice Roberts will be eighty years old on 21 July 2016. He has spent over half a century in penal institutions, a narrow, reduced existence for a human being. Devoid of freedom of choice, achievement and courage, self-sacrifice, generosity, compassion and love, he has imposed the bleakest limitations on himself. Having re-emerged into the world after forty-eight years behind prison walls, one way or another Roberts will remain ring-fenced for what remains of his life.

It is not always possible to understand why some people do terrible things, unthinkable, unimaginable things. But it is possible to observe the context, analyse what they do and what came before. If good and evil are intrinsic components of human nature, what then makes one person predominantly good and another evil?

In recent years, some ex-pupils of Roberts's former boarding school who were there during the two decades following the war have claimed that they were physically and sexually abused. Some members of the De La Salle Order of Christian Brothers, who founded and ran Roberts's old school, and their lay employees have since become notorious for sexually abusing children in their care at other institutions. Some have served and are still serving prison sentences. Historical allegations of child abuse against the De La Salle Brothers-run St William's Community Home near York referred to 142 individuals when they were aged between ten and sixteen, claiming damages totalling £8 million. The offences in schools and institutions run by the De La Salle order across the UK is now a matter of public record.

Harry Roberts was always at his best where structure and order were imposed. In the Army and even in prison he received glowing reports. But not when he was a pupil at boarding school. Having become a habitual truant, he was eventually expelled. Sixty-five-year-old Harry Roberts's remark to animal-sanctuary owner Joan Cartwright is most revealing: '*You can never trust honest people because they always let you down.*'

Male children particularly who develop attachment disorder and are then subjected to sexual trauma in early life have a tendency to become violent towards others as they grow up, and there is evidence to suggest that this is exacerbated by the development of any underlying personality disorder.

When these toxic ingredients are fused together in one individual it can produce the perfect storm: a human being whose behaviour indicates dissociative relationships, social and sexual dysfunction, suppressed anger and a sense of simmering injustice which manifest outwardly in volatile, unpredictable and violent actions against those who challenge or threaten them.

In 1966 the British nation's response to the victims' families was spontaneous and deeply felt. An anonymous donation of £100,000 was offered to establish a permanent trust to assist in cases where police officers were killed or injured on duty. It was later revealed that the donor was Sir Billy Butlin, founder and owner of the Butlin's Holiday Camp empire. As a result The Police Dependants' Trust was founded in 1966 and continues its vital work today. In its first year the Trust paid a total of £33,985 in grants. This year grants totalling over £1 million will have been paid. Since its inception the Trust has paid out in excess of £47 million to almost seven thousand beneficiaries.

Fifty years after the shootings in Braybrook Street, David Stanley Bertram Wombwell would have been seventy-five on 16 April 2016, Geoffrey Roger Fox ninety-two on 22 December and Christopher Tippet Head eighty-one years old on Christmas Eve. They might have lived to be old men, have seen their children grow to adults, known their grandchildren, had ordinary, fulfilling lives – had they not been cut down in their prime and had their hopes, dreams and future days stolen away.

If it is true that we are not really dead until there is no one left alive who remembers who we were, then those three young London policemen will survive a great deal longer than most of us. It is with that in mind that this book is written, for the remembrance of their sacrifice in public service and with enduring gratitude.

Appendix

Police Officer Biographies

The three police officers who lost their lives in the line of duty on a quiet street next to Wormwood Scrubs Park on that summer afternoon, 12 August 1966, were thirty-year-old Christopher Tippet Head, twenty-five-year-old David Stanley Bertram Wombwell and forty-one-year-old Geoffrey Roger Fox.

When policemen are killed in the line of duty, who they are is masked by the job they do. In news reports and memorials their names are prefaced by their rank, the circumstances always framed by the public service they were performing. That distances them, makes them seem less like human, vivid, three-dimensional people. Without knowing something of their background and lives, their untimely, violent deaths seem less horrific, shocking and painful.

Christopher Head was born to parents Fred and Phylia on Christmas Eve 1935 in Dartmouth, Devon. He was the youngest of five children. The family lived at 168 Victoria

Road, one of four modest terraced houses with sweeping views over the town and River Dart.

Fred and Phylia had their youngest son christened Christopher Tippet Head at St Clement's Church, a short walk from their home. His brother and three sisters had also been pushed up the steep hill in the same pram to St Clement's, wearing the family christening robe made by a great-grandmother on their mother's side, and had been given Phylia's maiden name, Tippet, as a second name.

At the time of Chris Head's birth his father, Fred, was fifty-one years old, the eldest of thirteen children. His mother, Phylia, was thirty-nine, the third of four children and his parents had been married for twelve years.

Chris's father began his working life with the Royal Navy in 1903. Fred Head left the Navy after nineteen years' service in 1922 and married seamstress Phylia the same year. The couple moved to Dartmouth when Fred found employment as a stoker at the hospital of the Britannia Royal Naval College. He was still doing the same job thirteen years later in 1935 when Chris was born.

When Chris was three the Head family moved from Victoria Road a short distance away to Townstall. Two years later the fortunes of the Head family were thrown off course when Chris's father, aged fifty-six, died unexpectedly from a stroke in 1940. His mother, who was by then in her mid-forties, brought up her two sons and three daughters single-handed, as well as nursing her seventy-six-year-old bedridden mother who moved from

Appendix

Torquay and lived with the family after the death of Chris's grandfather.

Unlike Harry Roberts, Jack Witney and John Duddy who were evacuated from London and Glasgow at the start of the war, the children of Dartmouth were not sent away. The danger of air raids in a provincial seaside town clearly was not so great, but Dartmouth and its inhabitants didn't escape unscathed. On 18 September 1942, when Chris Head was six years old, Nazi Luftwaffe planes bombed the harbour, hitting and sinking the river ferry in midstream, dropped two bombs on the Naval College and finally scored a direct hit on Philips & Sons, Shipbuilders and Engineers, killing twenty men and women.

Six weeks after Chris's seventh birthday, mid-morning on Saturday, 13 February 1943, there was another devastating raid on Dartmouth with scarcely time to sound the air-raid siren. One German aircraft swooped over the town and the first bombs hit Higher Street, narrowly missing the primary school and landing on a small shop and the Town Arms public house to the north of it, killing two people. Another bomb hit the Midland Bank, killing two more, and a third bomb hit the College. The corner of Foss Street and Duke Street collapsed from the blasts, including the old Tudor house and Flavel Church Hall. The Butterwalk was windowless and leaning so badly that it was feared it too would collapse. Local people searched through the rubble for survivors and dead bodies for twenty-one hours until all hope of finding anyone was exhausted. The final toll was fourteen dead, all civilians including women and children.

During the war years, with their night-time blackouts and the threat of bombing raids, Chris Head followed his older siblings into the local infants and primary school. Shortly after the war ended he got a place at Dartmouth Grammar School.

On 1 September 1952, after leaving school at seventeen Head became a police cadet in his parents' home town of Torquay. He applied himself with his usual focus and enthusiasm. His uniform was always neatly pressed, shoes gleaming and the peak of his cap pulled firmly down. He was a striking figure about the town. After eighteen months he had gained many useful experiences and insights into police work but at eighteen years old he was no longer eligible to be in the police cadets and left on 16 March 1954.

On 24 March, Head began his National Service and joined the Royal Air Force. Due to his police-cadet training he was posted to the RAF Police and stationed at Stranraer, Scotland where he served for two years. After being demobbed on 6 June 1956 Chris Head, now twenty years old, returned to Dartmouth and applied to join the Railway Police. He had no problem passing the entrance examination and interview at the selection board but was turned down on medical grounds as the doctor's report said he was colour-blind.

The rejection was devastating but Head found a job as a metal-polishing inspector at an aircraft factory twenty miles north of Dartmouth at Newton Abbot. He spent a restless eighteen months in civilian life before applying to the Metropolitan Police where his borderline colour-blindness would only exclude him from some specialist roles. He was accepted, left home and his native Devon once again and enrolled on 23 June 1958 at the Metropolitan Police training school at Peel House, 105 Regency Street, London SW1.

After her children left home Head's mother, Phylia, moved away from Dartmouth after thirty-six years and returned to her birthplace, Torquay. She later said that when her son visited her new home on free weekends she would find him lying in bed reading police instruction books. His training officers at Peel House found Chris Head unassuming, quiet and determined, with a natural aptitude for studying. It was no surprise to them that he passed the course well with a mark of a hundred and nineteen out of a possible hundred and twenty.

His training completed, Head was posted for a probationary period to 'B' District, Kensington and Chelsea, on 29 September 1958. Walking the streets of his beat he quickly grew to like and know the area and local people. The smart young bobby with his Devonshire accent was a popular figure among the cosmopolitan market traders of the area and grew privy to their gossip and concerns. But it wasn't all about policing: some of them had difficulty with correspondence and literacy and Chris Head was always ready to help them write letters and fill out forms.

It is a picture of community and innocence that could

have been borrowed from the BBC television series *Dixon of Dock Green* about daily life at an East London police station. But as gunfire echoed across Wormwood Scrubs Park at 3:17 on the afternoon of Friday, 12 August 1966 this illusion was shattered for ever.

Head's appointment as a PC in the Metropolitan Police was confirmed 1 July 1960. After six years in uniform on the beat he joined the CID as a Detective Constable at 'F' Division on 13 May 1963. Eight months later, on 10 February 1964, he moved to Scotland Yard's C10 and worked under Detective Superintendent Jack Knight in the Stolen Car Squad. On 19 October he went to 'C' Division in Westminster. On 1 April 1964 he moved to 'E' Division, Camden. Eighteen months later, on 25 October 1965, Head returned to Scotland Yard, this time to join the C1 Major Crime Squad. After passing the examination to become a sergeant he returned to 'F' Division at Shepherd's Bush on 28 February 1966, next door to the area of London where he'd begun his life as a policeman. Unusually for the time and for a man of Chris Head's age and family background, at thirty years old he was still unmarried and was living in bachelor police accommodation at Ravenscourt House, 3 Paddenswick Road, London W6.

David Stanley Bertram Wombwell was born on 16 April 1941 in Weston Way, Baldock, Hertfordshire and attended the primary school there, twenty-three miles north-west of the place where twenty-five years later his murderer would be arrested.

While David was still an infant his parents separated and he lived with his mother Daphne for three years during the war while his father Kenneth was in Canada with the Royal Air Force. Ken's version of events is that when he returned to Hertfordshire, Daphne contacted him and said, 'You have to come and pick up your son because if you don't I'm putting him in a home. Quite frankly, he bores me.'

David went to live with his father and his fifty-nine-year-old paternal grandmother, Mrs Ethel Wombwell, at Castle Farm, five miles south of Hitchin, where his older cousin Rob was also being brought up by his grandmother.

David later went to two other schools, one in Bedford and then to Broadmead School in Tennyson Road, Luton. After leaving Broadmead he went to the Luton School of Technology and took a course in motor engineering. This led him to his first job with Chater-Lea Motor Engineers at Letchworth.

But the idea of one day becoming a policeman took root in David Wombwell early in life. When his mother remarried, his stepfather Ben Scoot often told David stories about members of his family who were in the police force. David's mother later recalled: 'All Ben's people were in the police and David used to love to hear about the force when he was a boy'. While Wombwell was working at Chater-Lea he applied to join the Hertfordshire Constabulary Cadet Force but was informed that there were no vacancies.

When his father moved to Harpenden, David changed jobs and was employed at the Electric Hose and Rubber Company that made the high-pressure hoses used in submarines and mining. For two years he was the personal driver of managing director Don Taylor who in August 1966 wrote a heartfelt tribute to David that was published in the local press.

David Wombwell's love of cars led him to his next job in Harpenden as a trainee car salesman. His other great love took the form of local girl Gillian Hague who was training to become a hairdresser. Towards the end of 1962 David's young life was getting complicated. He applied to join the Metropolitan Police and asked Gillian's father for his permission for them to get engaged. But, disapproving of the way things were going, David's mother Daphne intervened and offered him a ticket to America so that he could spread his wings before settling down. The dilemma was finally resolved when Gillian announced that she was pregnant. Within days David's Metropolitan Police application was accepted, too.

And so it was that with Gillian four weeks pregnant at the age of sixteen the couple were married at St Albans Registry Office on 27 October 1962. It was a small family gathering with Gillian's parents, David's mother Daphne and her second husband Ben Scoot there. David's father Ken was not there to see his son married as he had decided not to attend because of the deep and long-standing differences that he had with David's mother. But after tea at Gillian's parents' house there was a large party in the evening at a local hotel and, with Daphne absent, Ken Wombwell was there to join in the celebrations.

The following year, on 11 February 1963, David Wombwell achieved his long-held ambition and joined the Metropolitan Police. He attended the training school at Hendon for three months. Gillian, now five months pregnant, went to live at Castle Farm under the wise and watchful eye of Grandma Wombwell. Gillian only saw David at weekends.

With his training completed on 12 May, Wombwell was posted to Hammersmith and Fulham, 'F' Division, as a Police Constable, a month after his twenty-first birthday. A few weeks later and twenty-four days before her seventeenth birthday Gillian gave birth to a son, Daen, on 2 June 1963.

As a married officer with a child, PC Wombwell was allocated a flat above Brentford police station and here David, Gillian and their new baby son had their first family home together. By December 1963 Gillian was pregnant again and the following year they moved to police accommodation at Eastfield Court in East Acton where their second child Melanie was born at home on 6 September 1964.

The young Wombwell family settled in quickly to living in the company of other police families at Eastfield Court. Looking back at that happy time fifty years later Gillian recalls: '. . . there were a lot of children of that sort of age and young couples. Mums would sit out on the step drinking tea or coffee as the kids played. There was a great sense of comradeship, none of us had much money, we made wine, made beer, had cheese-and-wine parties which was literally French bread and cheese on your lap at each others' flats and it was a close community because of the shift work.' The shifts meant that fathers were often around during the day and Gillian said that when David was home he was always a hands-on dad. He and Daen were inseparable to such an extent that when Melanie was born Gillian remembers saying to him 'Keep your hands off her, this one's mine.'

With a wife and family to support David Wombwell was driven, ambitious and aiming for higher things at work – after just three years on the beat he applied to join the CID. At twenty-four he became a Temporary Detective Constable at Shepherd's Bush on 2 January 1966.

Wombwell was considered by his superiors to be very keen and promising. A tribute to him that still hangs on the walls of the Braybrook Suite at Hammersmith police station says: *He had packed a great deal of experience into his brief period of service having given invaluable assistance to the Regional Crime Squad and to the team investigating the 'nude murders'.*

Chris Head too had been involved in the investigation of the 'Nude Murders' along with numerous CID and uniformed officers across 'F' Division. Between 1964 and 1965 six women had been found dead at various locations in West London, several of them next to or near the River Thames. All the victims had worked as prostitutes and had been left strangled and naked, leading to the murders being called the 'Nude Murders' (also the Hammersmith Murders) and the man responsible dubbed 'Jack the Stripper'.

Among Head and Wombwell's older, more experienced colleagues was Geoffrey Fox. He'd been a PC at Shepherd's Bush since 6 November 1950 and was one of the most popular men at the station. During sixteen years on the beat he had become well-known on the local streets and had gained a considerable reputation, both inside and outside the police station. With an enviable network of local contacts who supplied him with invaluable insights and information, Fox's legendary memory for faces and his instinct for always being in the right place at the right time meant that he received three commendations from the Metropolitan Police Commissioner.

Geoffrey Roger Fox was born on Monday, 22 December 1924 at Godstone, Surrey. He left school at the end of his elementary education and was called up two weeks before his eighteenth birthday for National Service on 7 December 1942. He went on to see four years' active service in the Royal Navy during the Second World War until he was demobbed on 27 August 1946. At the age of twenty-two Geoff Fox married his wife, Margaret, the following year, 29 November 1947. They had their first child, Ann Margaret, on 29 August 1948, followed by a son,

Appendix

Paul Geoffrey, on 30 April 1950. Thirteen years later they had a third child, Mandy Ann, born on 3 December 1963.

Fox had been working as a bus conductor when he joined the Metropolitan Police on 24 July 1950. After training school PC Fox was sent to 'F' Division for a probationary period and his appointment was confirmed on 29 July 1952 while he was at Shepherd's Bush, where he remained. On 24 November 1963 Fox passed the prestigious Class 1 Police Advanced Driver course at the world-famous Metropolitan Police Motor Driving School at Hendon. During the six-month course (costing £20,000 per pupil) he learnt high-performance driving skills on the public highway, including pursuit driving, 999 driving, high-speed cornering and night driving. One of his prized possessions was the pennant he won at the driving school for being the best driver on his course. Combined with his extensive local knowledge, this coveted qualification meant that he was always in demand as a Q-car driver.

Fox is remembered by colleagues for the willing, friendly help he always gave at social activities and his wit in presentation speeches to mark transfers or retirements. They recall: *'No one ever went in vain to Geoff for help or advice and he was a great ambassador for the Service because of his kindness and concern for others.'* In his spare time Geoffrey Fox was fond of fishing and often invited younger colleagues to join him, saying it was a good way to unwind from police work. It no doubt also helped him to develop the fortitude and patience that was needed to catch criminals.

Head of The Police Investigation

Fifty-one-year-old Richard Claude Chitty had joined the Metropolitan Police in 1939 after working for his father, a market gardener. The career change for young Dick Chitty was prompted by his father saying: 'I don't know how you would get a job if it wasn't for me.'

Chitty said, later 'I was a cocky lad at the time so I decided to join the police. I was enrolled and went to training school at Peel House. It was all drill, discipline and learning. Once I got there I wished I'd never joined. But after the ten-week course I was posted to Putney to walk the beat.'

Three years later he went to West End Central in Saville Row, the busiest police station in London. After volunteering for the RAF and serving as a navigator in a bomber squadron from 1943-45, Chitty rejoined the police at the end of the war. He was soon promoted to sergeant and over the next ten years progressed to Detective Inspector at Hammersmith, the HQ of 'F' Division. By 1966 he had risen to the rank of Detective Superintendent at Scotland Yard on a salary of £185 per month and was a veteran of fourteen murder investigations.

Appendix

OFFICERS ARRESTING

John Edward WITNEY
Detective Inspector STEVENTON, 'S' Division
Detective Sergeant BURROWS, 'S' Division
Detective Sergeant HARVEY, 'S' Division

John DUDDY
Detective Chief Inspector Robert BROWN, Glasgow City Police
Detective Chief Inspector HENSLEY, 'T' Division
Detective Inspector SLIPPER, C.O.C.8 Flying Squad

Harry Maurice ROBERTS
Police Sergeant SMITH, Hertfordshire Constabulary
Police Sergeant THORNE, Hertfordshire Constabulary
Detective Chief Superintendent NEWMAN
Detective Superintendent CHITTY, C1 Murder Squad, Scotland Yard

Sources and Bibliography

The National Archives (some files and closed pages opened after Freedom of Information Act application for this book):
DPP2/4276; DPP2/4277; DPP2/4279/1; DPP2/4279/2; DPP2/4280; CRIM1/3139; MEPO2/11031; MEPO2/11037.

Newspapers:
British Newspaper Archive
The Times Digital Archive
www.ukpressonline.co.uk

Independent Television News:
www.itnsource.com

Bibliography:
No Answer From Foxtrot Eleven by Tom Tullett, published by Michael Joseph Ltd 1967.

Sources and Bibliography

The Neophiliacs: The Revolution in English Life in the 1950s and 1960s by Christopher Booker, published by Wm Collins 1969. Pimlico edition with new introduction 1992.

Specialist in Crime by Ernest Millen CBE, formerly Deputy Assistant Commissioner at Scotland Yard and Commander of the CID, published by George G. Harrap & Co Ltd 1972.

Slipper of the Yard by Jack Slipper, published by Sidgwick and Jackson Ltd 1981.

Natural Born Killers by Kate Kray, published by Blake Publishing Ltd 1999.

Death on the Beat by Dick Kirby, published by Pen & Sword Ltd 2012.

Interviews with Dorothy Roberts, June Howard and Lillian Perry in chapters 38 and 39, of *No Answer From Foxtrot Eleven* by Tom Tullet, 1967, reprinted by kind permission of Michael Joseph Ltd, London, an imprint of Penguin Group UK.

Police killer Harry Roberts's five-year terror campaign to silence woman who kept him behind bars by Ian Gallagher, from *Mail on Sunday*, 19 April 2009, reprinted by kind permission of Associated Newspapers Ltd, London.